UNCANNY X-MEN: SUPERIOR VOL. 2 — APOCALYPSE WARS. Contains material originally published in magazine form as UNCANNY X-MEN #6-10. First printing 2016. ISBN# 978-0-7851-9608-2. Published by MARVEL WORLDWIDE, INC., a subsidiary of MARVEL ENTERTAINMENT, LLC. OFFICE OF PUBLICATION: 135 West 50th Street, New York, NY 10020. Copyright © 2016 MARVEL No similarity between any of the names, characters, persons, and/or institutions in this magazine with those of any living or dead person or institution is intended, and any such similarity which may exist is purely coincidental. **Printed in Canada.** ALAN FINE, President, Marvel Entertainment; DAN BUCKLEY, President, TV, Publishing & Brand Management; JOE QUESADA, Chief Creative Officer; TOM BREVOORT, SVP of Publishing; DAVID BOGART, SVP of Business Affairs & Operations, Publishing & Partnership; C.B. CEBULSKI, VP of Brand Management & Development, Asia; DAVID GABRIEL, SVP of Sales & Marketing, Publishing; JEFF YOUNGQUIST, VP of Production & Special Projects; DAN CARR, Executive Director of Publishing Technology; ALEX MORALES, Director of Publishing Operations; SUSAN CRESPI, Production Manager; STAN LEE, Chairman Emeritus. For information regarding advertising in Marvel Comics or on Marvel.com, please contact Vit DeBellis, Integrated Sales Manager, at vdebellis@marvel.com. For Marvel subscription inquiries, please call 888-511-5480. **Manufactured between 9/23/2016 and 10/31/2016 by SOLISCO PRINTERS, SCOTT, QC, CANADA.**

10 9 8 7 6 5 4 3 2 1

TERRIGEN MISTS CIRCLE THE GLOBE, WHITTLING DOWN MUTANTKIND'S NUMBERS AND SUPPRESSING ANY NEW MUTANT MANIFESTATIONS. BELIEVING BIGGER THREATS REQUIRE MORE THREATENING X-MEN, MAGNETO IS JOINED BY A TEAM OF THE MOST RUTHLESS MUTANTS ALIVE TO STEM THE THREAT OF EXTINCTION…

UNCANNY X-MEN

APOCALYPSE WARS

WHILE INVESTIGATING A STRING OF MURDERS INVOLVING MUTANT HEALERS, MAGNETO AND HIS TEAM OF X-MEN UNCOVERED THE GROUP RESPONSIBLE — THE DARK RIDERS. USING A HEALER TO LURE THEM TO THE ISLAND OF GENOSHA, MAGNETO LAID AND ACTIVATED A TRAP, DETONATING THE ISLAND AND SEEMINGLY OBLITERATING HIS ENEMIES.

NOW, THE UNCANNY X-MEN — MAGNETO, PSYLOCKE, SABRETOOTH, M AND THE DISTANT, DRONE-LIKE ARCHANGEL — SCOUR THE GLOBE, STAMPING OUT ANYONE WHO WOULD STAND IN THE WAY OF MUTANTKIND'S CONTINUED SURVIVAL.

CULLEN BUNN
WRITER

KEN LASHLEY
ARTIST

NOLAN WOODARD
COLORIST

"GOING PUBLIC"

PACO MEDINA
PENCILER

JUAN VLASCO
INKER

JESUS ABURTOV
COLOR ARTIST

VC's JOE CARAMAGNA
LETTERER

GREG LAND & NOLAN WOODARD
COVER ART

CHRISTINA HARRINGTON & CHRIS ROBINSON
ASSISTANT EDITORS

DANIEL KETCHUM
EDITOR

MARK PANICCIA
X-MEN GROUP EDITOR

X-MEN CREATED BY *STAN LEE* & *JACK KIRBY*

COLLECTION EDITOR: *JENNIFER GRÜNWALD*
ASSOCIATE MANAGING EDITOR: *KATERI WOODY*
ASSOCIATE EDITOR: *SARAH BRUNSTAD*
EDITOR, SPECIAL PROJECTS: *MARK D. BEAZLEY*
VP PRODUCTION & SPECIAL PROJECTS: *JEFF YOUNGQUIST*
SVP PRINT, SALES & MARKETING: *DAVID GABRIEL*
BOOK DESIGNER: *JAY BOWEN*

EDITOR IN CHIEF: *AXEL ALONSO*
CHIEF CREATIVE OFFICER: *JOE QUESADA*
PUBLISHER: *DAN BUCKLEY*
EXECUTIVE PRODUCER: *ALAN FINE*

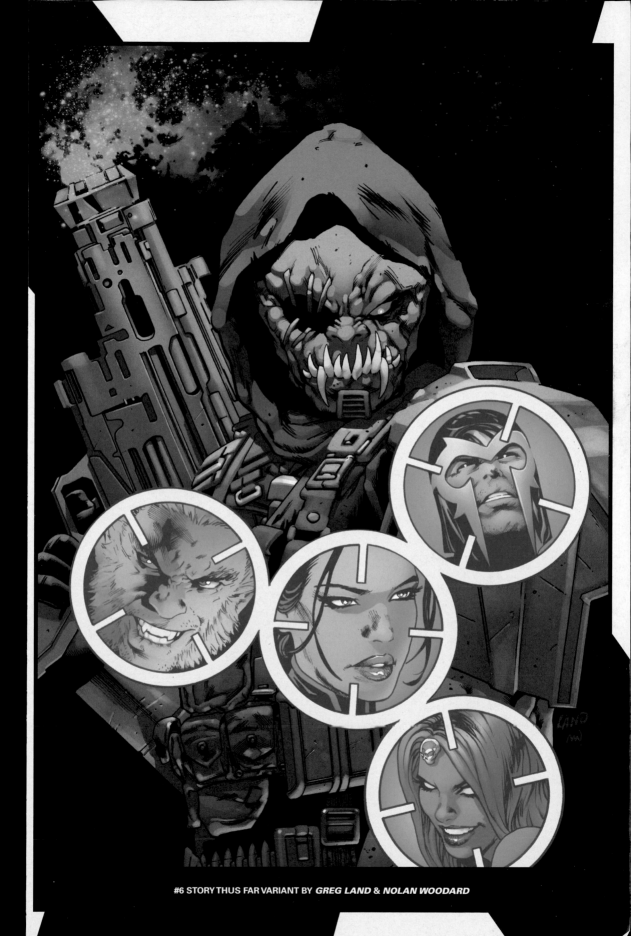

#6 STORY THUS FAR VARIANT BY *GREG LAND* & *NOLAN WOODARD*

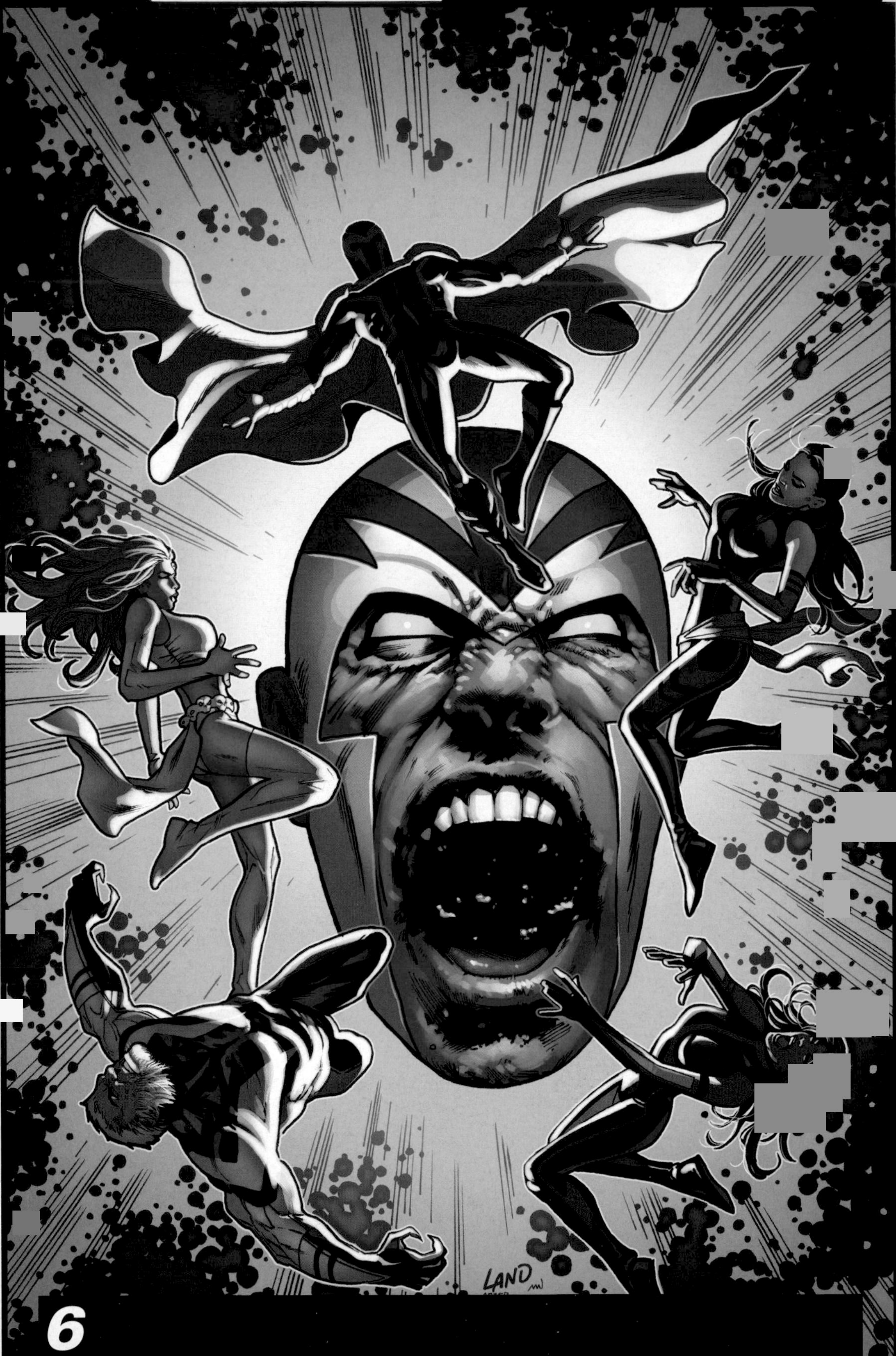
LAND
6

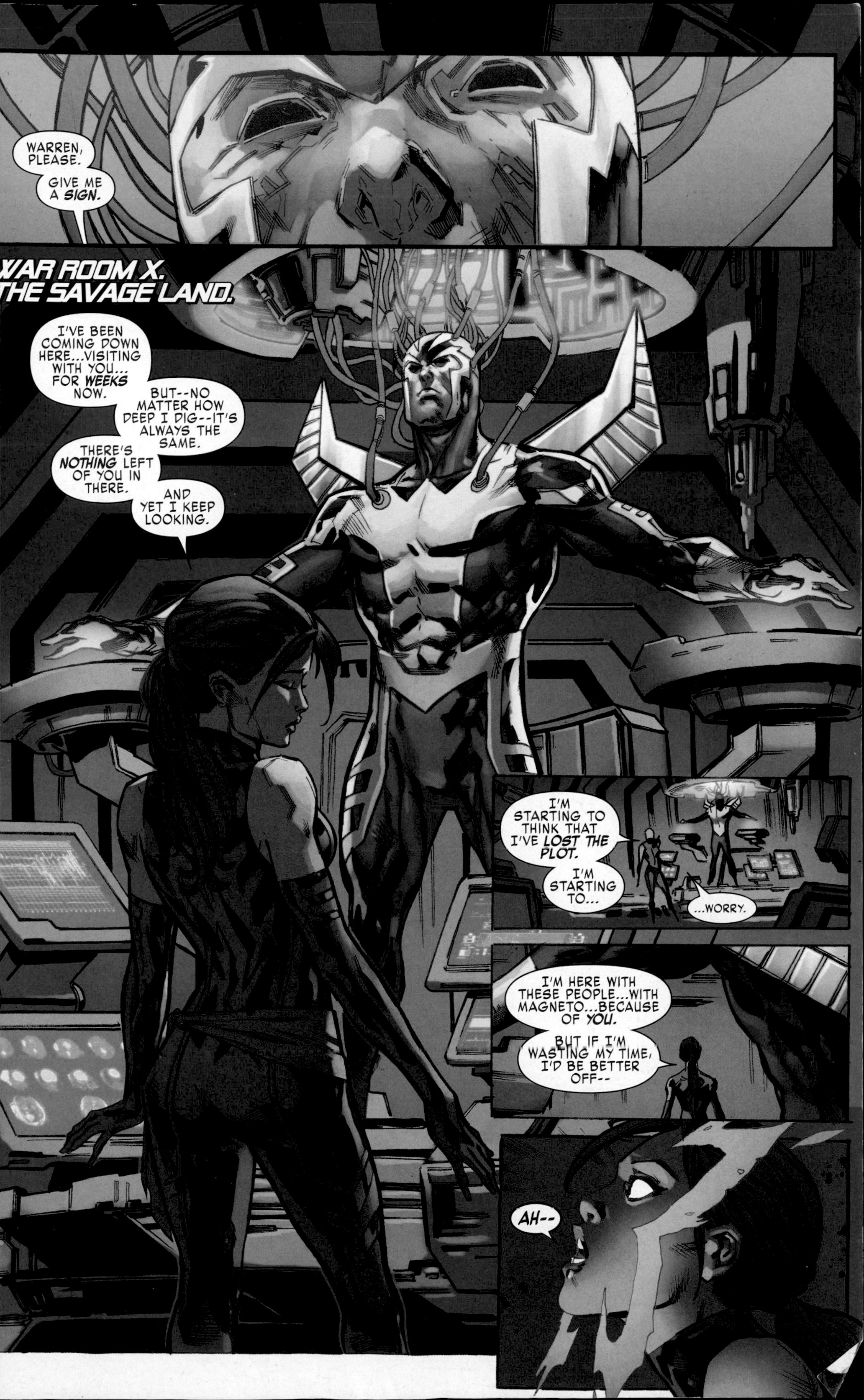
WARREN, PLEASE.
GIVE ME A SIGN.
WAR ROOM X. THE SAVAGE LAND.
I'VE BEEN COMING DOWN HERE...VISITING WITH YOU... FOR WEEKS NOW.
BUT--NO MATTER HOW DEEP I DIG--IT'S ALWAYS THE SAME.
THERE'S NOTHING LEFT OF YOU IN THERE.
AND YET I KEEP LOOKING.
I'M STARTING TO THINK THAT I'VE LOST THE PLOT.
I'M STARTING TO...
...WORRY.
I'M HERE WITH THESE PEOPLE...WITH MAGNETO...BECAUSE OF YOU.
BUT IF I'M WASTING MY TIME, I'D BE BETTER OFF--
AH--

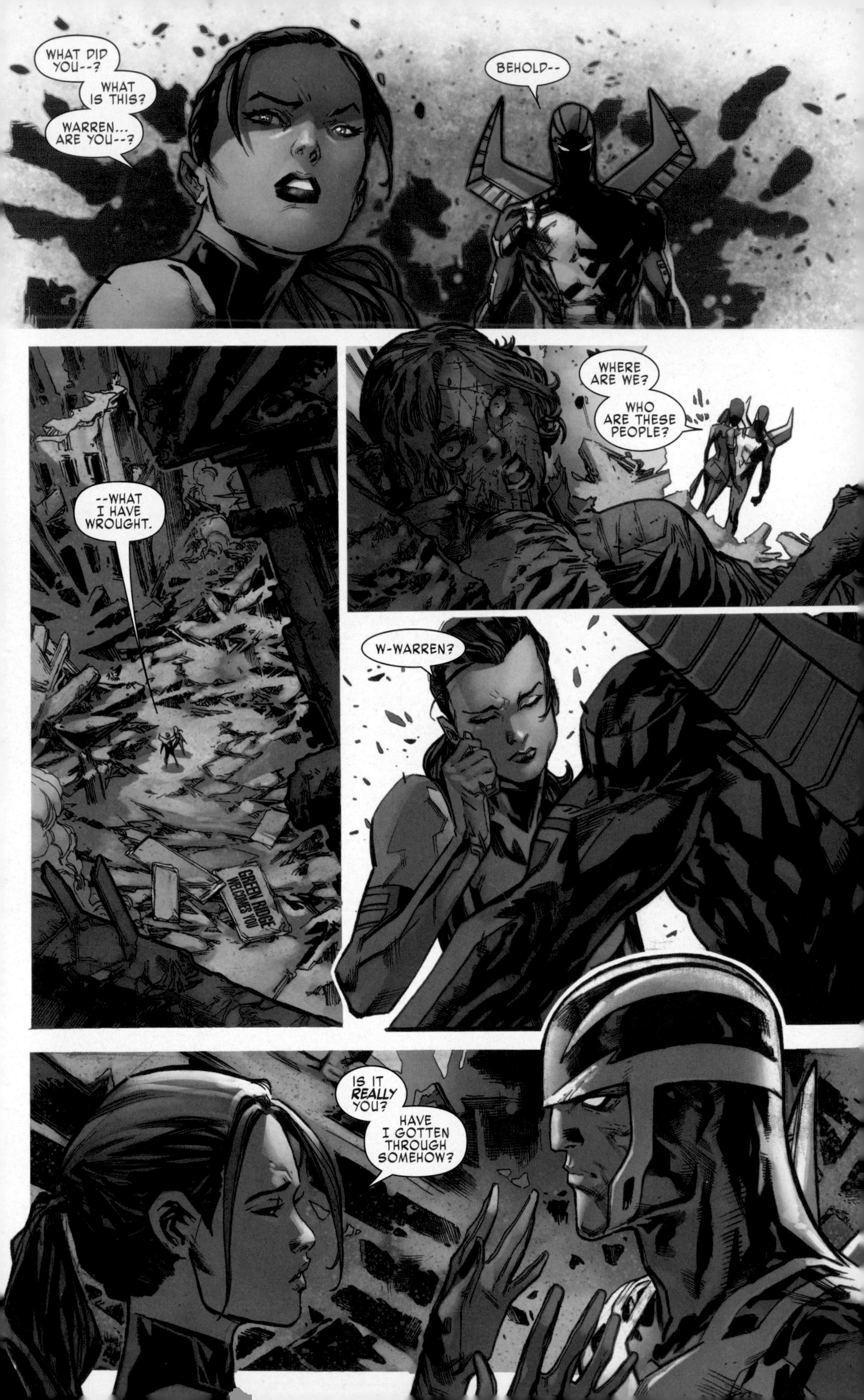
WHAT DID YOU--?
WHAT IS THIS?
WARREN... ARE YOU--?
BEHOLD--
--WHAT I HAVE WROUGHT.
GREEN RIDGE WELCOMES YOU
WHERE ARE WE?
WHO ARE THESE PEOPLE?
W-WARREN?
IS IT REALLY YOU?
HAVE I GOTTEN THROUGH SOMEHOW?

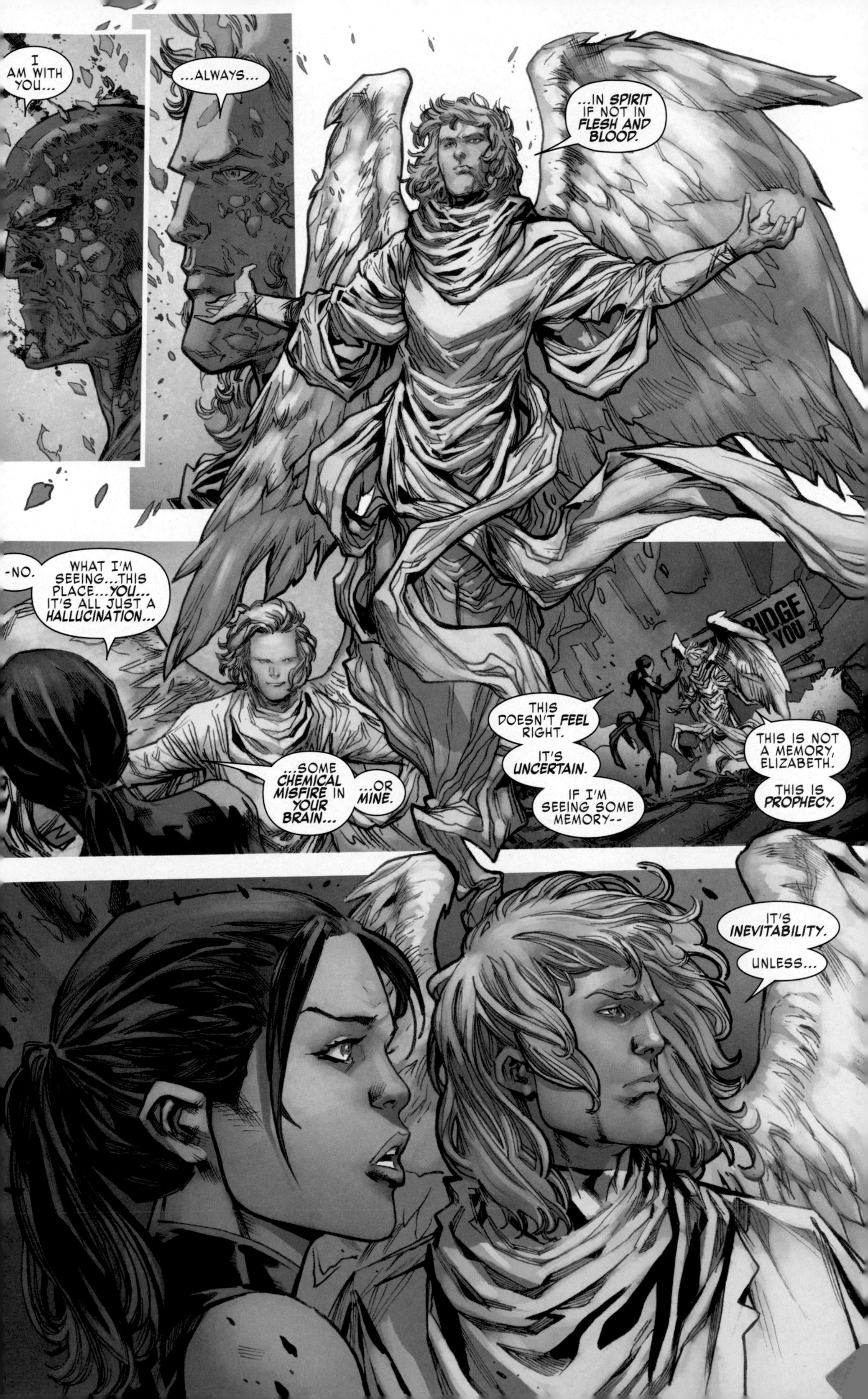
I AM WITH YOU...
...ALWAYS...
...IN SPIRIT IF NOT IN FLESH AND BLOOD.
-NO.
WHAT I'M SEEING...THIS PLACE...YOU... IT'S ALL JUST A HALLUCINATION...
...SOME CHEMICAL MISFIRE IN YOUR BRAIN...
...OR MINE.
THIS DOESN'T FEEL RIGHT.
IT'S UNCERTAIN.
IF I'M SEEING SOME MEMORY--
RIDGE
YOU
THIS IS NOT A MEMORY, ELIZABETH.
THIS IS PROPHECY.
IT'S INEVITABILITY.
UNLESS...

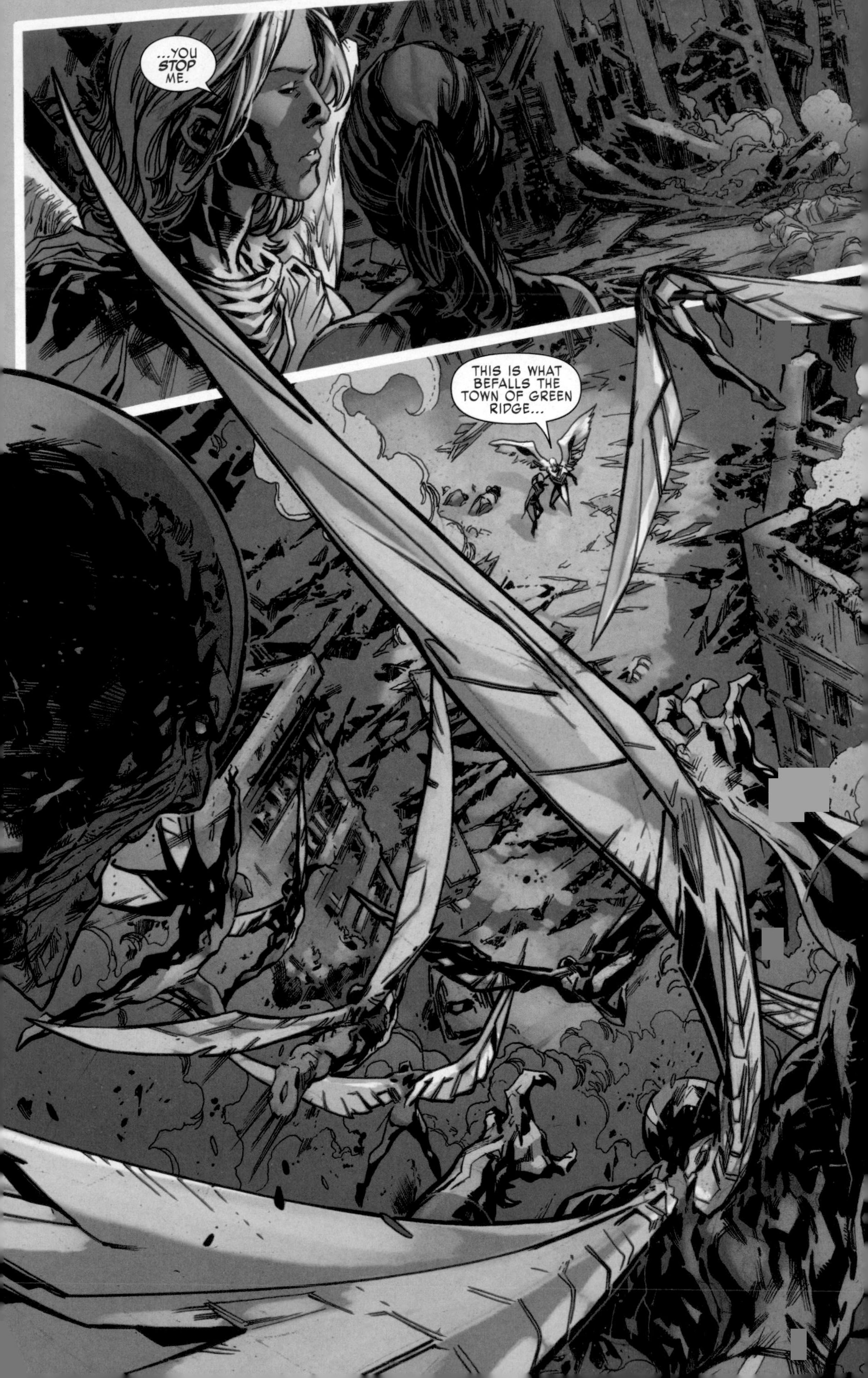
...YOU STOP ME.
THIS IS WHAT BEFALLS THE TOWN OF GREEN RIDGE...

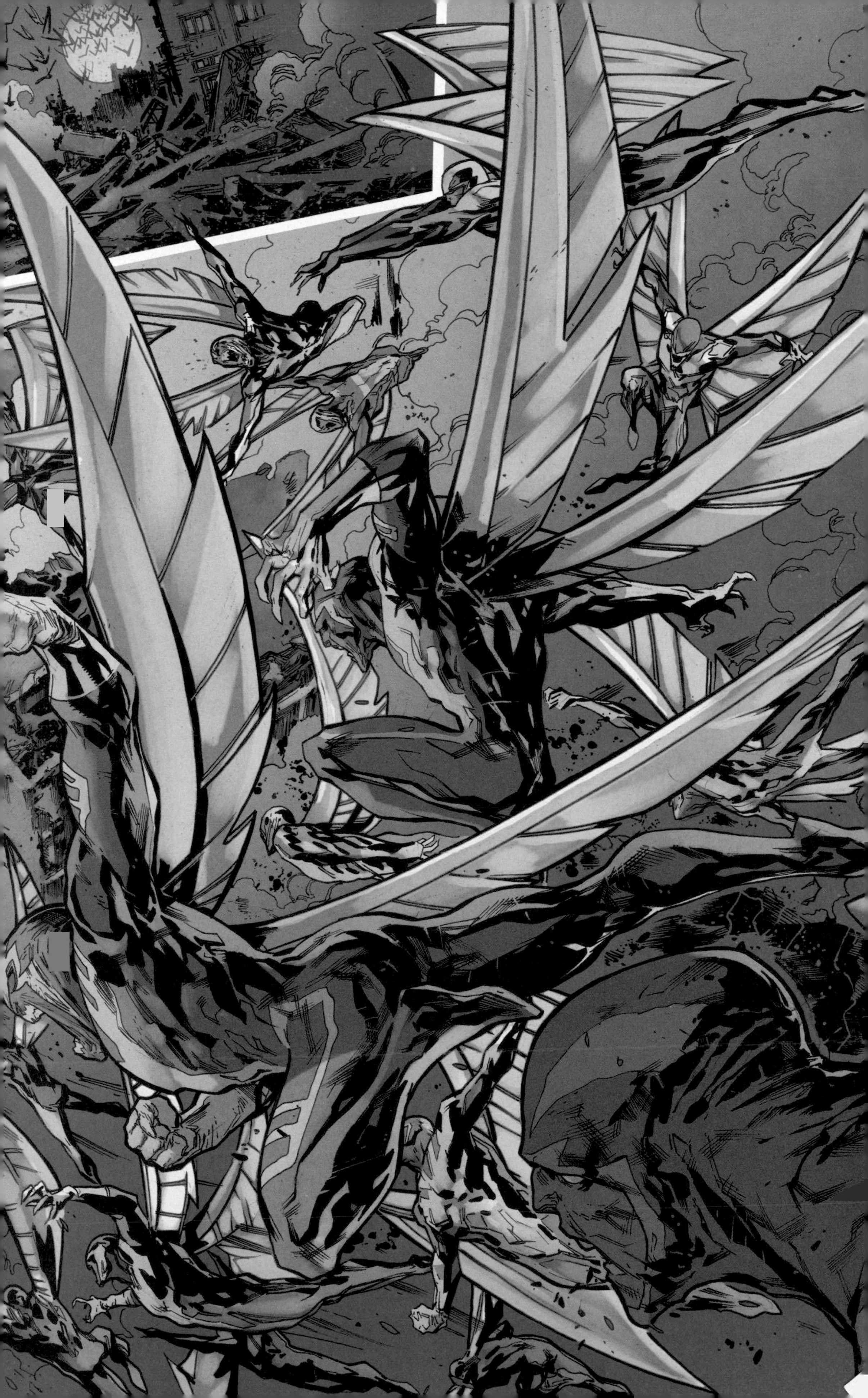

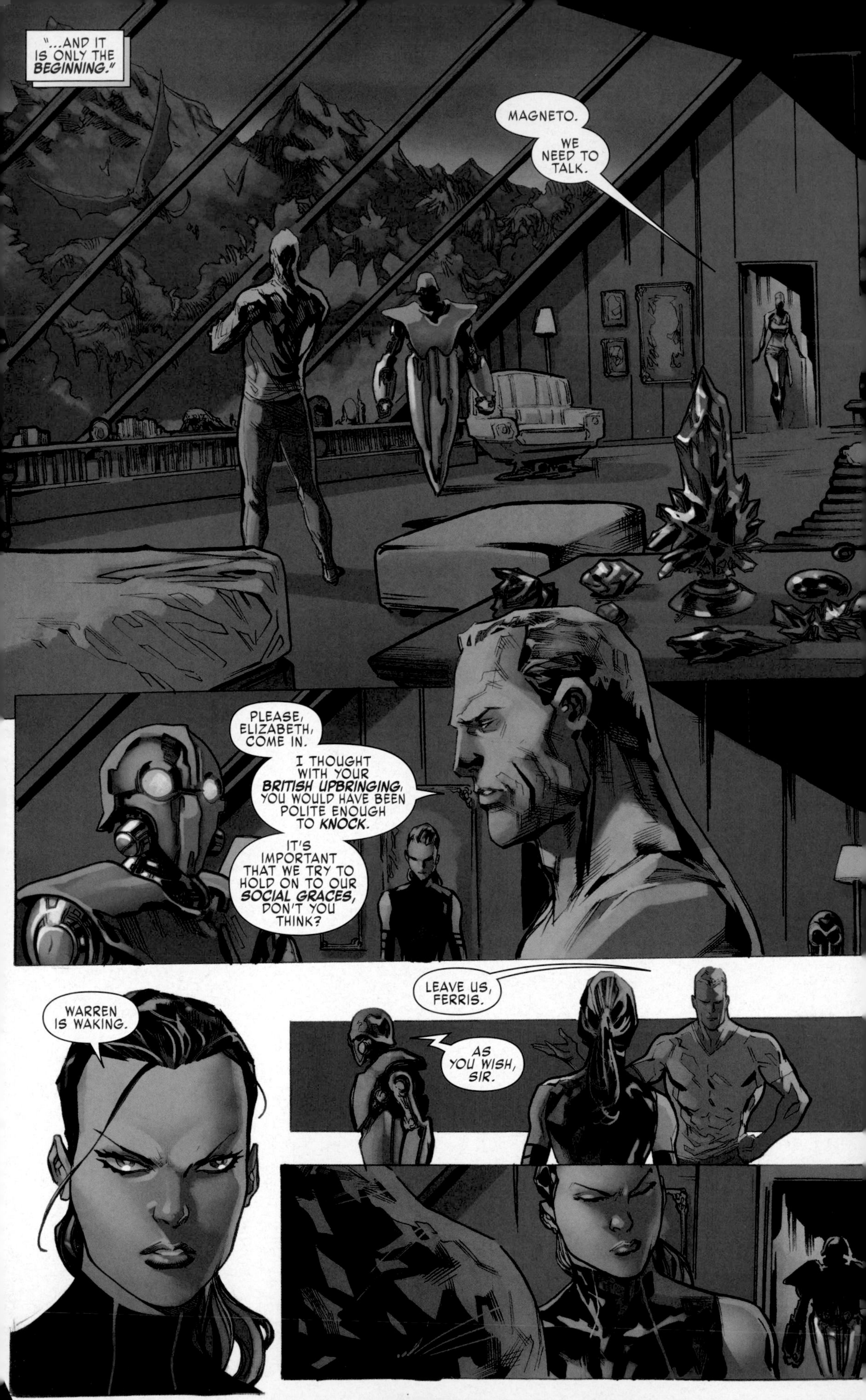
"...AND IT IS ONLY THE BEGINNING."
MAGNETO.
WE NEED TO TALK.
PLEASE, ELIZABETH, COME IN.
I THOUGHT WITH YOUR BRITISH UPBRINGING, YOU WOULD HAVE BEEN POLITE ENOUGH TO KNOCK.
IT'S IMPORTANT THAT WE TRY TO HOLD ON TO OUR SOCIAL GRACES, DON'T YOU THINK?
WARREN IS WAKING.
LEAVE US, FERRIS.
AS YOU WISH, SIR.

SO...

...ARCHANGEL.

AS YOU KNOW, I'VE BEEN WORKING WITH HIM...

...TRYING TO FIGURE OUT IF WE WERE DEALING WITH WARREN...

...OR THE DARK ANGEL PERSONA...

...THE VERSION OF ARCHANGEL THAT WAS TWISTED INTO THE GENOCIDAL HEIR TO APOCALYPSE.

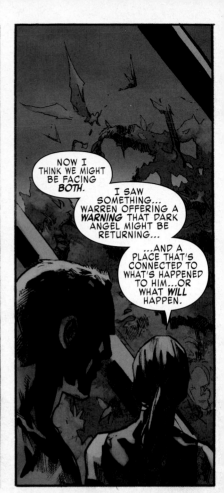

NOW I THINK WE MIGHT BE FACING BOTH.

I SAW SOMETHING... WARREN OFFERING A WARNING THAT DARK ANGEL MIGHT BE RETURNING...

...AND A PLACE THAT'S CONNECTED TO WHAT'S HAPPENED TO HIM...OR WHAT WILL HAPPEN.

I'VE BEEN READING THIS MOMENT.

IF THE DARK ANGEL RETURNS, I'M NOT SURE IF I'M STRONG ENOUGH TO KILL HIM AGAIN.

AND IF IT'S NOT DARK ANGEL...IF IT'S WARREN...

...HOW CAN I FACE HIM?

THIS TIME, I AM HERE TO HELP YOU.

YOU DON'T UNDERSTAND.

YOU CAN'T POSSIBLY.

YOU'VE SEEN HORRORS, BUT THIS--

SHOW ME.

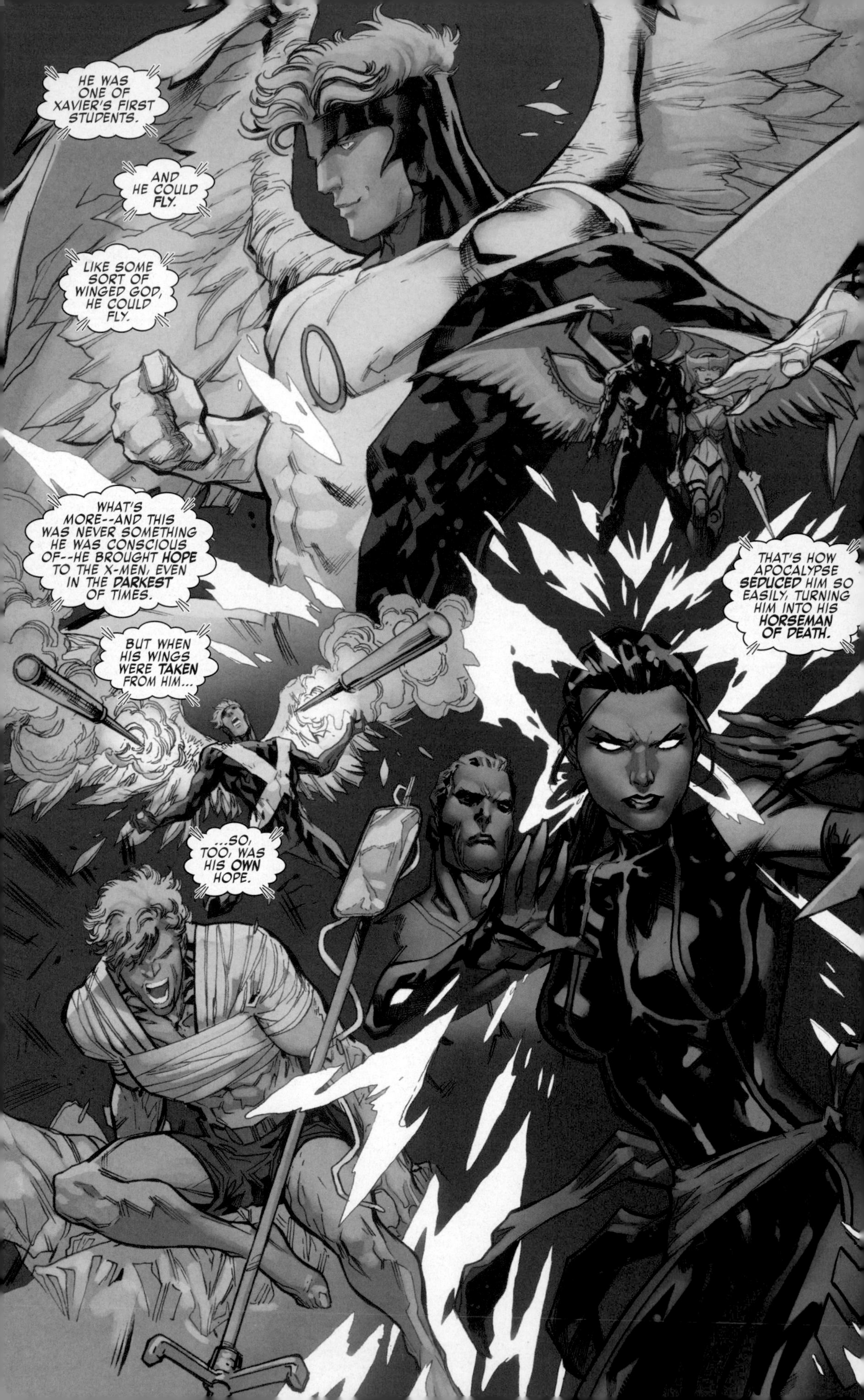
HE WAS ONE OF XAVIER'S FIRST STUDENTS.
AND HE COULD **FLY**.
LIKE SOME SORT OF WINGED GOD, HE COULD FLY.
WHAT'S MORE--AND THIS WAS NEVER SOMETHING HE WAS CONSCIOUS OF--HE BROUGHT **HOPE** TO THE X-MEN, EVEN IN THE **DARKEST** OF TIMES.
BUT WHEN HIS WINGS WERE **TAKEN** FROM HIM...
...SO, TOO, WAS HIS **OWN** HOPE.
THAT'S HOW APOCALYPSE **SEDUCED** HIM SO EASILY, TURNING HIM INTO HIS **HORSEMAN OF DEATH.**

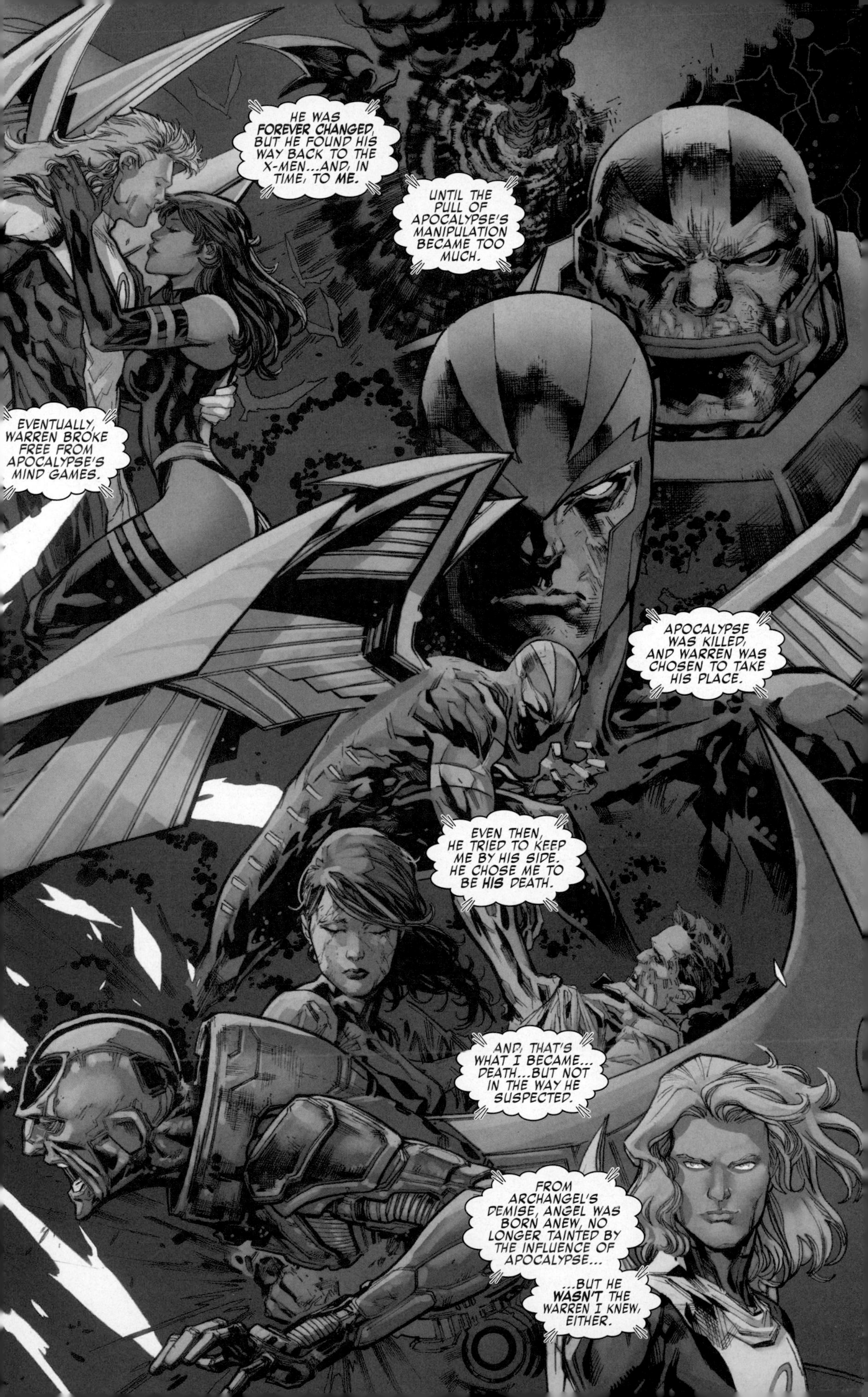
HE WAS **FOREVER CHANGED**, BUT HE FOUND HIS WAY BACK TO THE X-MEN...AND, IN TIME, TO **ME**.
UNTIL THE PULL OF APOCALYPSE'S MANIPULATION BECAME TOO MUCH.
EVENTUALLY, WARREN BROKE FREE FROM APOCALYPSE'S MIND GAMES.
APOCALYPSE WAS KILLED, AND WARREN WAS CHOSEN TO TAKE HIS PLACE.
EVEN THEN, HE TRIED TO KEEP ME BY HIS SIDE. HE CHOSE ME TO BE **HIS** DEATH.
AND THAT'S WHAT I BECAME... DEATH...BUT NOT IN THE WAY HE SUSPECTED.
FROM ARCHANGEL'S DEMISE, ANGEL WAS BORN ANEW, NO LONGER TAINTED BY THE INFLUENCE OF APOCALYPSE...
...BUT HE **WASN'T** THE WARREN I KNEW, EITHER.

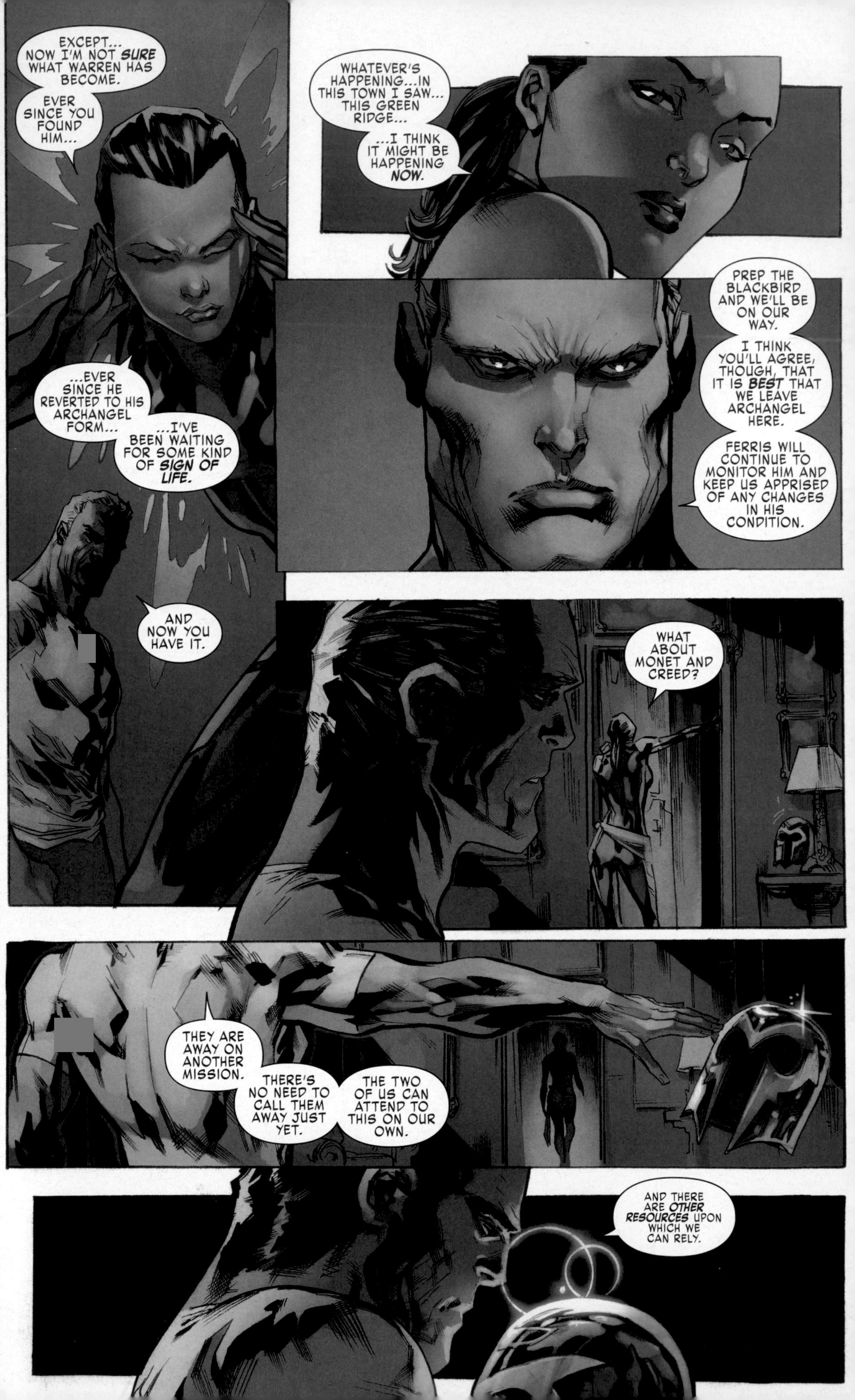
EXCEPT... NOW I'M NOT SURE WHAT WARREN HAS BECOME.
EVER SINCE YOU FOUND HIM...
...EVER SINCE HE REVERTED TO HIS ARCHANGEL FORM...
...I'VE BEEN WAITING FOR SOME KIND OF SIGN OF LIFE.
AND NOW YOU HAVE IT.
WHATEVER'S HAPPENING...IN THIS TOWN I SAW... THIS GREEN RIDGE...
...I THINK IT MIGHT BE HAPPENING NOW.
PREP THE BLACKBIRD AND WE'LL BE ON OUR WAY.
I THINK YOU'LL AGREE, THOUGH, THAT IT IS BEST THAT WE LEAVE ARCHANGEL HERE.
FERRIS WILL CONTINUE TO MONITOR HIM AND KEEP US APPRISED OF ANY CHANGES IN HIS CONDITION.
WHAT ABOUT MONET AND CREED?
THEY ARE AWAY ON ANOTHER MISSION.
THERE'S NO NEED TO CALL THEM AWAY JUST YET.
THE TWO OF US CAN ATTEND TO THIS ON OUR OWN.
AND THERE ARE OTHER RESOURCES UPON WHICH WE CAN RELY.

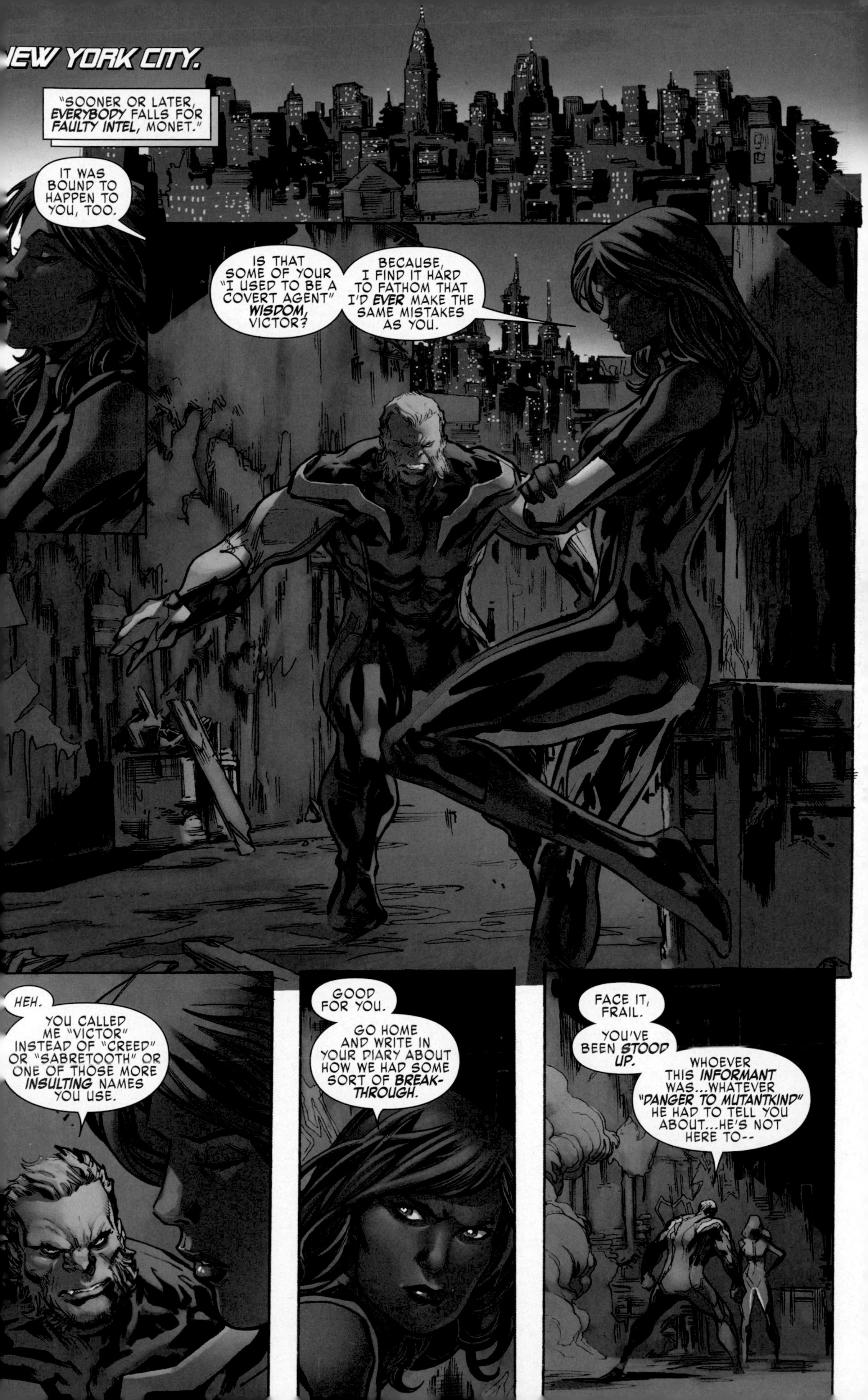
NEW YORK CITY.
"SOONER OR LATER, EVERYBODY FALLS FOR FAULTY INTEL, MONET."
IT WAS BOUND TO HAPPEN TO YOU, TOO.
IS THAT SOME OF YOUR "I USED TO BE A COVERT AGENT" WISDOM, VICTOR?
BECAUSE, I FIND IT HARD TO FATHOM THAT I'D EVER MAKE THE SAME MISTAKES AS YOU.
HEH.
YOU CALLED ME "VICTOR" INSTEAD OF "CREED" OR "SABRETOOTH" OR ONE OF THOSE MORE INSULTING NAMES YOU USE.
GOOD FOR YOU.
GO HOME AND WRITE IN YOUR DIARY ABOUT HOW WE HAD SOME SORT OF BREAK-THROUGH.
FACE IT, FRAIL.
YOU'VE BEEN STOOD UP.
WHOEVER THIS INFORMANT WAS...WHATEVER "DANGER TO MUTANTKIND" HE HAD TO TELL YOU ABOUT...HE'S NOT HERE TO--

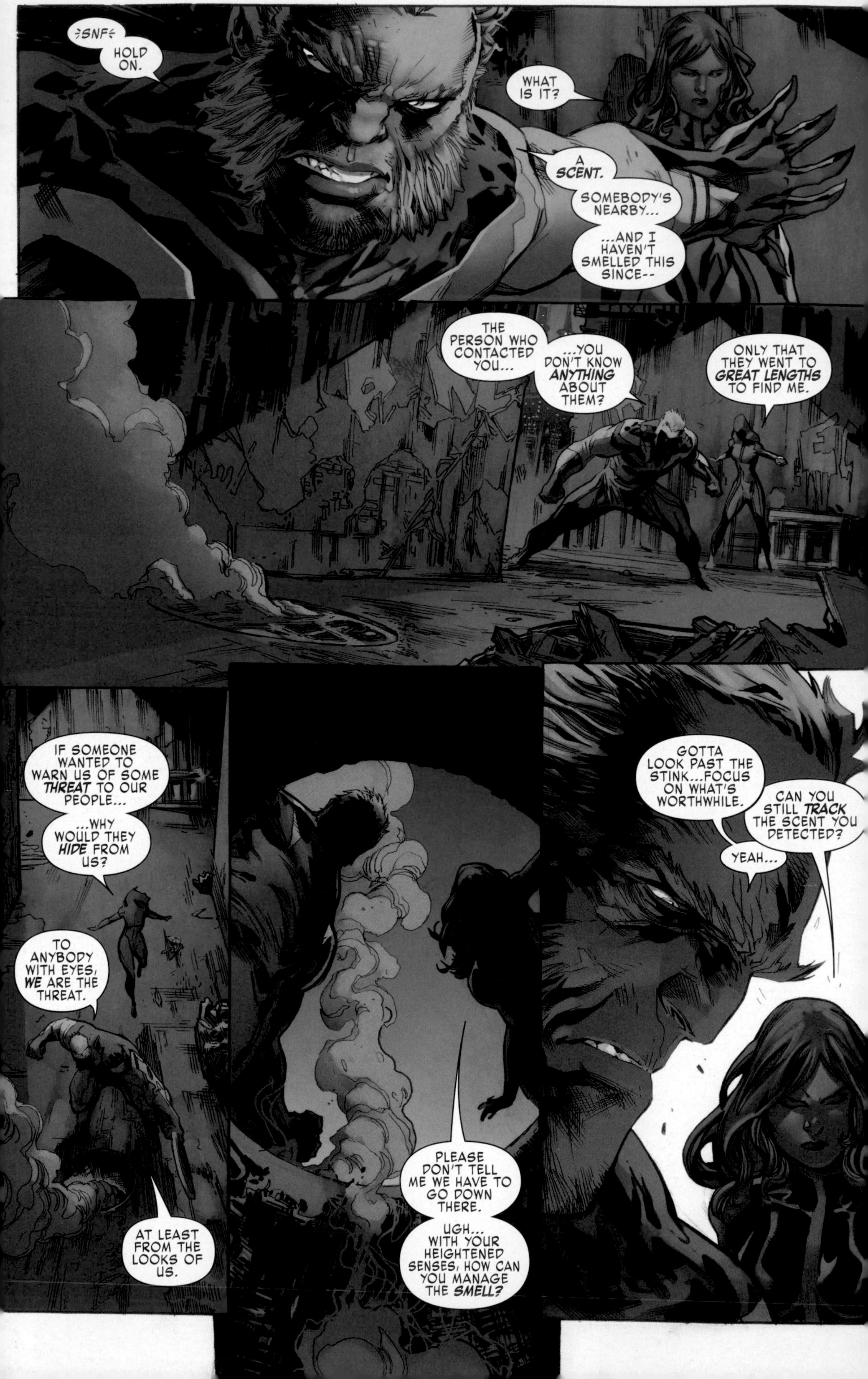

⁼SNF⁼
HOLD ON.
WHAT IS IT?
A SCENT.
SOMEBODY'S NEARBY...
...AND I HAVEN'T SMELLED THIS SINCE--
THE PERSON WHO CONTACTED YOU...
...YOU DON'T KNOW ANYTHING ABOUT THEM?
ONLY THAT THEY WENT TO GREAT LENGTHS TO FIND ME.
IF SOMEONE WANTED TO WARN US OF SOME THREAT TO OUR PEOPLE...
...WHY WOULD THEY HIDE FROM US?
TO ANYBODY WITH EYES, WE ARE THE THREAT.
AT LEAST FROM THE LOOKS OF US.
PLEASE DON'T TELL ME WE HAVE TO GO DOWN THERE.
UGH... WITH YOUR HEIGHTENED SENSES, HOW CAN YOU MANAGE THE SMELL?
GOTTA LOOK PAST THE STINK...FOCUS ON WHAT'S WORTHWHILE.
CAN YOU STILL TRACK THE SCENT YOU DETECTED?
YEAH...

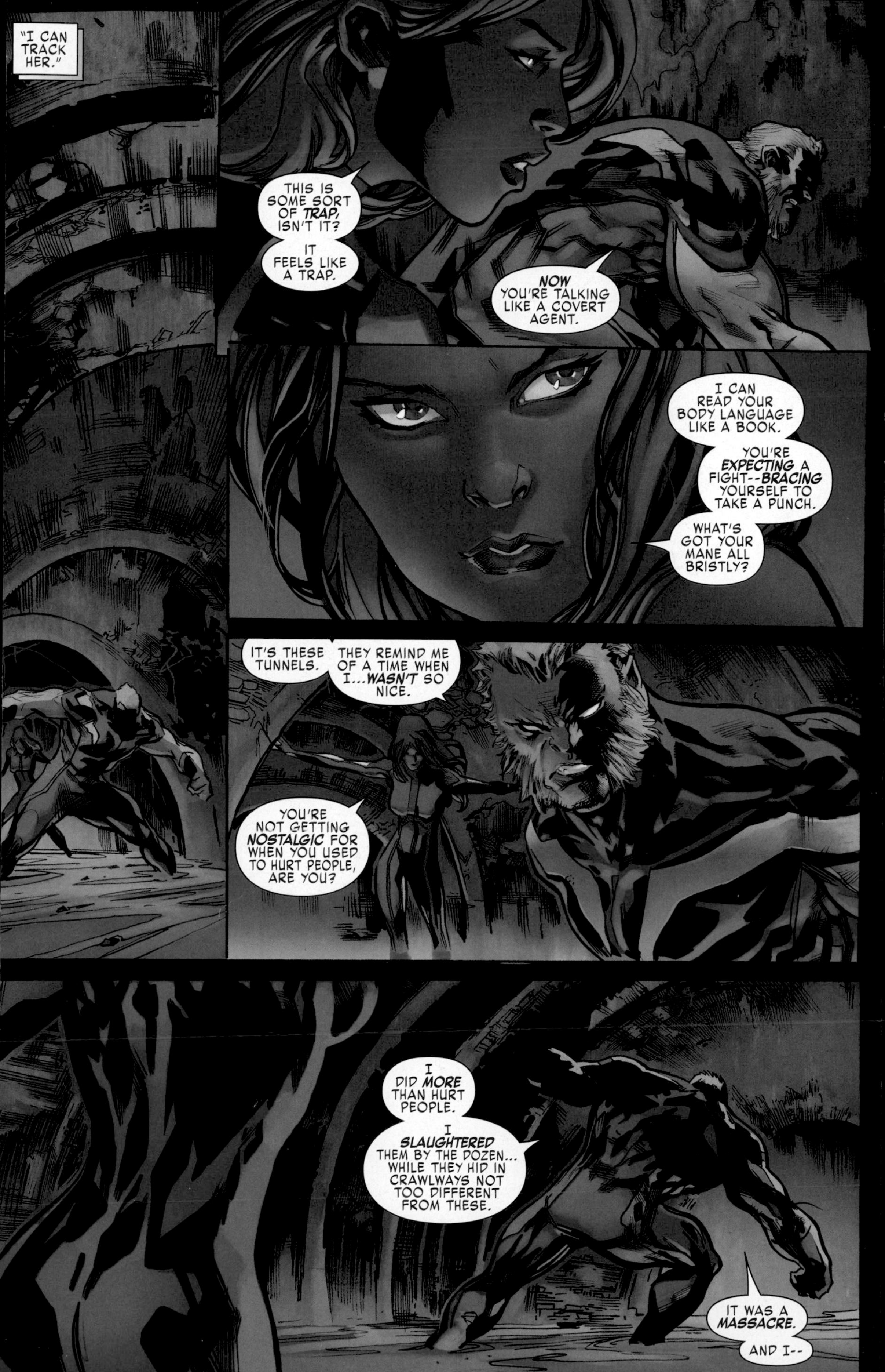

"I CAN TRACK HER."
THIS IS SOME SORT OF TRAP, ISN'T IT?
IT FEELS LIKE A TRAP.
NOW YOU'RE TALKING LIKE A COVERT AGENT.
I CAN READ YOUR BODY LANGUAGE LIKE A BOOK.
YOU'RE EXPECTING A FIGHT--BRACING YOURSELF TO TAKE A PUNCH.
WHAT'S GOT YOUR MANE ALL BRISTLY?
IT'S THESE TUNNELS.
THEY REMIND ME OF A TIME WHEN I...WASN'T SO NICE.
YOU'RE NOT GETTING NOSTALGIC FOR WHEN YOU USED TO HURT PEOPLE, ARE YOU?
I DID MORE THAN HURT PEOPLE.
I SLAUGHTERED THEM BY THE DOZEN... WHILE THEY HID IN CRAWLWAYS NOT TOO DIFFERENT FROM THESE.
IT WAS A MASSACRE.
AND I--

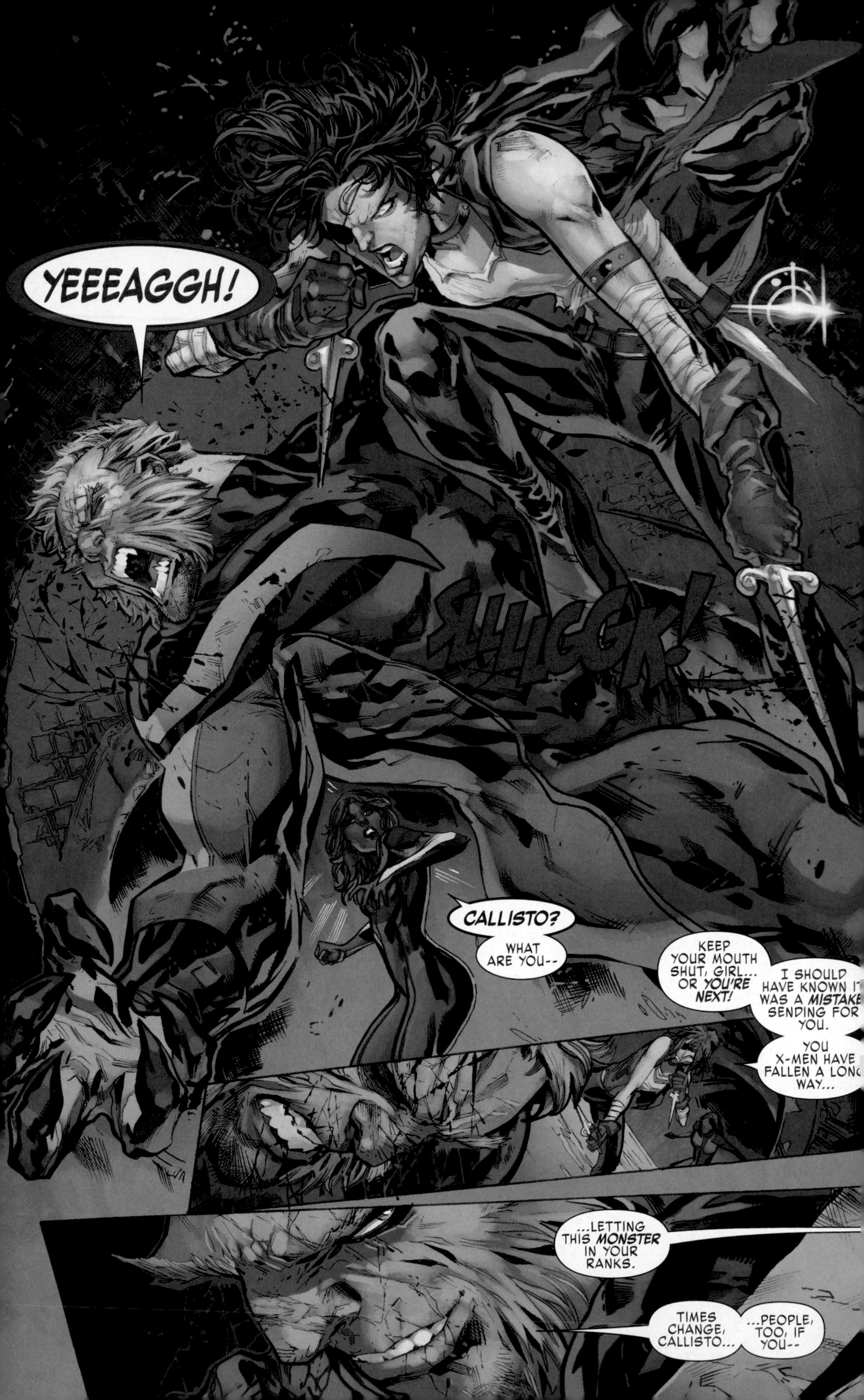
YEEEAGGH!
SHLLICGGK!
CALLISTO?
WHAT ARE YOU--
KEEP YOUR MOUTH SHUT, GIRL... OR YOU'RE NEXT!
I SHOULD HAVE KNOWN IT WAS A MISTAKE SENDING FOR YOU.
YOU X-MEN HAVE FALLEN A LONG WAY...
...LETTING THIS MONSTER IN YOUR RANKS.
TIMES CHANGE, CALLISTO...
...PEOPLE, TOO, IF YOU--

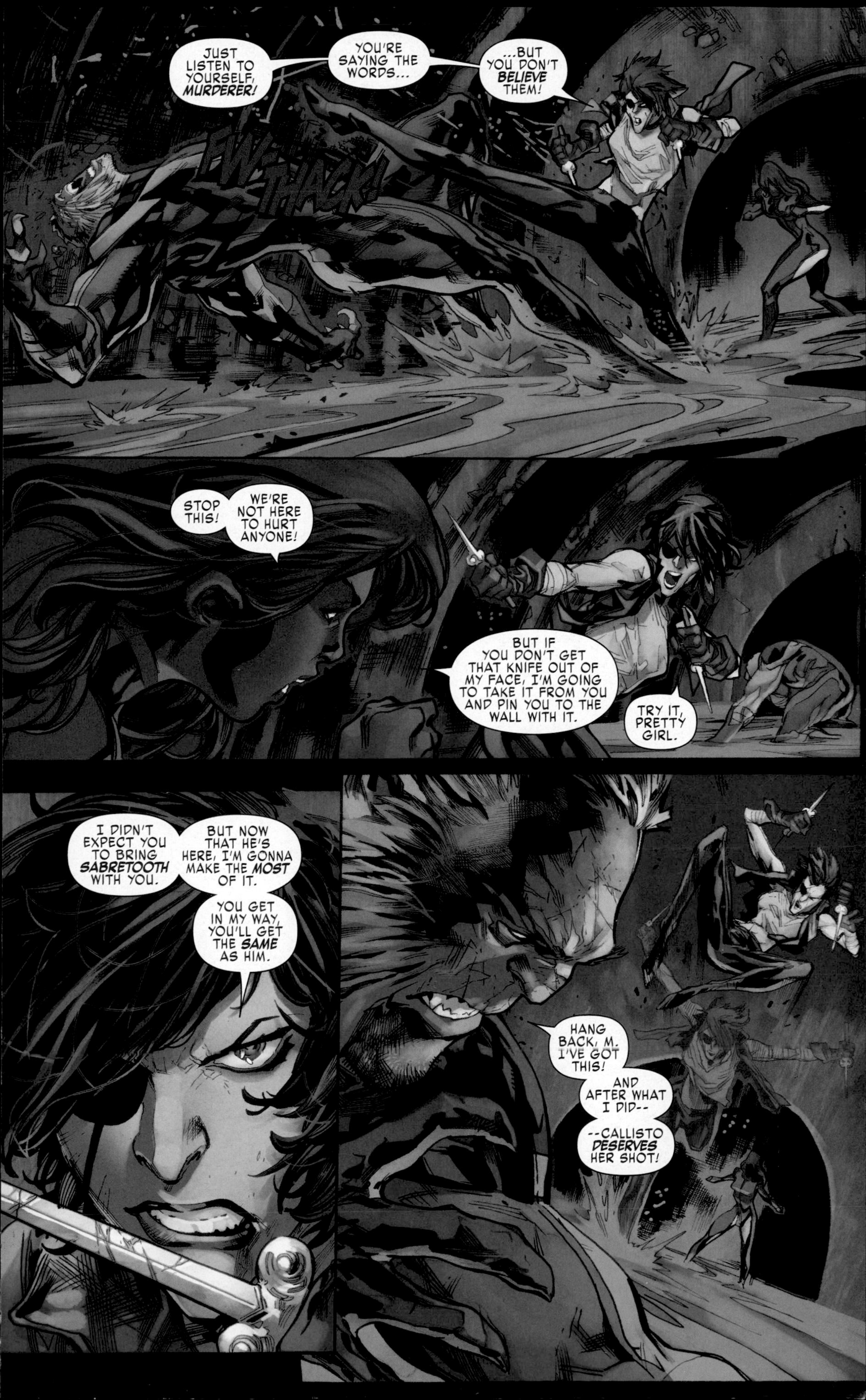

JUST LISTEN TO YOURSELF, MURDERER!
YOU'RE SAYING THE WORDS...
...BUT YOU DON'T BELIEVE THEM!
FW-THACK!
STOP THIS!
WE'RE NOT HERE TO HURT ANYONE!
BUT IF YOU DON'T GET THAT KNIFE OUT OF MY FACE, I'M GOING TO TAKE IT FROM YOU AND PIN YOU TO THE WALL WITH IT.
TRY IT, PRETTY GIRL.
I DIDN'T EXPECT YOU TO BRING SABRETOOTH WITH YOU.
BUT NOW THAT HE'S HERE, I'M GONNA MAKE THE MOST OF IT.
YOU GET IN MY WAY, YOU'LL GET THE SAME AS HIM.
HANG BACK, M. I'VE GOT THIS!
AND AFTER WHAT I DID--
--CALLISTO DESERVES HER SHOT!

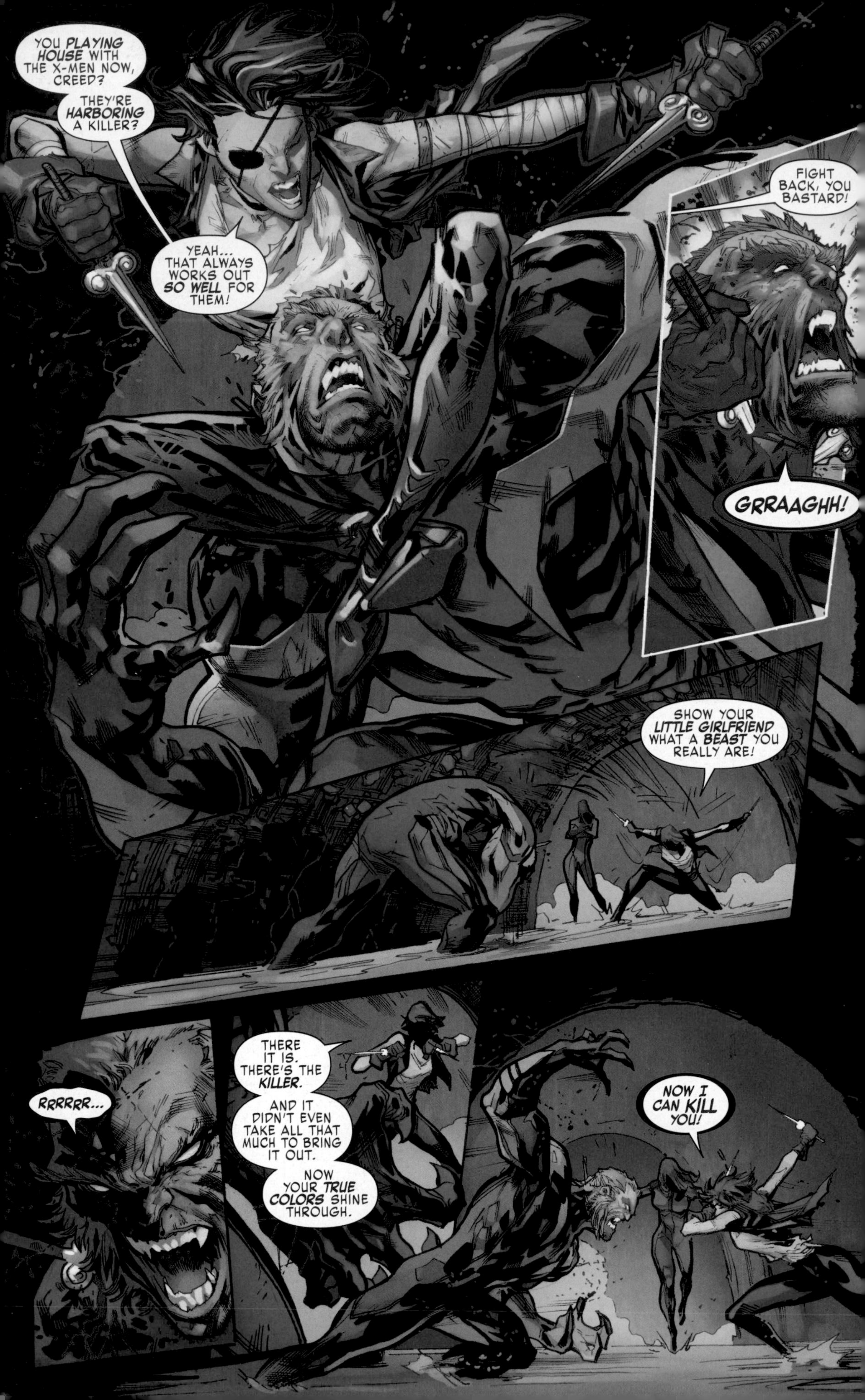
YOU PLAYING HOUSE WITH THE X-MEN NOW, CREED?
THEY'RE HARBORING A KILLER?
YEAH... THAT ALWAYS WORKS OUT SO WELL FOR THEM!
FIGHT BACK, YOU BASTARD!
GRRAAGHH!
SHOW YOUR LITTLE GIRLFRIEND WHAT A BEAST YOU REALLY ARE!
RRRRRR...
THERE IT IS. THERE'S THE KILLER.
AND IT DIDN'T EVEN TAKE ALL THAT MUCH TO BRING IT OUT.
NOW YOUR TRUE COLORS SHINE THROUGH.
NOW I CAN KILL YOU!

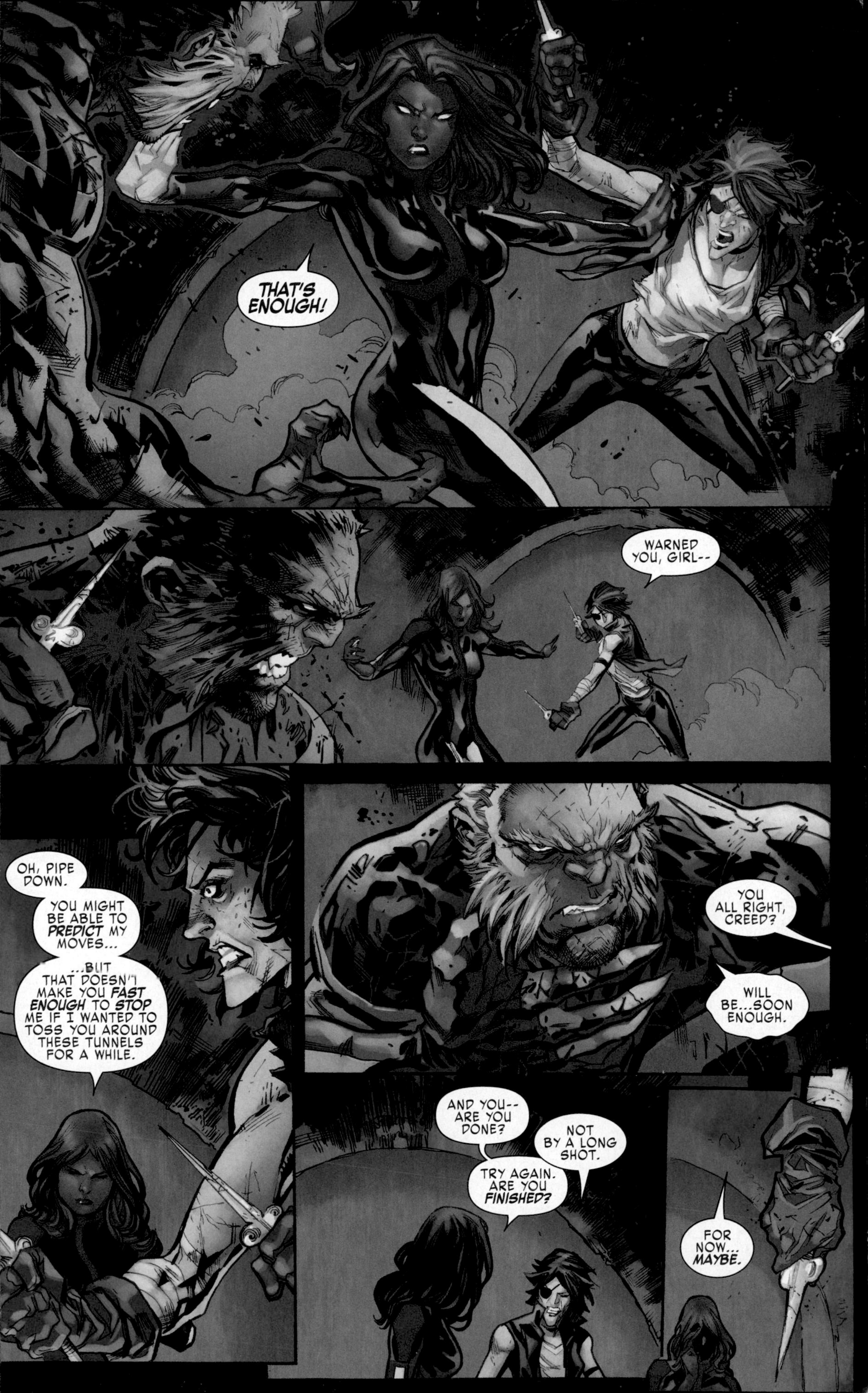
THAT'S ENOUGH!
WARNED YOU, GIRL--
OH, PIPE DOWN.
YOU MIGHT BE ABLE TO PREDICT MY MOVES...
...BUT THAT DOESN'T MAKE YOU FAST ENOUGH TO STOP ME IF I WANTED TO TOSS YOU AROUND THESE TUNNELS FOR A WHILE.
YOU ALL RIGHT, CREED?
WILL BE...SOON ENOUGH.
AND YOU-- ARE YOU DONE?
NOT BY A LONG SHOT.
TRY AGAIN. ARE YOU FINISHED?
FOR NOW... MAYBE.

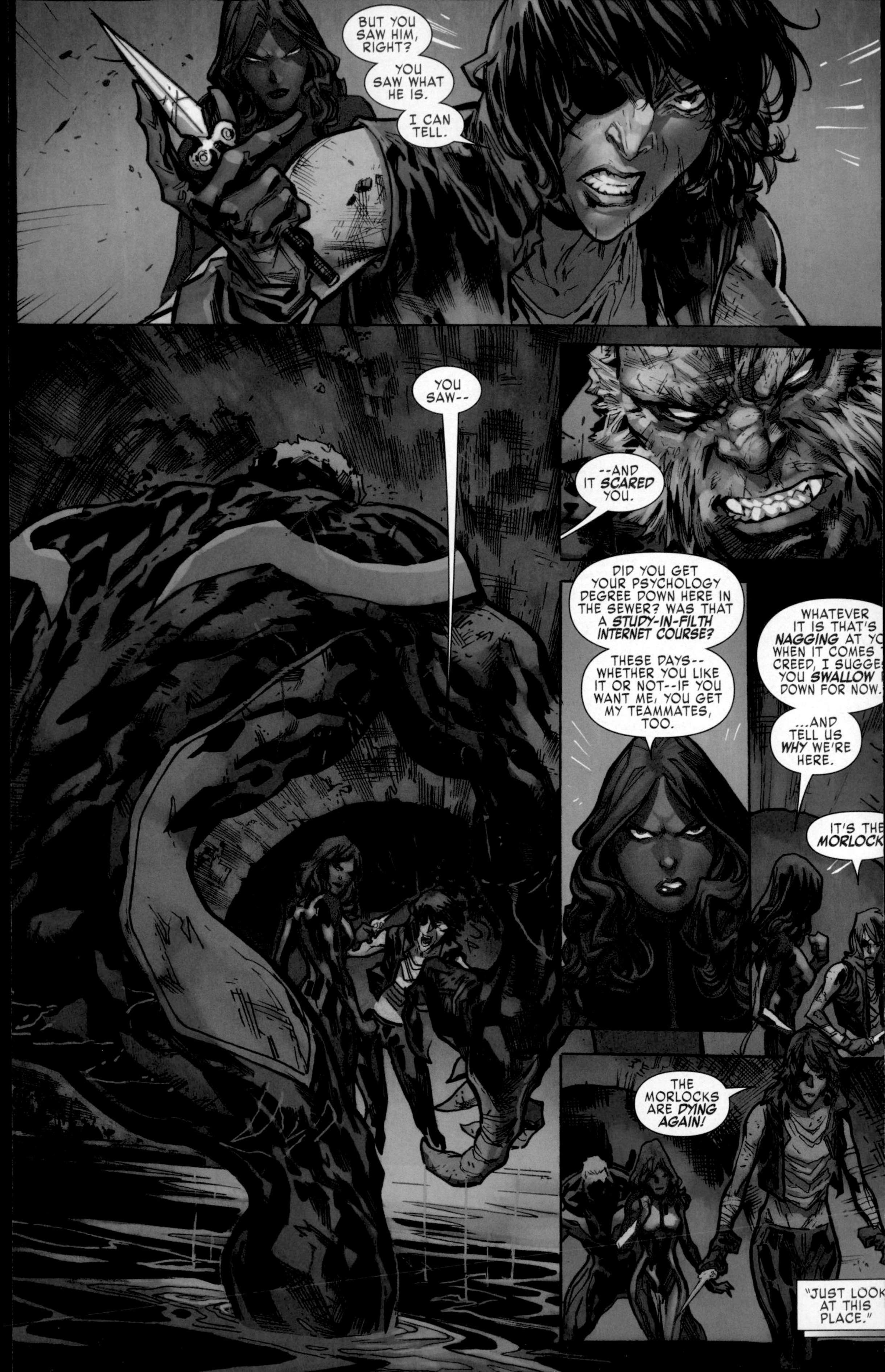

BUT YOU SAW HIM, RIGHT?
YOU SAW WHAT HE IS.
I CAN TELL.
YOU SAW--
--AND IT SCARED YOU.
DID YOU GET YOUR PSYCHOLOGY DEGREE DOWN HERE IN THE SEWER? WAS THAT A STUDY-IN-FILTH INTERNET COURSE?
THESE DAYS--WHETHER YOU LIKE IT OR NOT--IF YOU WANT ME, YOU GET MY TEAMMATES, TOO.
...AND TELL US WHY WE'RE HERE.
THE MORLOCKS ARE DYING AGAIN!
"JUST LOOK AT THIS PLACE."

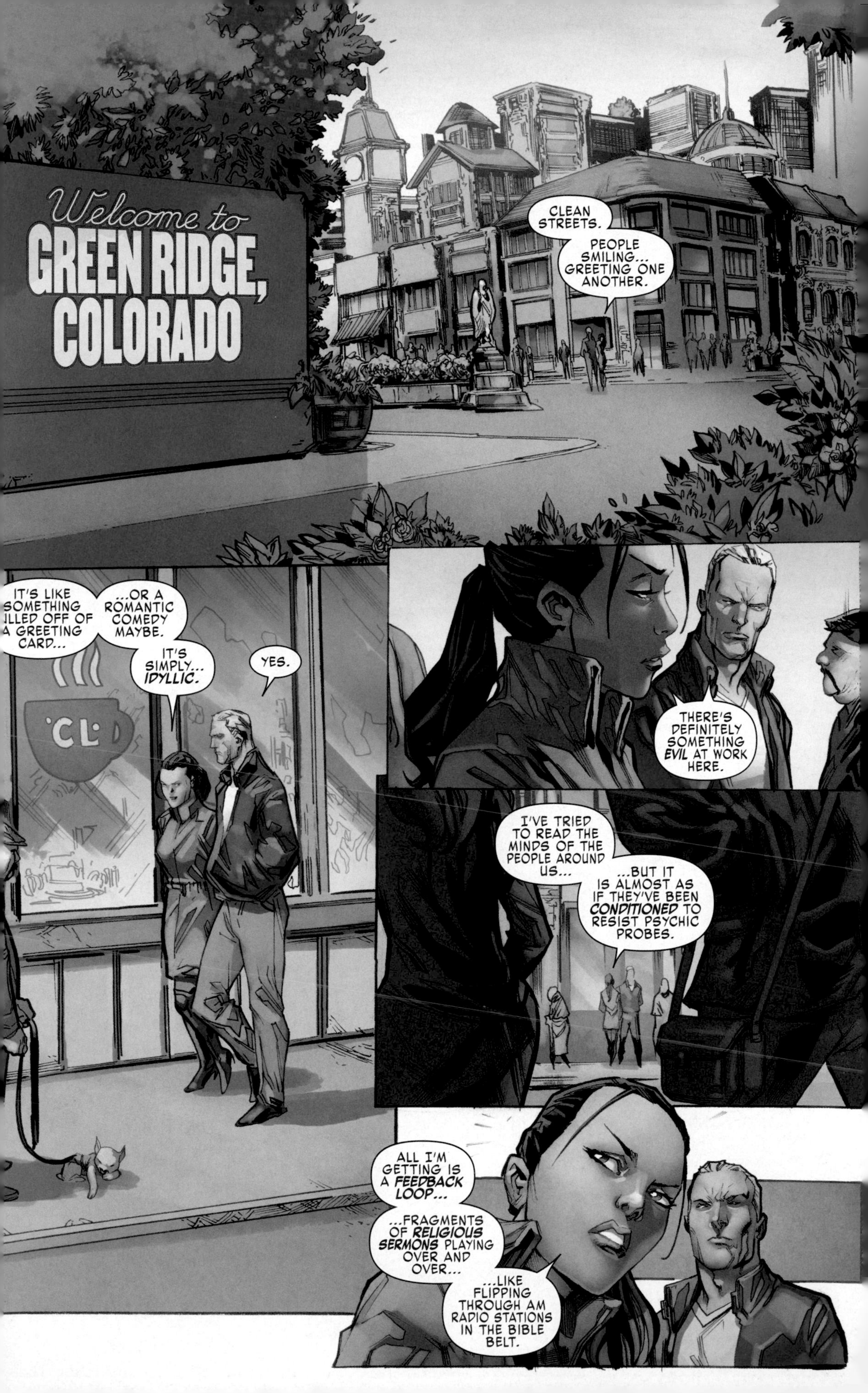
Welcome to
GREEN RIDGE, COLORADO
CLEAN STREETS.
PEOPLE SMILING... GREETING ONE ANOTHER.
IT'S LIKE SOMETHING ULLED OFF OF A GREETING CARD...
...OR A ROMANTIC COMEDY MAYBE.
IT'S SIMPLY... IDYLLIC.
YES.
THERE'S DEFINITELY SOMETHING EVIL AT WORK HERE.
I'VE TRIED TO READ THE MINDS OF THE PEOPLE AROUND US...
...BUT IT IS ALMOST AS IF THEY'VE BEEN CONDITIONED TO RESIST PSYCHIC PROBES.
ALL I'M GETTING IS A FEEDBACK LOOP...
...FRAGMENTS OF RELIGIOUS SERMONS PLAYING OVER AND OVER...
...LIKE FLIPPING THROUGH AM RADIO STATIONS IN THE BIBLE BELT.

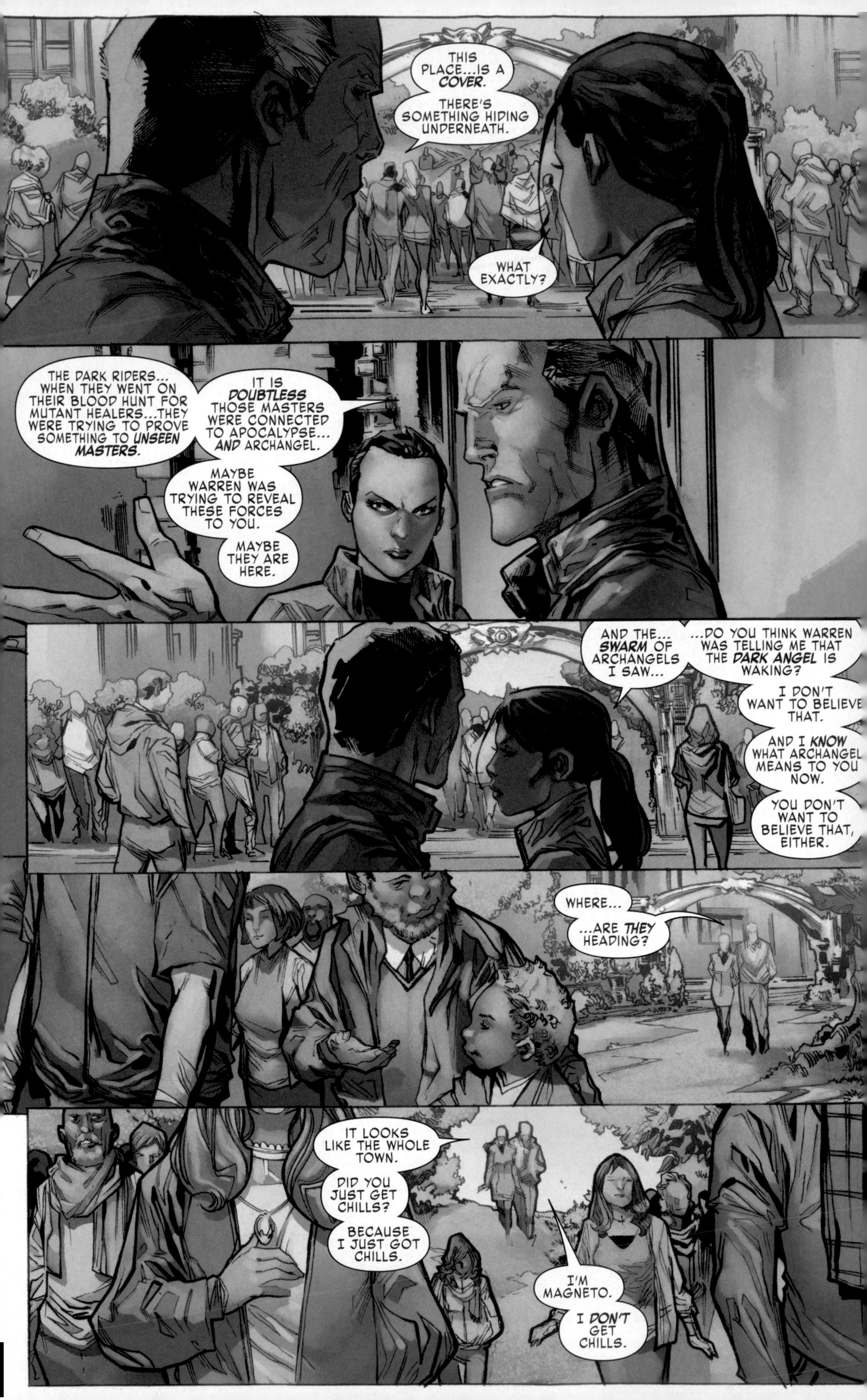
THIS PLACE...IS A COVER.
THERE'S SOMETHING HIDING UNDERNEATH.
WHAT EXACTLY?
THE DARK RIDERS... WHEN THEY WENT ON THEIR BLOOD HUNT FOR MUTANT HEALERS...THEY WERE TRYING TO PROVE SOMETHING TO UNSEEN MASTERS.
IT IS DOUBTLESS THOSE MASTERS WERE CONNECTED TO APOCALYPSE... AND ARCHANGEL.
MAYBE WARREN WAS TRYING TO REVEAL THESE FORCES TO YOU.
MAYBE THEY ARE HERE.
AND THE... SWARM OF ARCHANGELS I SAW...
...DO YOU THINK WARREN WAS TELLING ME THAT THE DARK ANGEL IS WAKING?
I DON'T WANT TO BELIEVE THAT.
AND I KNOW WHAT ARCHANGEL MEANS TO YOU NOW.
YOU DON'T WANT TO BELIEVE THAT, EITHER.
WHERE...
...ARE THEY HEADING?
IT LOOKS LIKE THE WHOLE TOWN.
DID YOU JUST GET CHILLS?
BECAUSE I JUST GOT CHILLS.
I'M MAGNETO.
I DON'T GET CHILLS.

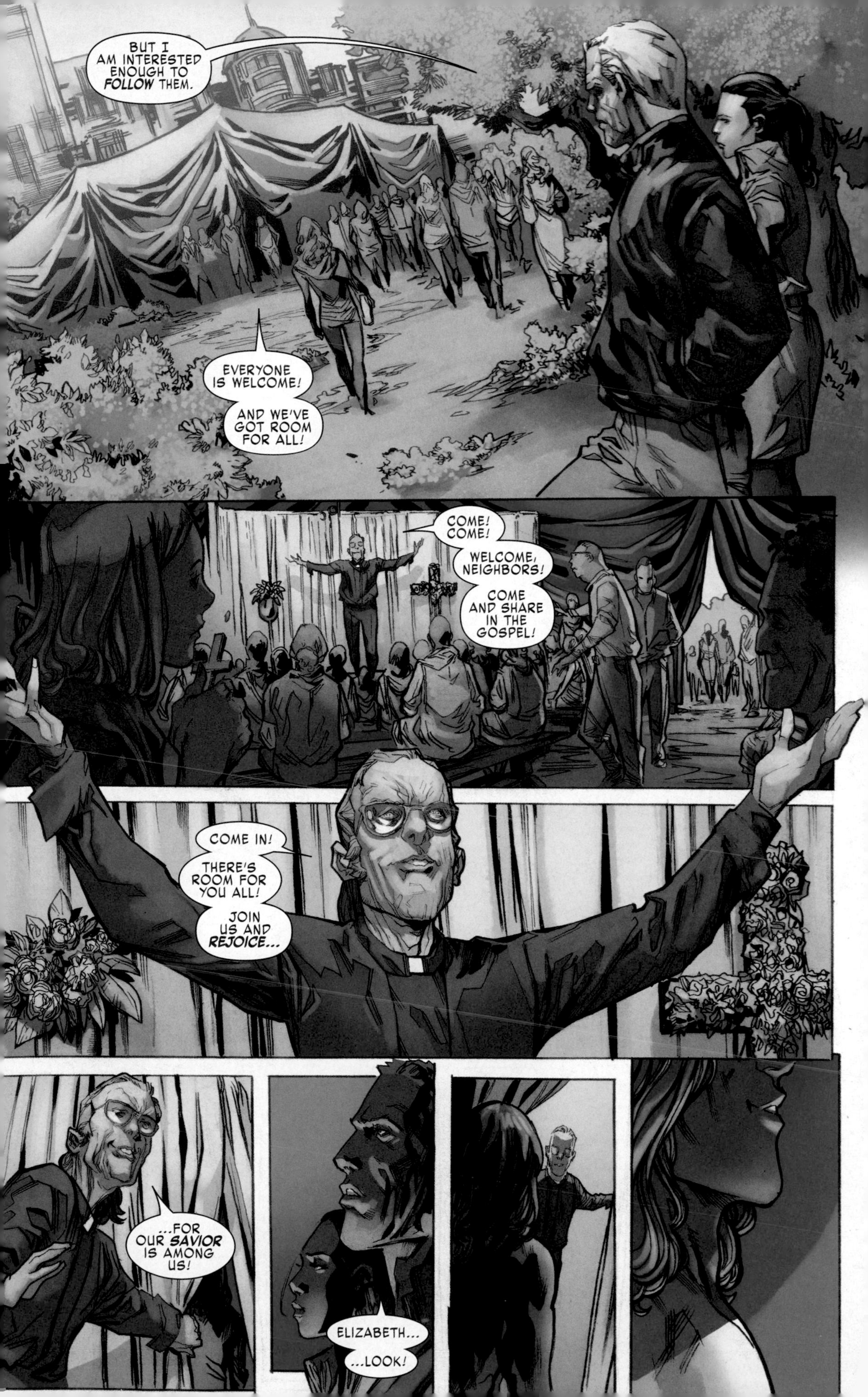
BUT I AM INTERESTED ENOUGH TO *FOLLOW* THEM.
EVERYONE IS WELCOME!
AND WE'VE GOT ROOM FOR ALL!
COME! COME!
WELCOME, NEIGHBORS!
COME AND SHARE IN THE GOSPEL!
COME IN!
THERE'S ROOM FOR YOU ALL!
JOIN US AND *REJOICE*...
...FOR OUR *SAVIOR* IS AMONG US!
ELIZABETH...
...LOOK!

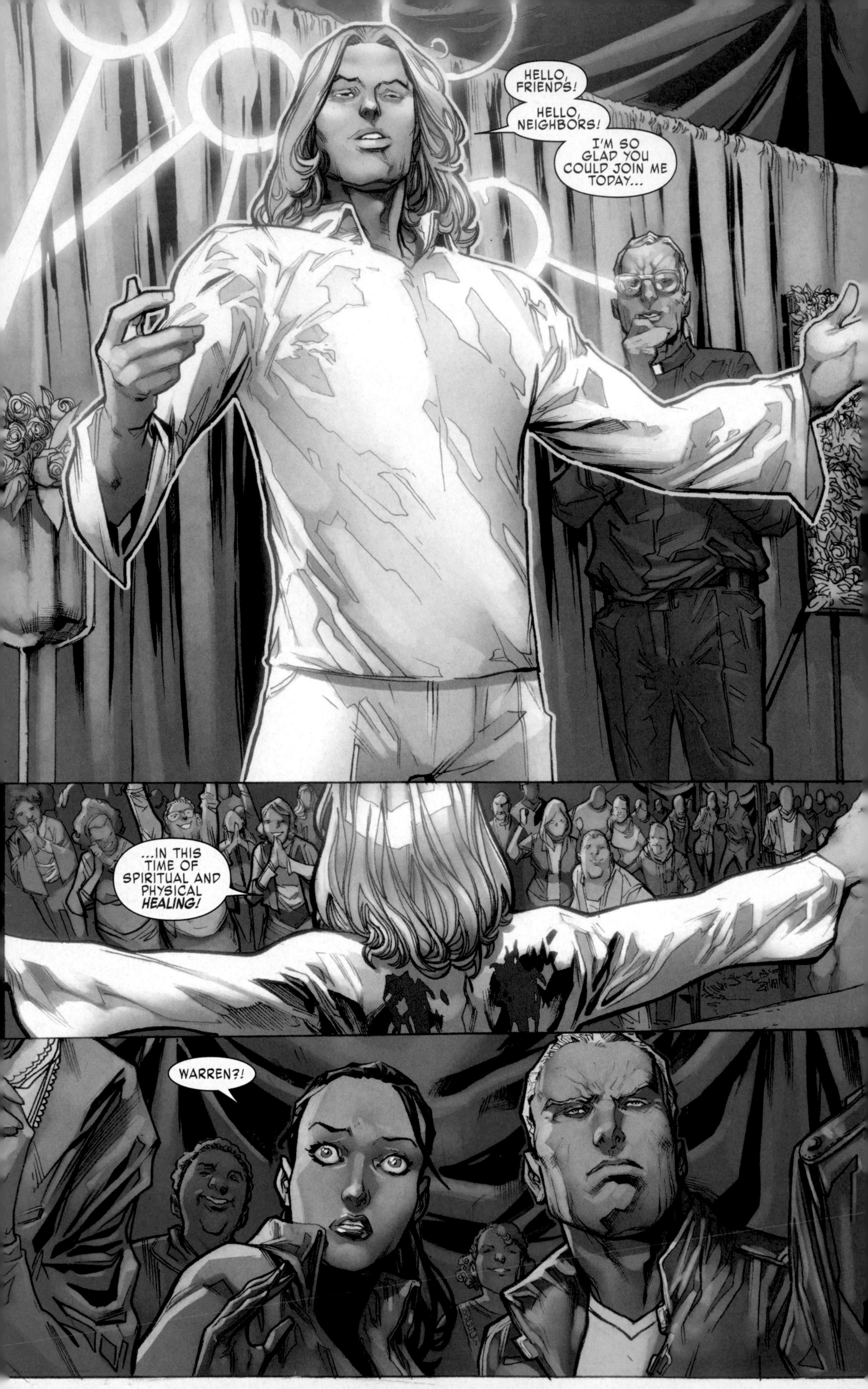
HELLO, FRIENDS!
HELLO, NEIGHBORS!
I'M SO GLAD YOU COULD JOIN ME TODAY...
...IN THIS TIME OF SPIRITUAL AND PHYSICAL *HEALING!*
WARREN?!

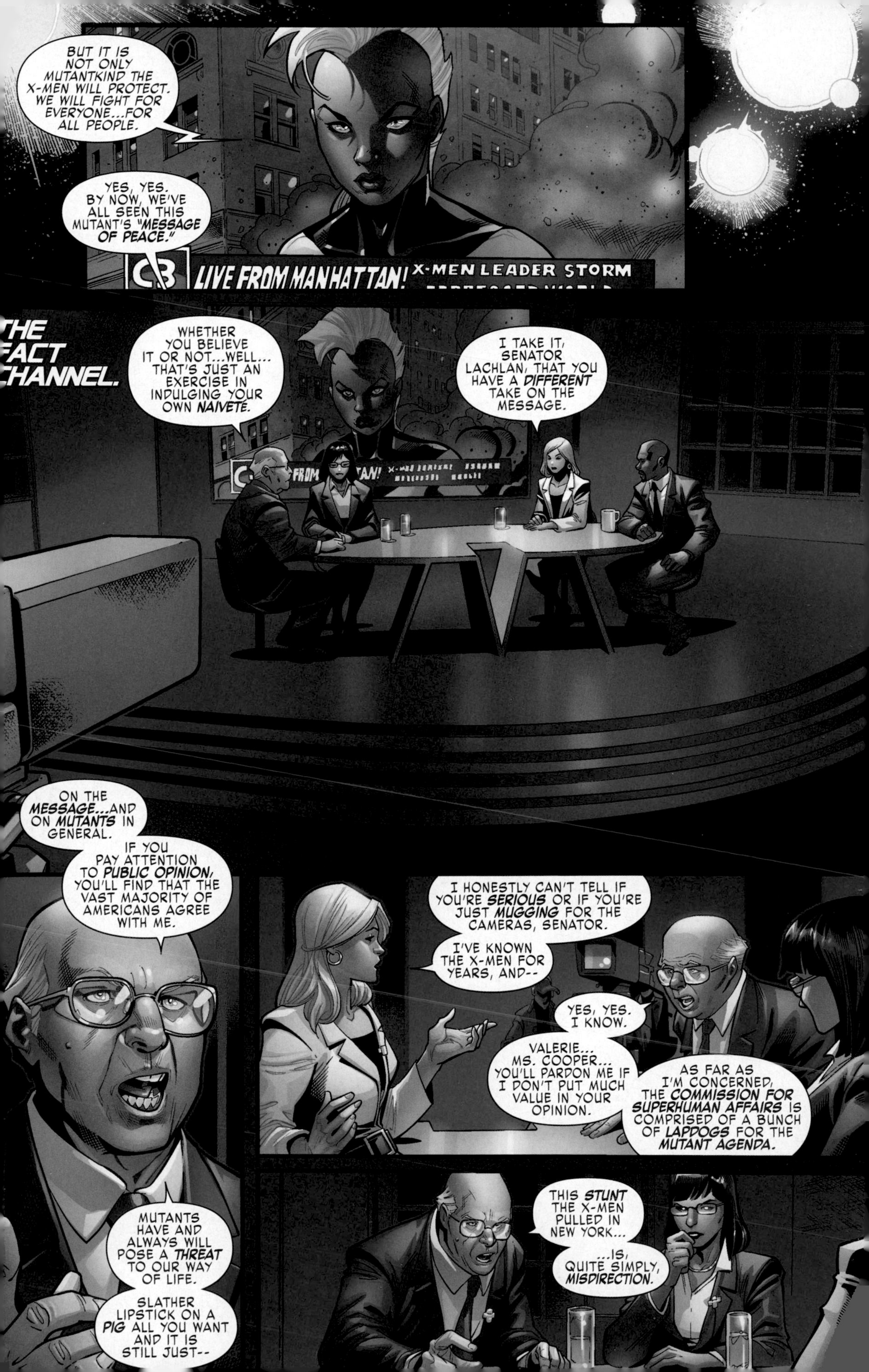
BUT IT IS NOT ONLY MUTANTKIND THE X-MEN WILL PROTECT. WE WILL FIGHT FOR EVERYONE...FOR ALL PEOPLE.
YES, YES. BY NOW, WE'VE ALL SEEN THIS MUTANT'S "MESSAGE OF PEACE."
LIVE FROM MANHATTAN! X-MEN LEADER STORM
THE
ACT
HANNEL.
WHETHER YOU BELIEVE IT OR NOT...WELL... THAT'S JUST AN EXERCISE IN INDULGING YOUR OWN NAIVETÉ.
I TAKE IT, SENATOR LACHLAN, THAT YOU HAVE A DIFFERENT TAKE ON THE MESSAGE.
ON THE MESSAGE...AND ON MUTANTS IN GENERAL.
IF YOU PAY ATTENTION TO PUBLIC OPINION, YOU'LL FIND THAT THE VAST MAJORITY OF AMERICANS AGREE WITH ME.
MUTANTS HAVE AND ALWAYS WILL POSE A THREAT TO OUR WAY OF LIFE.
SLATHER LIPSTICK ON A PIG ALL YOU WANT AND IT IS STILL JUST--
I HONESTLY CAN'T TELL IF YOU'RE SERIOUS OR IF YOU'RE JUST MUGGING FOR THE CAMERAS, SENATOR.
I'VE KNOWN THE X-MEN FOR YEARS, AND--
YES, YES. I KNOW.
VALERIE... MS. COOPER... YOU'LL PARDON ME IF I DON'T PUT MUCH VALUE IN YOUR OPINION.
AS FAR AS I'M CONCERNED, THE COMMISSION FOR SUPERHUMAN AFFAIRS IS COMPRISED OF A BUNCH OF LAPDOGS FOR THE MUTANT AGENDA.
THIS STUNT THE X-MEN PULLED IN NEW YORK...
...IS, QUITE SIMPLY, MISDIRECTION.

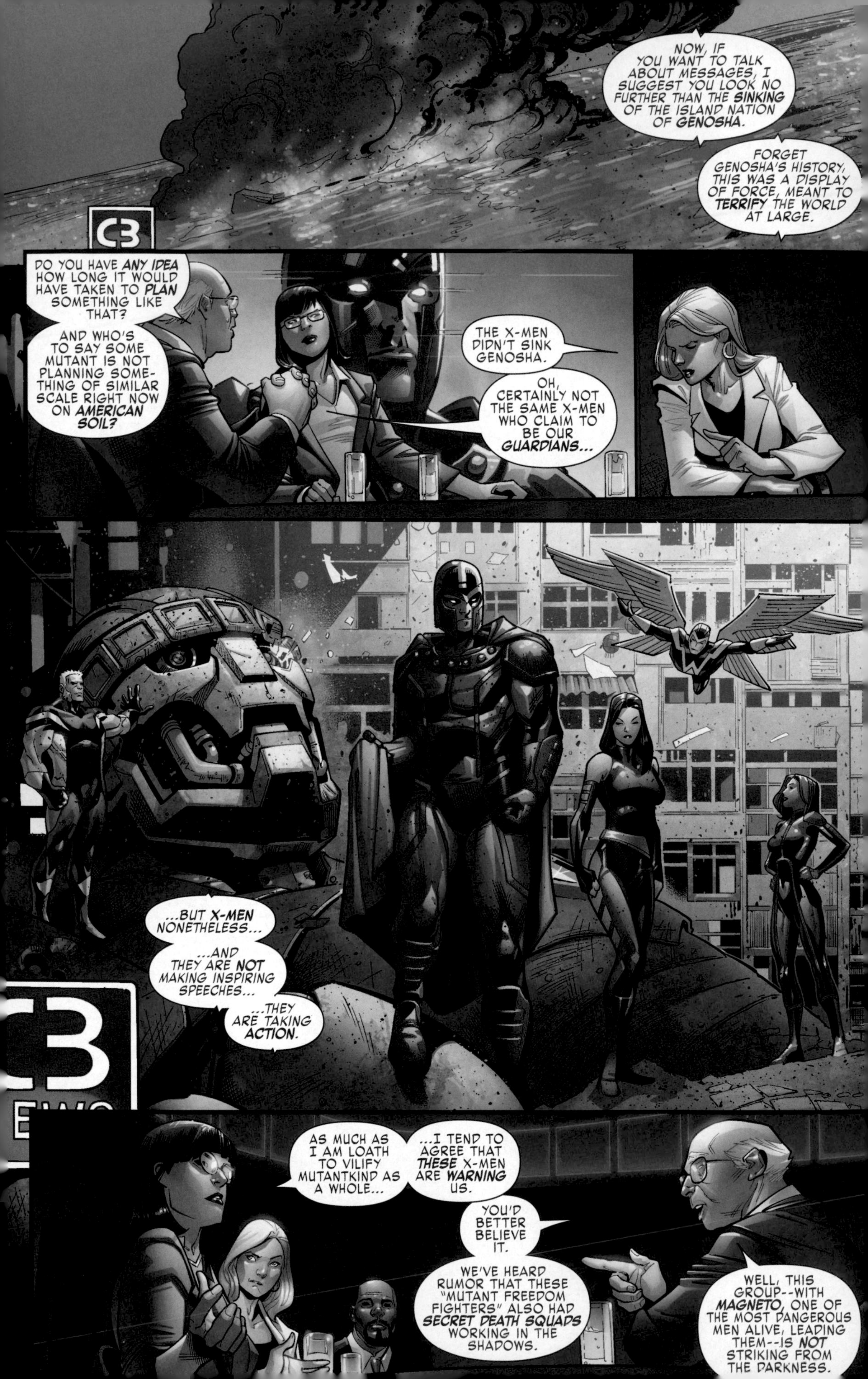
NOW, IF YOU WANT TO TALK ABOUT MESSAGES, I SUGGEST YOU LOOK NO FURTHER THAN THE SINKING OF THE ISLAND NATION OF GENOSHA.
FORGET GENOSHA'S HISTORY, THIS WAS A DISPLAY OF FORCE, MEANT TO TERRIFY THE WORLD AT LARGE.
C3
DO YOU HAVE ANY IDEA HOW LONG IT WOULD HAVE TAKEN TO PLAN SOMETHING LIKE THAT?
AND WHO'S TO SAY SOME MUTANT IS NOT PLANNING SOMETHING OF SIMILAR SCALE RIGHT NOW ON AMERICAN SOIL?
THE X-MEN DIDN'T SINK GENOSHA.
OH, CERTAINLY NOT THE SAME X-MEN WHO CLAIM TO BE OUR GUARDIANS...
...BUT X-MEN NONETHELESS...
...AND THEY ARE NOT MAKING INSPIRING SPEECHES...
...THEY ARE TAKING ACTION.
C3
AS MUCH AS I AM LOATH TO VILIFY MUTANTKIND AS A WHOLE...
...I TEND TO AGREE THAT THESE X-MEN ARE WARNING US.
YOU'D BETTER BELIEVE IT.
WE'VE HEARD RUMOR THAT THESE "MUTANT FREEDOM FIGHTERS" ALSO HAD SECRET DEATH SQUADS WORKING IN THE SHADOWS.
WELL, THIS GROUP--WITH MAGNETO, ONE OF THE MOST DANGEROUS MEN ALIVE, LEADING THEM--IS NOT STRIKING FROM THE DARKNESS.

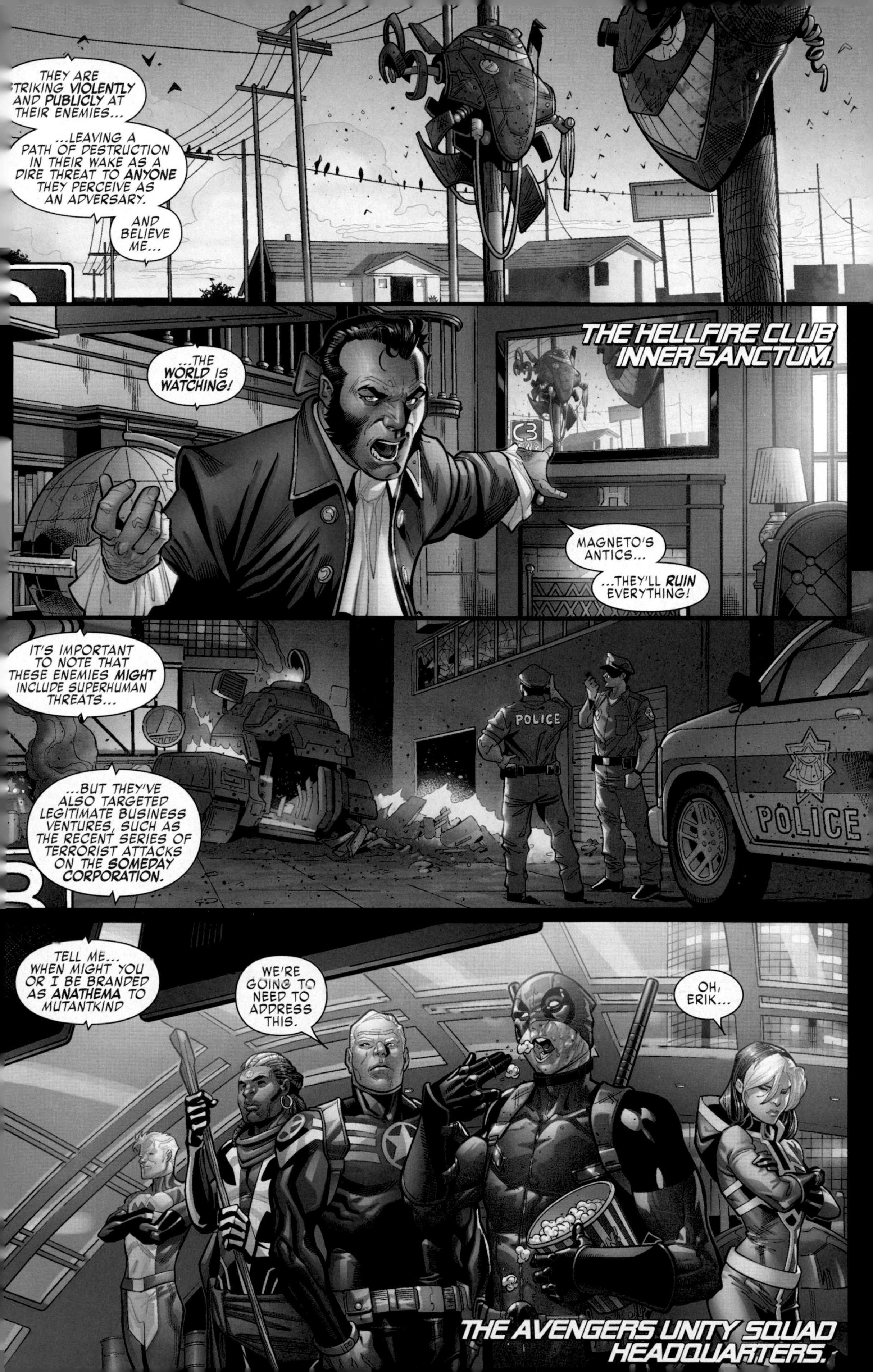
THEY ARE STRIKING VIOLENTLY AND PUBLICLY AT THEIR ENEMIES...
...LEAVING A PATH OF DESTRUCTION IN THEIR WAKE AS A DIRE THREAT TO ANYONE THEY PERCEIVE AS AN ADVERSARY.
AND BELIEVE ME...
THE HELLFIRE CLUB INNER SANCTUM.
...THE WORLD IS WATCHING!
MAGNETO'S ANTICS...
...THEY'LL RUIN EVERYTHING!
IT'S IMPORTANT TO NOTE THAT THESE ENEMIES MIGHT INCLUDE SUPERHUMAN THREATS...
...BUT THEY'VE ALSO TARGETED LEGITIMATE BUSINESS VENTURES, SUCH AS THE RECENT SERIES OF TERRORIST ATTACKS ON THE SOMEDAY CORPORATION.
POLICE
POLICE
TELL ME... WHEN MIGHT YOU OR I BE BRANDED AS ANATHEMA TO MUTANTKIND
WE'RE GOING TO NEED TO ADDRESS THIS.
OH, ERIK...
THE AVENGERS UNITY SQUAD HEADQUARTERS.

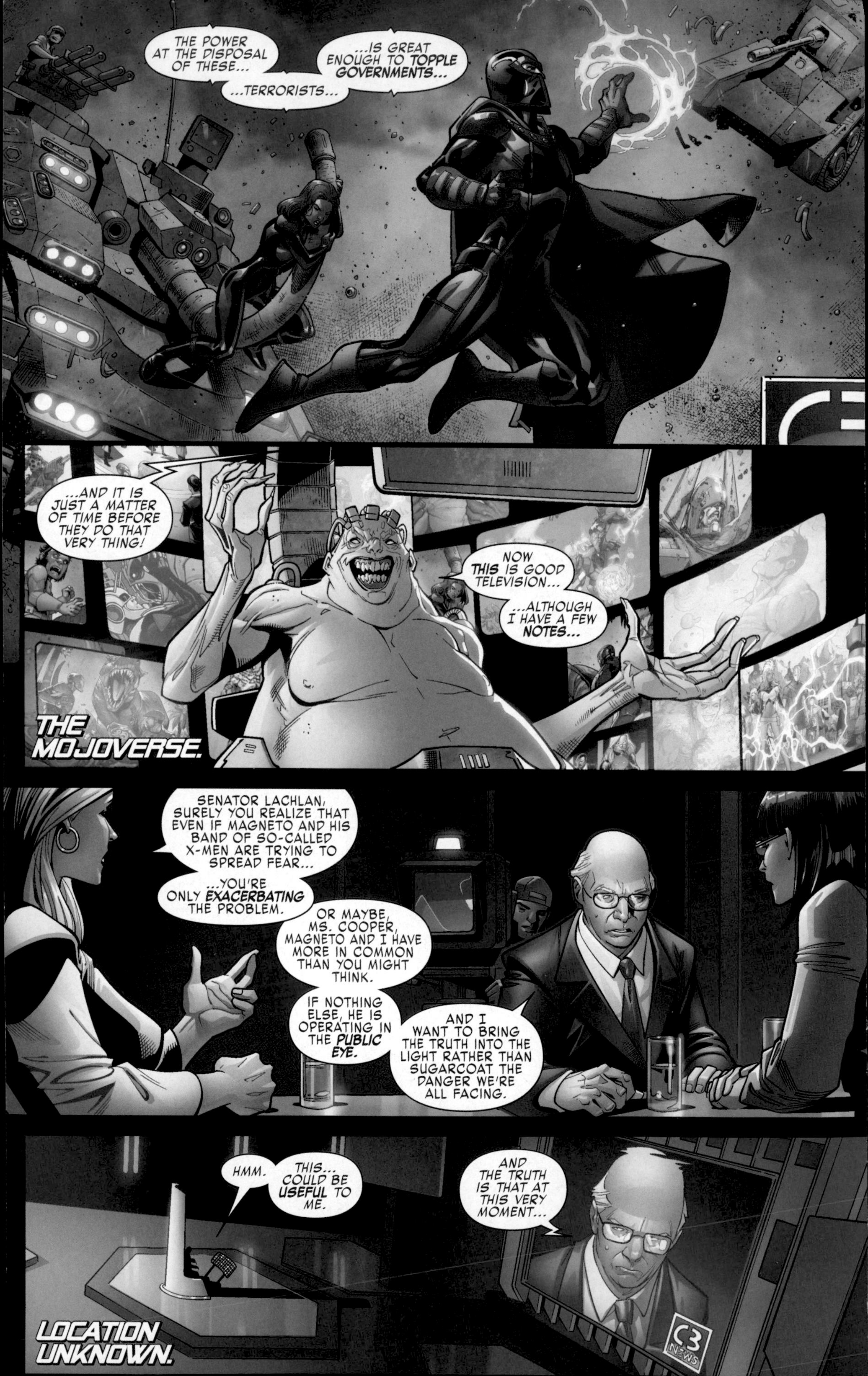
THE POWER AT THE DISPOSAL OF THESE...
...TERRORISTS...
...IS GREAT ENOUGH TO TOPPLE GOVERNMENTS...
...AND IT IS JUST A MATTER OF TIME BEFORE THEY DO THAT VERY THING!
NOW THIS IS GOOD TELEVISION...
...ALTHOUGH I HAVE A FEW NOTES...
THE MOJOVERSE.
SENATOR LACHLAN, SURELY YOU REALIZE THAT EVEN IF MAGNETO AND HIS BAND OF SO-CALLED X-MEN ARE TRYING TO SPREAD FEAR...
...YOU'RE ONLY EXACERBATING THE PROBLEM.
OR MAYBE, MS. COOPER, MAGNETO AND I HAVE MORE IN COMMON THAN YOU MIGHT THINK.
IF NOTHING ELSE, HE IS OPERATING IN THE PUBLIC EYE.
AND I WANT TO BRING THE TRUTH INTO THE LIGHT RATHER THAN SUGARCOAT THE DANGER WE'RE ALL FACING.
LOCATION UNKNOWN.
HMM.
THIS... COULD BE USEFUL TO ME.
AND THE TRUTH IS THAT AT THIS VERY MOMENT...
C3 NEWS

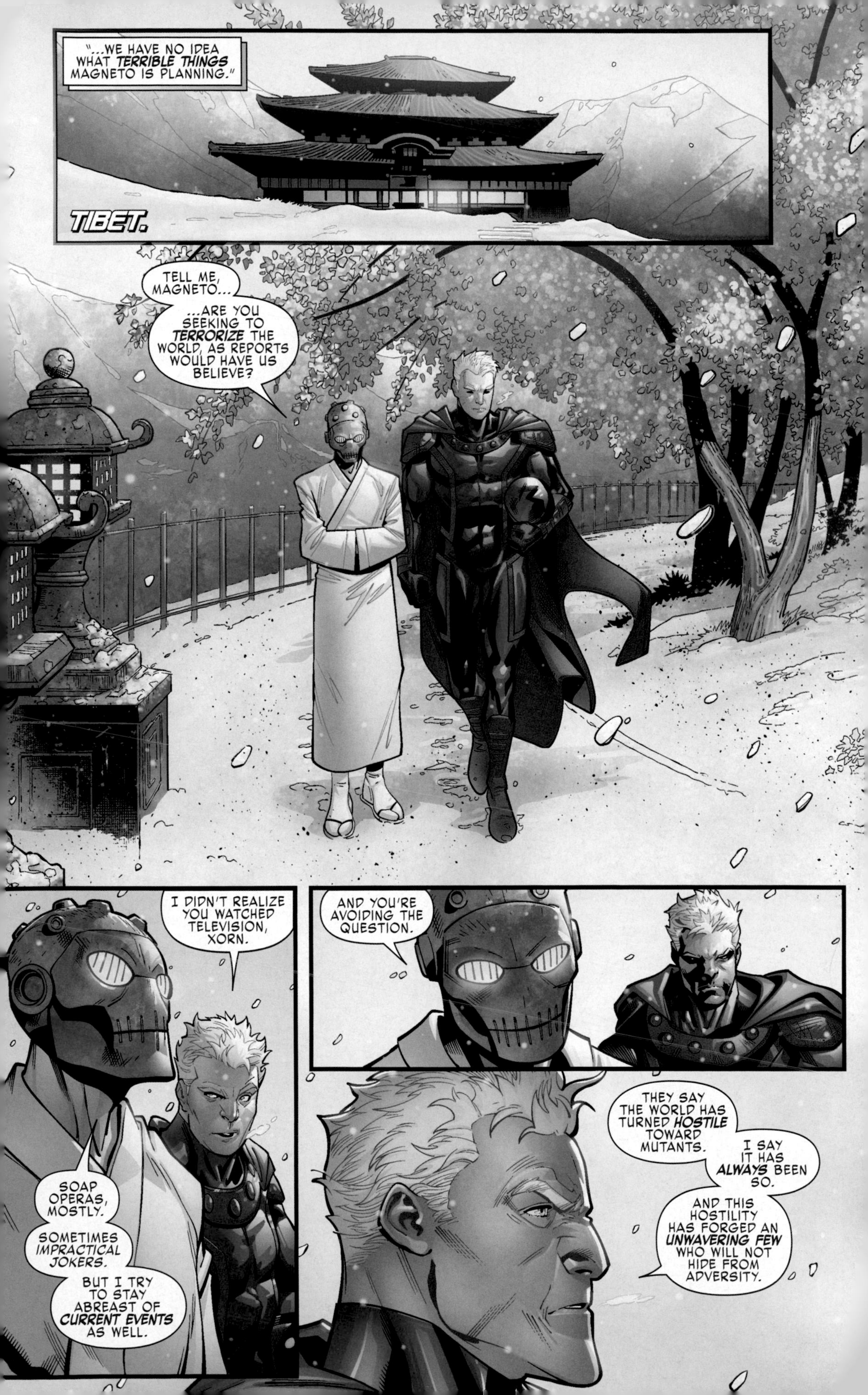
"...WE HAVE NO IDEA WHAT TERRIBLE THINGS MAGNETO IS PLANNING."
TIBET.
TELL ME, MAGNETO...
...ARE YOU SEEKING TO TERRORIZE THE WORLD, AS REPORTS WOULD HAVE US BELIEVE?
I DIDN'T REALIZE YOU WATCHED TELEVISION, XORN.
SOAP OPERAS, MOSTLY.
SOMETIMES IMPRACTICAL JOKERS.
BUT I TRY TO STAY ABREAST OF CURRENT EVENTS AS WELL.
AND YOU'RE AVOIDING THE QUESTION.
THEY SAY THE WORLD HAS TURNED HOSTILE TOWARD MUTANTS.
I SAY IT HAS ALWAYS BEEN SO.
AND THIS HOSTILITY HAS FORGED AN UNWAVERING FEW WHO WILL NOT HIDE FROM ADVERSITY.

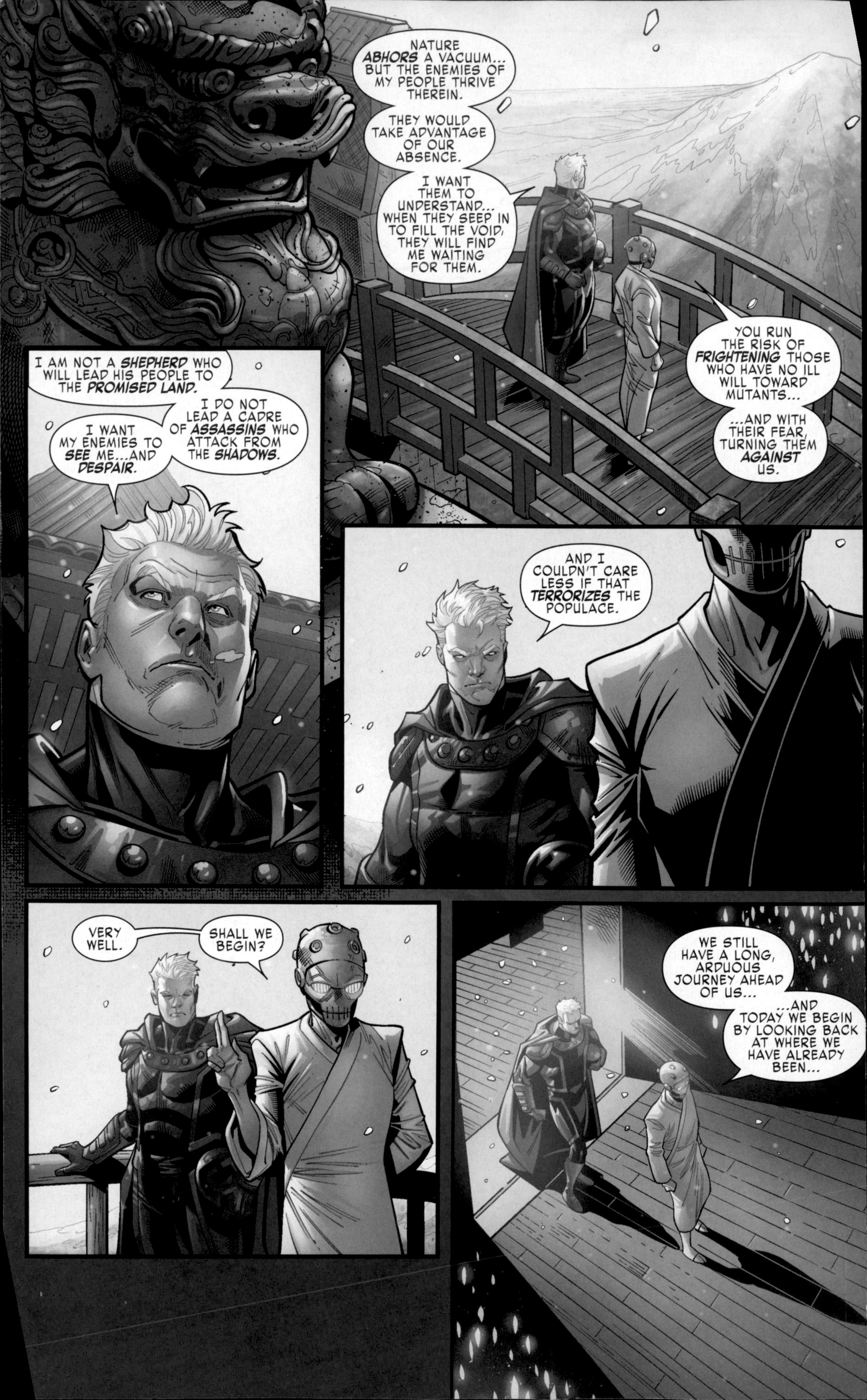
NATURE ABHORS A VACUUM... BUT THE ENEMIES OF MY PEOPLE THRIVE THEREIN.
THEY WOULD TAKE ADVANTAGE OF OUR ABSENCE.
I WANT THEM TO UNDERSTAND... WHEN THEY SEEP IN TO FILL THE VOID, THEY WILL FIND ME WAITING FOR THEM.
YOU RUN THE RISK OF FRIGHTENING THOSE WHO HAVE NO ILL WILL TOWARD MUTANTS...
...AND WITH THEIR FEAR, TURNING THEM AGAINST US.
I AM NOT A SHEPHERD WHO WILL LEAD HIS PEOPLE TO THE PROMISED LAND.
I DO NOT LEAD A CADRE OF ASSASSINS WHO ATTACK FROM THE SHADOWS.
I WANT MY ENEMIES TO SEE ME...AND DESPAIR.
AND I COULDN'T CARE LESS IF THAT TERRORIZES THE POPULACE.
VERY WELL.
SHALL WE BEGIN?
WE STILL HAVE A LONG, ARDUOUS JOURNEY AHEAD OF US...
...AND TODAY WE BEGIN BY LOOKING BACK AT WHERE WE HAVE ALREADY BEEN...

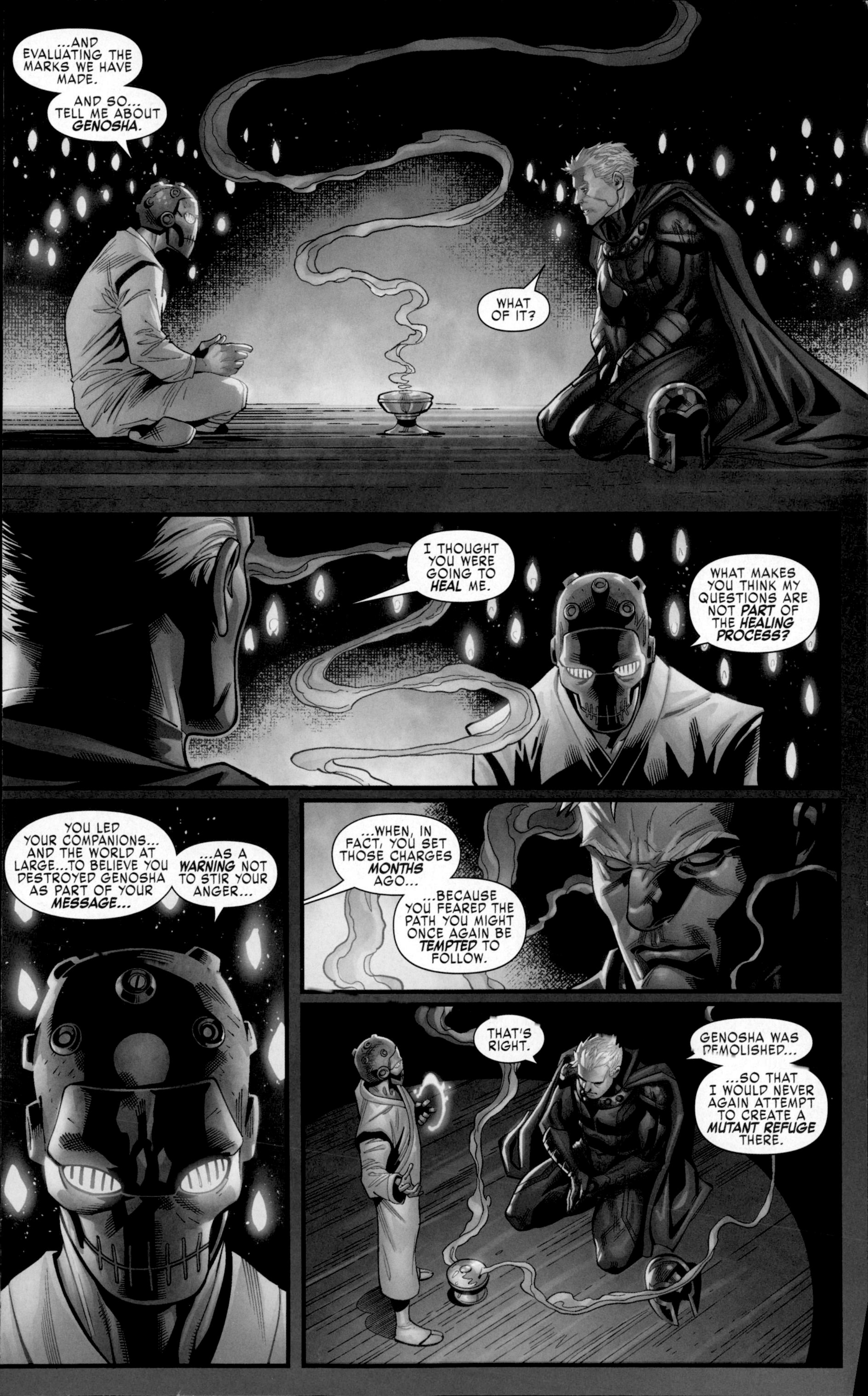
...AND EVALUATING THE MARKS WE HAVE MADE.
AND SO... TELL ME ABOUT GENOSHA.
WHAT OF IT?
I THOUGHT YOU WERE GOING TO HEAL ME.
WHAT MAKES YOU THINK MY QUESTIONS ARE NOT PART OF THE HEALING PROCESS?
YOU LED YOUR COMPANIONS... AND THE WORLD AT LARGE...TO BELIEVE YOU DESTROYED GENOSHA AS PART OF YOUR MESSAGE...
...AS A WARNING NOT TO STIR YOUR ANGER...
...WHEN, IN FACT, YOU SET THOSE CHARGES MONTHS AGO...
...BECAUSE YOU FEARED THE PATH YOU MIGHT ONCE AGAIN BE TEMPTED TO FOLLOW.
THAT'S RIGHT.
GENOSHA WAS DEMOLISHED...
...SO THAT I WOULD NEVER AGAIN ATTEMPT TO CREATE A MUTANT REFUGE THERE.

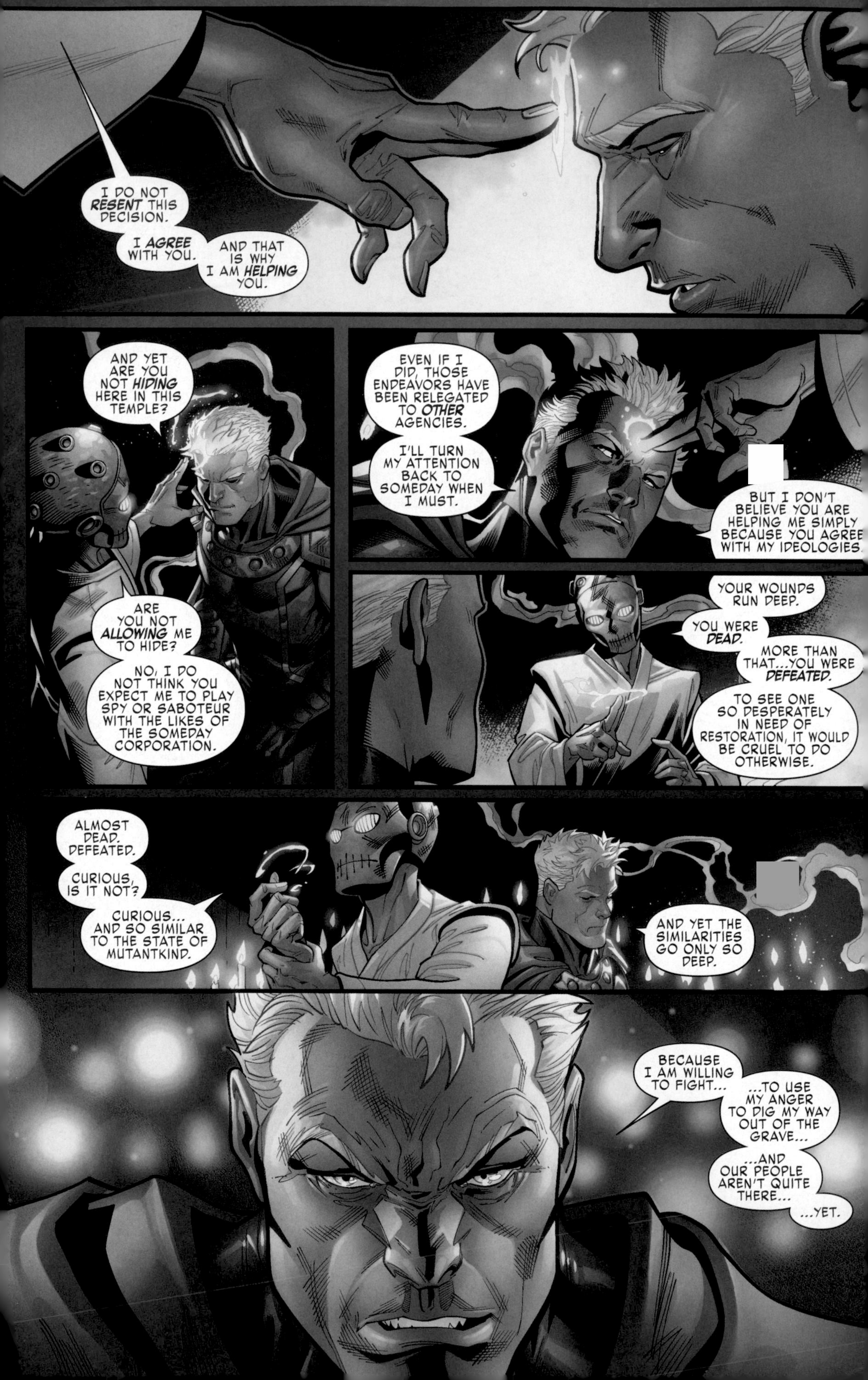
I DO NOT RESENT THIS DECISION.
I AGREE WITH YOU.
AND THAT IS WHY I AM HELPING YOU.
AND YET ARE YOU NOT HIDING HERE IN THIS TEMPLE?
ARE YOU NOT ALLOWING ME TO HIDE?
NO, I DO NOT THINK YOU EXPECT ME TO PLAY SPY OR SABOTEUR WITH THE LIKES OF THE SOMEDAY CORPORATION.
EVEN IF I DID, THOSE ENDEAVORS HAVE BEEN RELEGATED TO OTHER AGENCIES.
I'LL TURN MY ATTENTION BACK TO SOMEDAY WHEN I MUST.
BUT I DON'T BELIEVE YOU ARE HELPING ME SIMPLY BECAUSE YOU AGREE WITH MY IDEOLOGIES.
YOUR WOUNDS RUN DEEP.
YOU WERE DEAD.
MORE THAN THAT...YOU WERE DEFEATED.
TO SEE ONE SO DESPERATELY IN NEED OF RESTORATION, IT WOULD BE CRUEL TO DO OTHERWISE.
ALMOST DEAD. DEFEATED.
CURIOUS, IS IT NOT?
CURIOUS... AND SO SIMILAR TO THE STATE OF MUTANTKIND.
AND YET THE SIMILARITIES GO ONLY SO DEEP.
BECAUSE I AM WILLING TO FIGHT...
...TO USE MY ANGER TO DIG MY WAY OUT OF THE GRAVE...
...AND OUR PEOPLE AREN'T QUITE THERE...
...YET.

#6 VARIANT BY
KEN LASHLEY & NOLAN WOODARD

#6 VARIANT BY
WHILCE PORTACIO

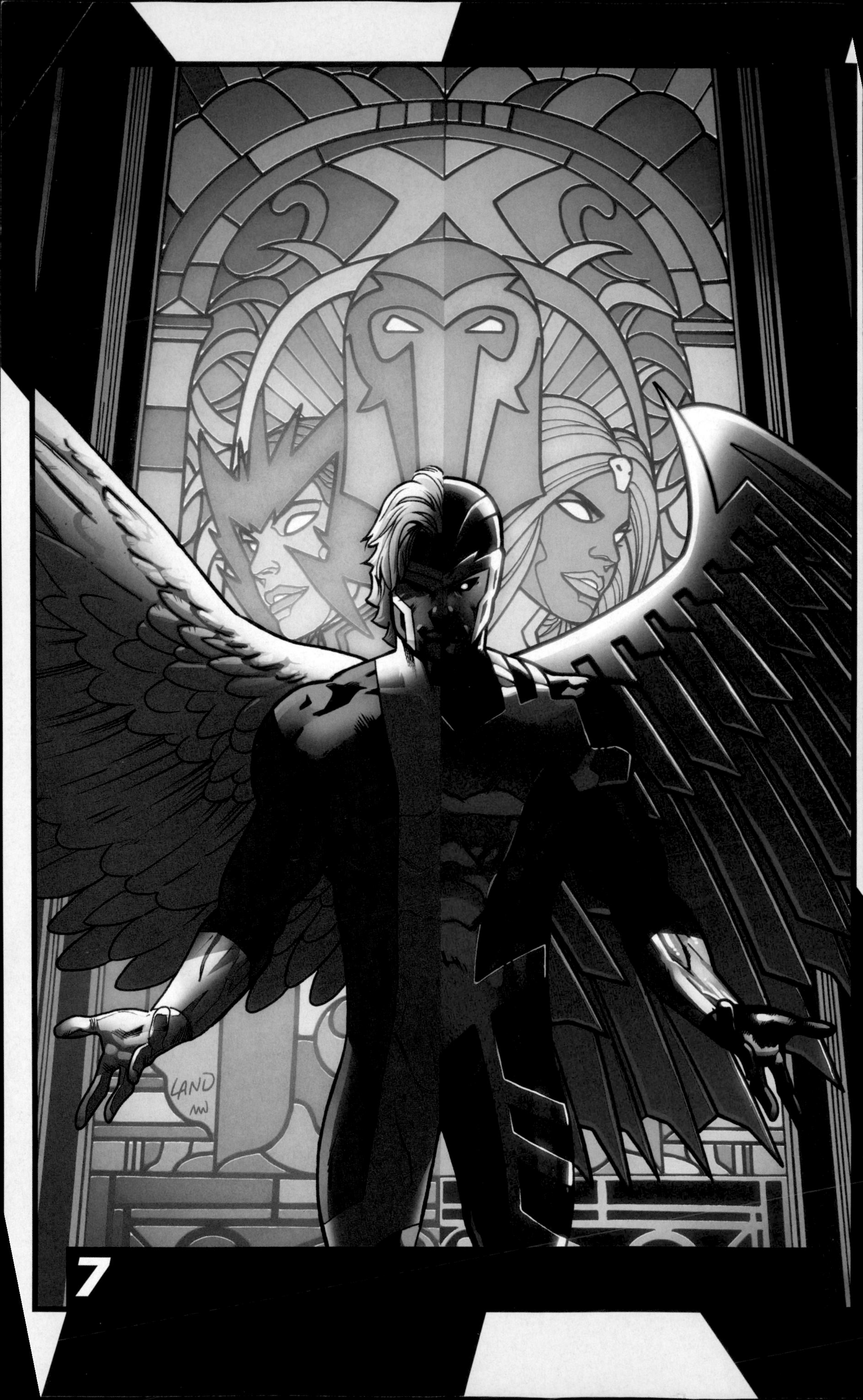
7

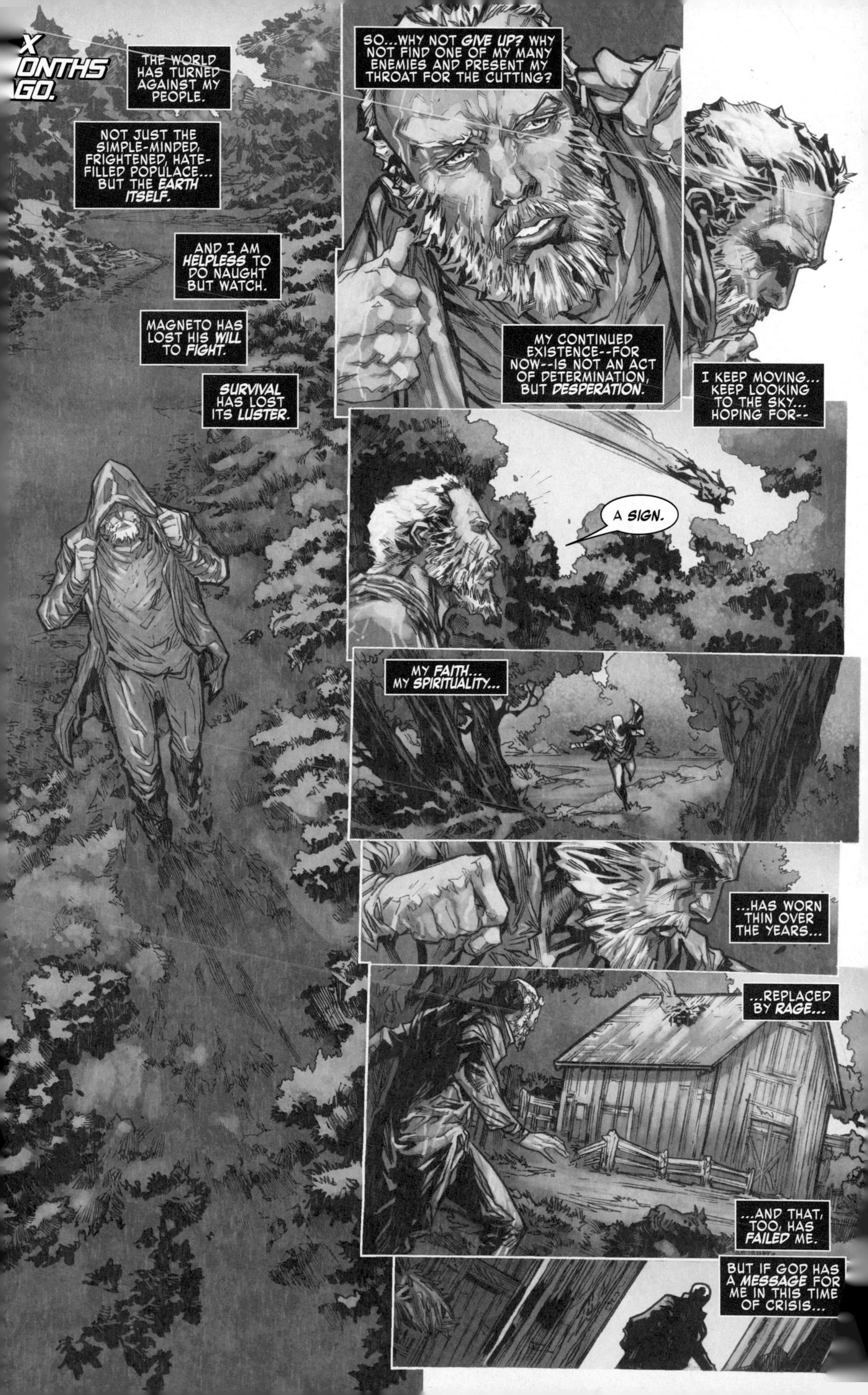
X ONTHS GO.
THE WORLD HAS TURNED AGAINST MY PEOPLE.
NOT JUST THE SIMPLE-MINDED, FRIGHTENED, HATE-FILLED POPULACE... BUT THE EARTH ITSELF.
AND I AM HELPLESS TO DO NAUGHT BUT WATCH.
MAGNETO HAS LOST HIS WILL TO FIGHT.
SURVIVAL HAS LOST ITS LUSTER.
SO...WHY NOT GIVE UP? WHY NOT FIND ONE OF MY MANY ENEMIES AND PRESENT MY THROAT FOR THE CUTTING?
MY CONTINUED EXISTENCE--FOR NOW--IS NOT AN ACT OF DETERMINATION, BUT DESPERATION.
I KEEP MOVING... KEEP LOOKING TO THE SKY... HOPING FOR--
A SIGN.
MY FAITH... MY SPIRITUALITY...
...HAS WORN THIN OVER THE YEARS...
...REPLACED BY RAGE...
...AND THAT, TOO, HAS FAILED ME.
BUT IF GOD HAS A MESSAGE FOR ME IN THIS TIME OF CRISIS...

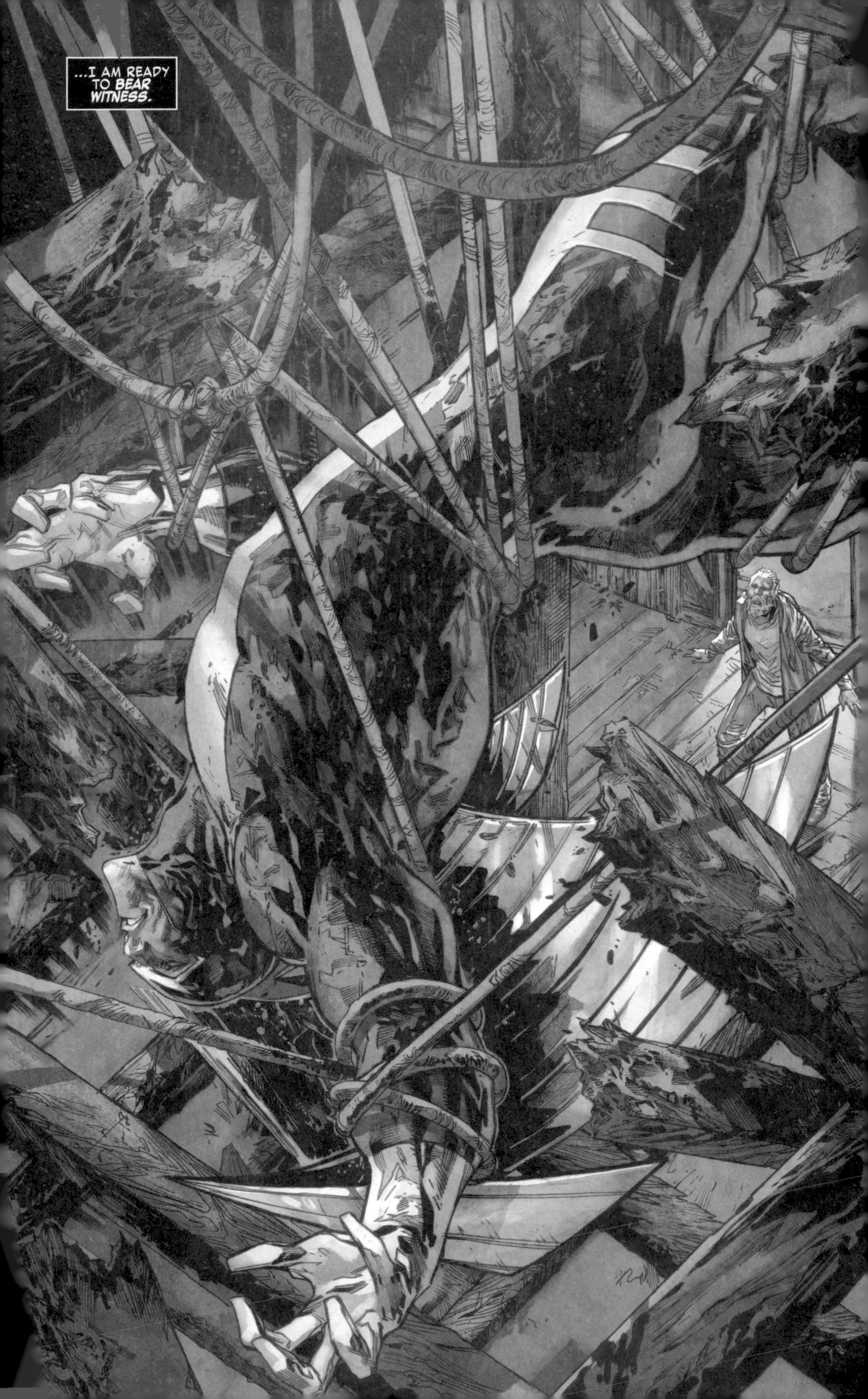
...I AM READY TO BEAR WITNESS.

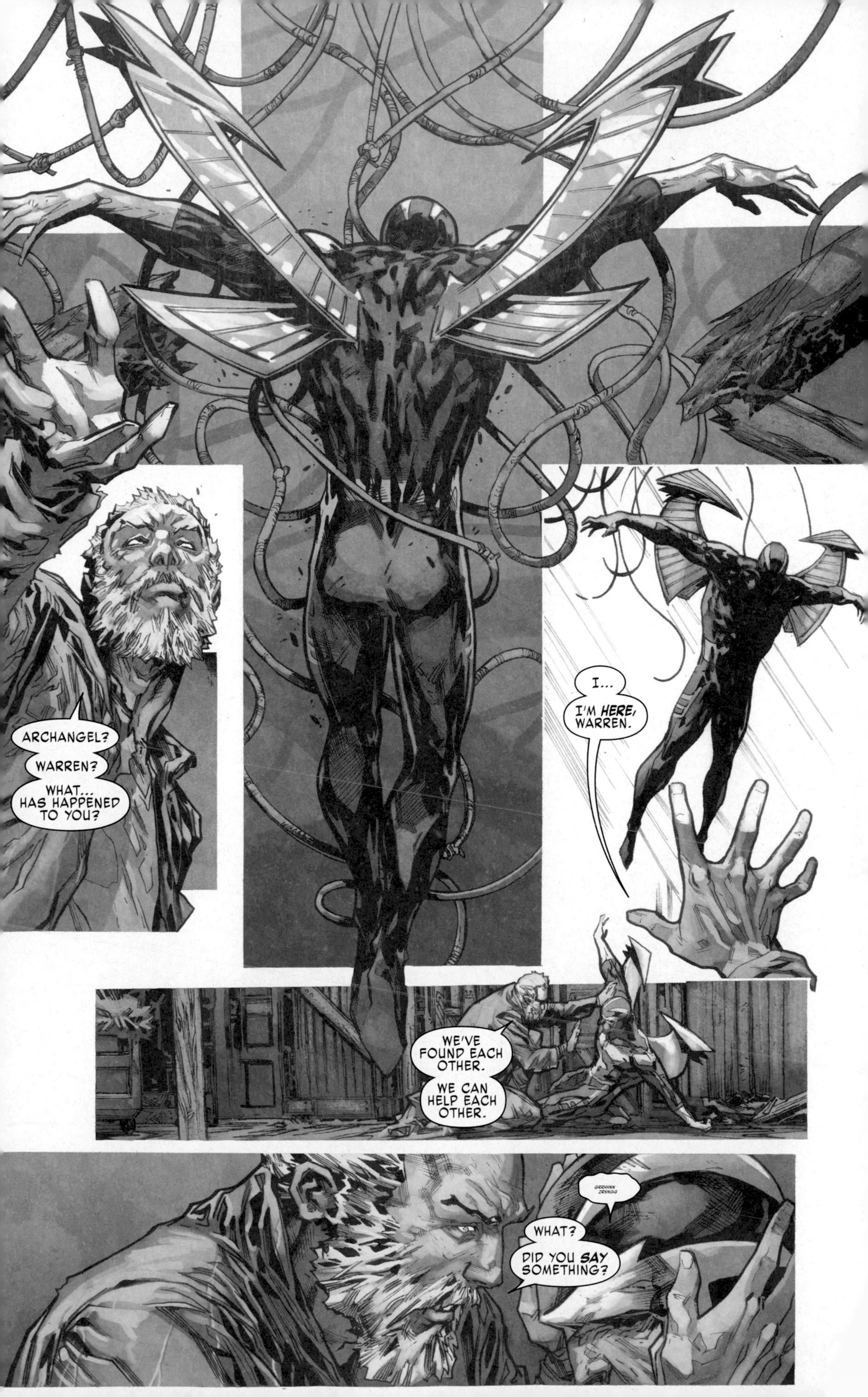
ARCHANGEL?
WARREN?
WHAT... HAS HAPPENED TO YOU?
I...
I'M **HERE**, WARREN.
WE'VE FOUND EACH OTHER.
WE CAN HELP EACH OTHER.
GRRHHNN ZRNNGG
WHAT?
DID YOU **SAY** SOMETHING?

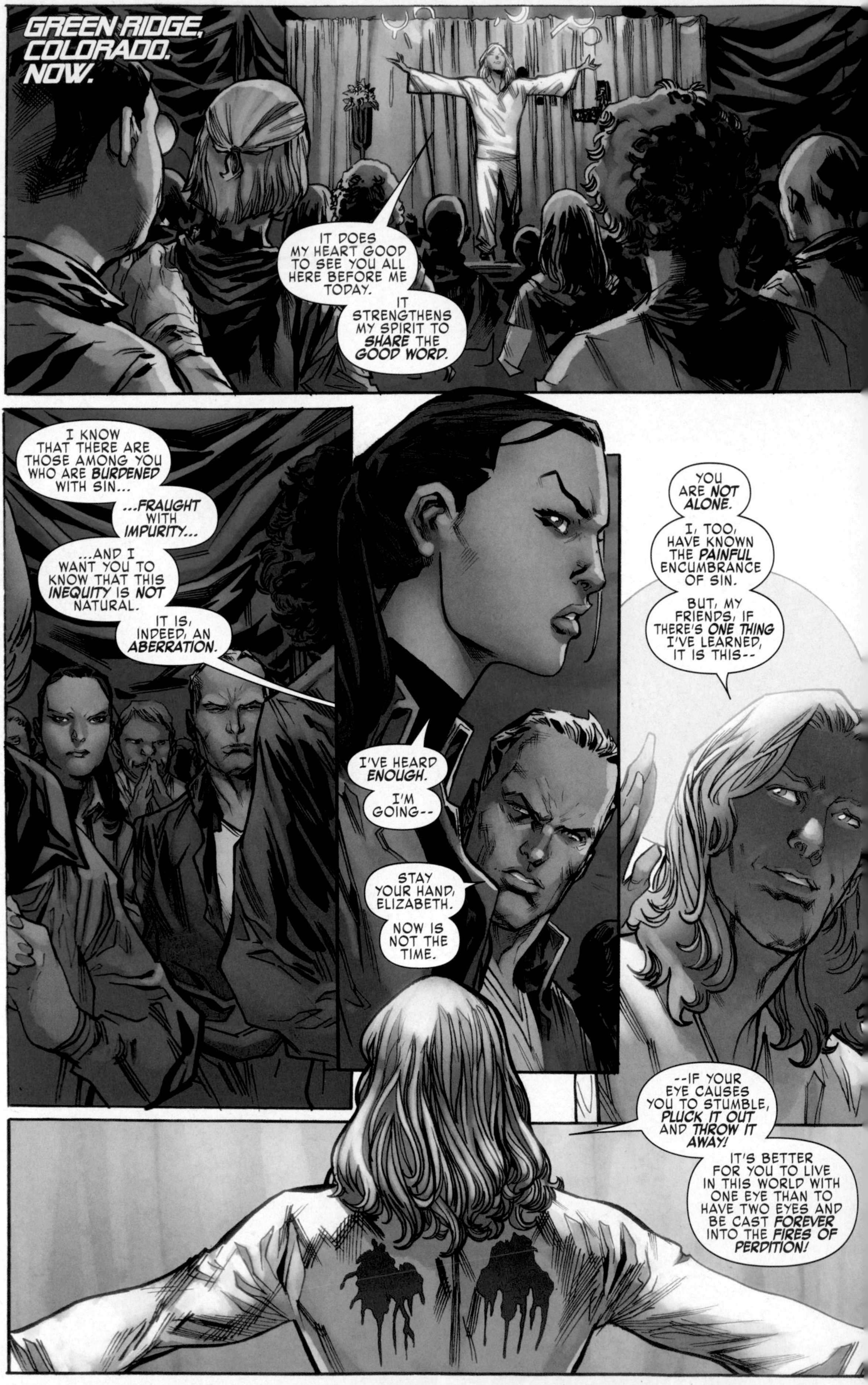
GREEN RIDGE, COLORADO. NOW.
IT DOES MY HEART GOOD TO SEE YOU ALL HERE BEFORE ME TODAY.
IT STRENGTHENS MY SPIRIT TO SHARE THE GOOD WORD.
I KNOW THAT THERE ARE THOSE AMONG YOU WHO ARE BURDENED WITH SIN...
...FRAUGHT WITH IMPURITY...
...AND I WANT YOU TO KNOW THAT THIS INEQUITY IS NOT NATURAL.
IT IS, INDEED, AN ABERRATION.
I'VE HEARD ENOUGH.
I'M GOING--
STAY YOUR HAND, ELIZABETH.
NOW IS NOT THE TIME.
YOU ARE NOT ALONE.
I, TOO, HAVE KNOWN THE PAINFUL ENCUMBRANCE OF SIN.
BUT, MY FRIENDS, IF THERE'S ONE THING I'VE LEARNED, IT IS THIS--
--IF YOUR EYE CAUSES YOU TO STUMBLE, PLUCK IT OUT AND THROW IT AWAY!
IT'S BETTER FOR YOU TO LIVE IN THIS WORLD WITH ONE EYE THAN TO HAVE TWO EYES AND BE CAST FOREVER INTO THE FIRES OF PERDITION!

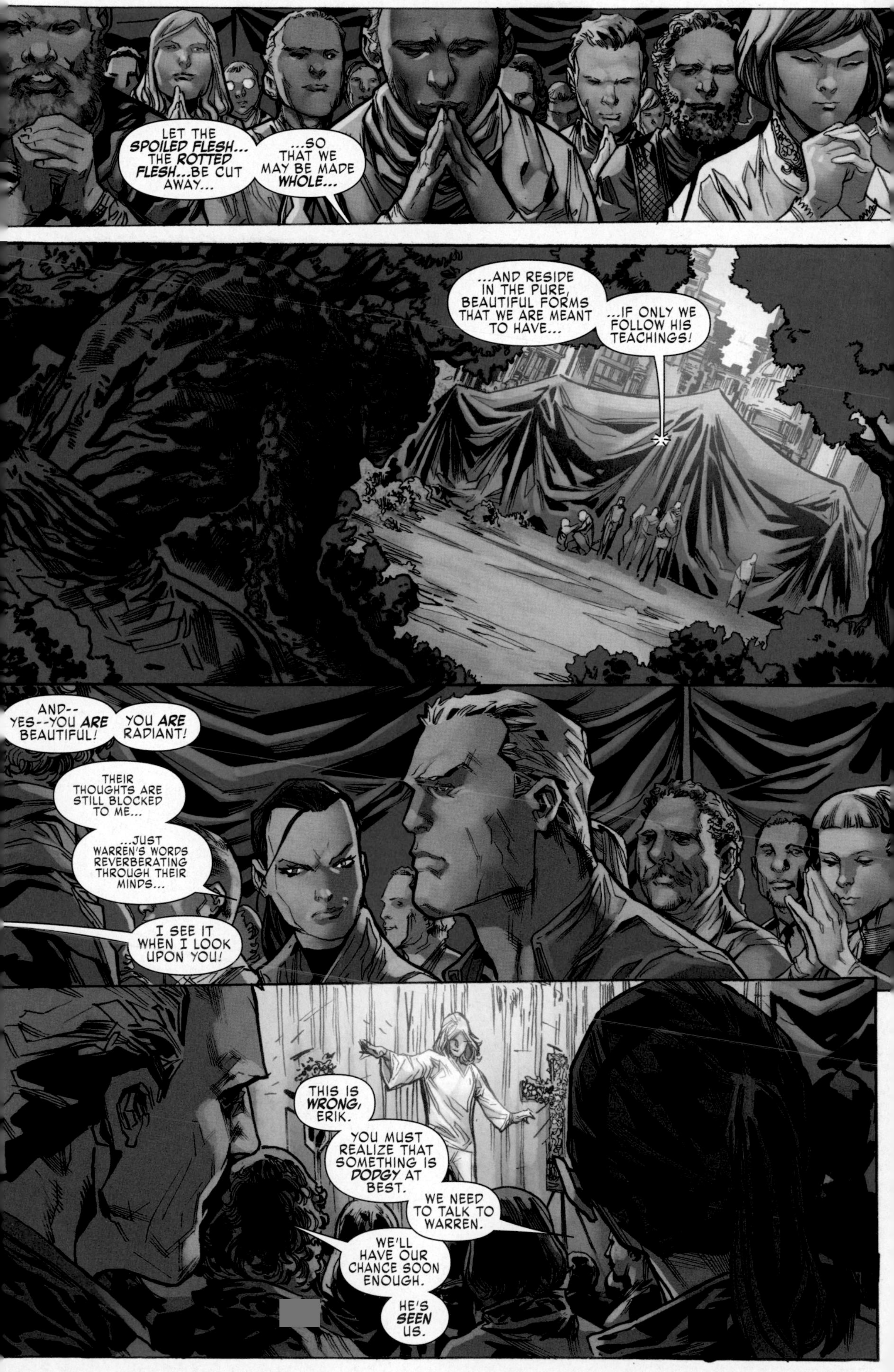
LET THE SPOILED FLESH... THE ROTTED FLESH...BE CUT AWAY...
...SO THAT WE MAY BE MADE WHOLE...
...AND RESIDE IN THE PURE, BEAUTIFUL FORMS THAT WE ARE MEANT TO HAVE...
...IF ONLY WE FOLLOW HIS TEACHINGS!
AND-- YES--YOU ARE BEAUTIFUL!
YOU ARE RADIANT!
THEIR THOUGHTS ARE STILL BLOCKED TO ME...
...JUST WARREN'S WORDS REVERBERATING THROUGH THEIR MINDS...
I SEE IT WHEN I LOOK UPON YOU!
THIS IS WRONG, ERIK.
YOU MUST REALIZE THAT SOMETHING IS DODGY AT BEST.
WE NEED TO TALK TO WARREN.
WE'LL HAVE OUR CHANCE SOON ENOUGH.
HE'S SEEN US.

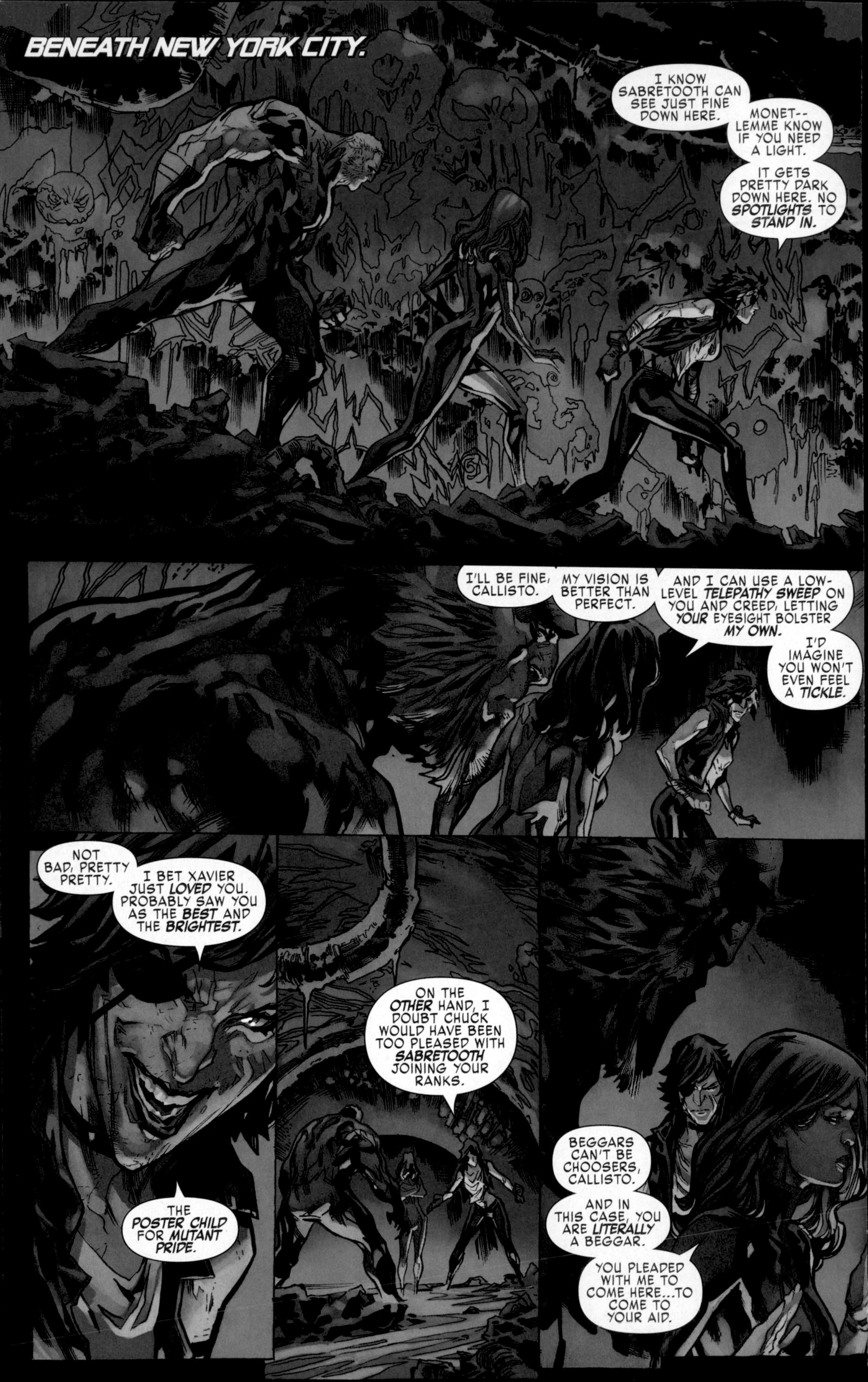
BENEATH NEW YORK CITY.
I KNOW SABRETOOTH CAN SEE JUST FINE DOWN HERE.
MONET-- LEMME KNOW IF YOU NEED A LIGHT.
IT GETS PRETTY DARK DOWN HERE. NO SPOTLIGHTS TO STAND IN.
I'LL BE FINE, CALLISTO.
MY VISION IS BETTER THAN PERFECT.
AND I CAN USE A LOW-LEVEL TELEPATHY SWEEP ON YOU AND CREED, LETTING YOUR EYESIGHT BOLSTER MY OWN.
I'D IMAGINE YOU WON'T EVEN FEEL A TICKLE.
NOT BAD, PRETTY PRETTY.
I BET XAVIER JUST LOVED YOU. PROBABLY SAW YOU AS THE BEST AND THE BRIGHTEST.
THE POSTER CHILD FOR MUTANT PRIDE.
ON THE OTHER HAND, I DOUBT CHUCK WOULD HAVE BEEN TOO PLEASED WITH SABRETOOTH JOINING YOUR RANKS.
BEGGARS CAN'T BE CHOOSERS, CALLISTO.
AND IN THIS CASE, YOU ARE LITERALLY A BEGGAR.
YOU PLEADED WITH ME TO COME HERE...TO COME TO YOUR AID.

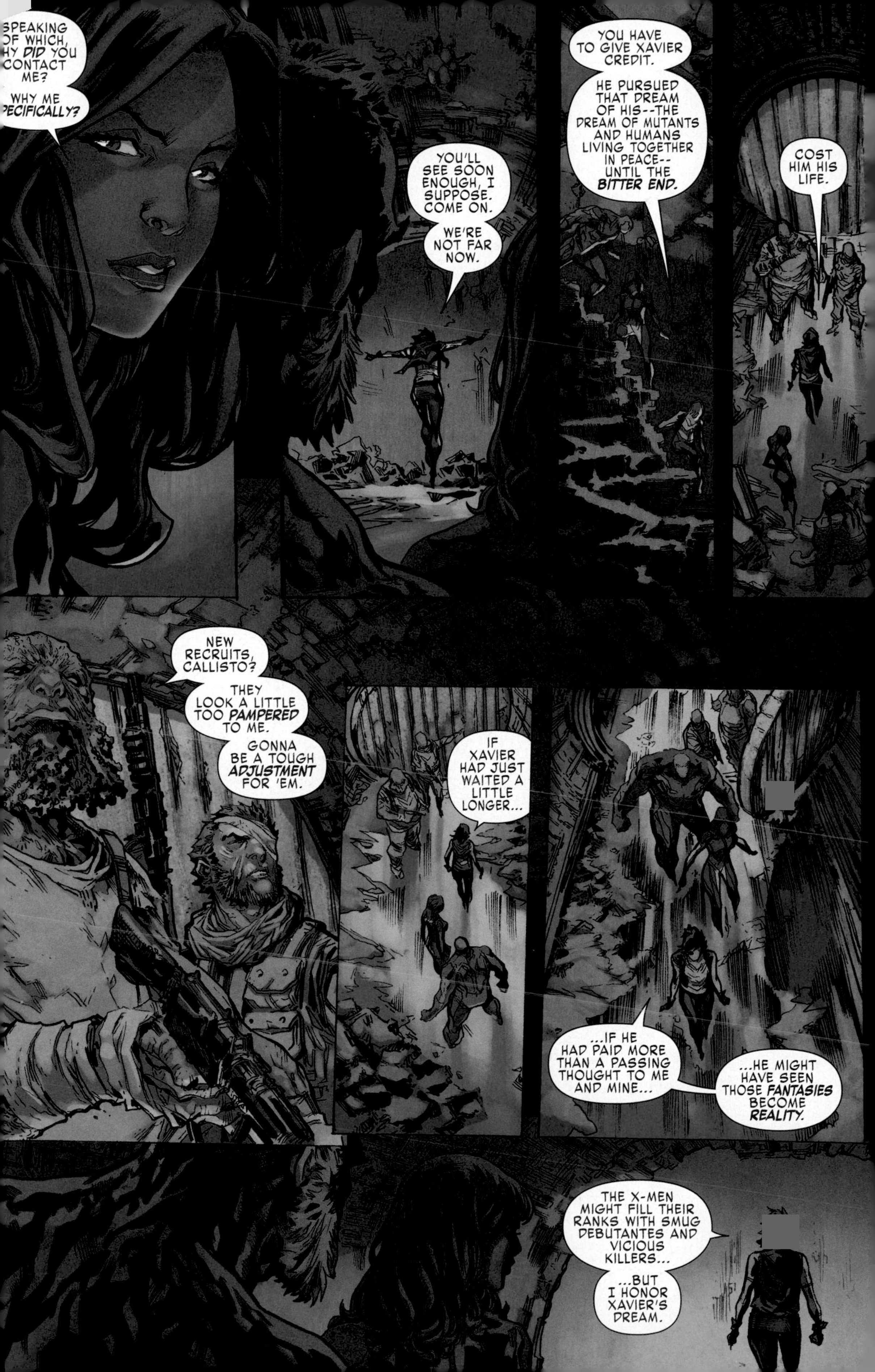
SPEAKING OF WHICH, HY DID YOU CONTACT ME?
WHY ME PECIFICALLY?
YOU'LL SEE SOON ENOUGH, I SUPPOSE. COME ON.
WE'RE NOT FAR NOW.
YOU HAVE TO GIVE XAVIER CREDIT.
HE PURSUED THAT DREAM OF HIS--THE DREAM OF MUTANTS AND HUMANS LIVING TOGETHER IN PEACE--UNTIL THE BITTER END.
COST HIM HIS LIFE.
NEW RECRUITS, CALLISTO?
THEY LOOK A LITTLE TOO PAMPERED TO ME.
GONNA BE A TOUGH ADJUSTMENT FOR 'EM.
IF XAVIER HAD JUST WAITED A LITTLE LONGER...
...IF HE HAD PAID MORE THAN A PASSING THOUGHT TO ME AND MINE...
...HE MIGHT HAVE SEEN THOSE FANTASIES BECOME REALITY.
THE X-MEN MIGHT FILL THEIR RANKS WITH SMUG DEBUTANTES AND VICIOUS KILLERS...
...BUT I HONOR XAVIER'S DREAM.

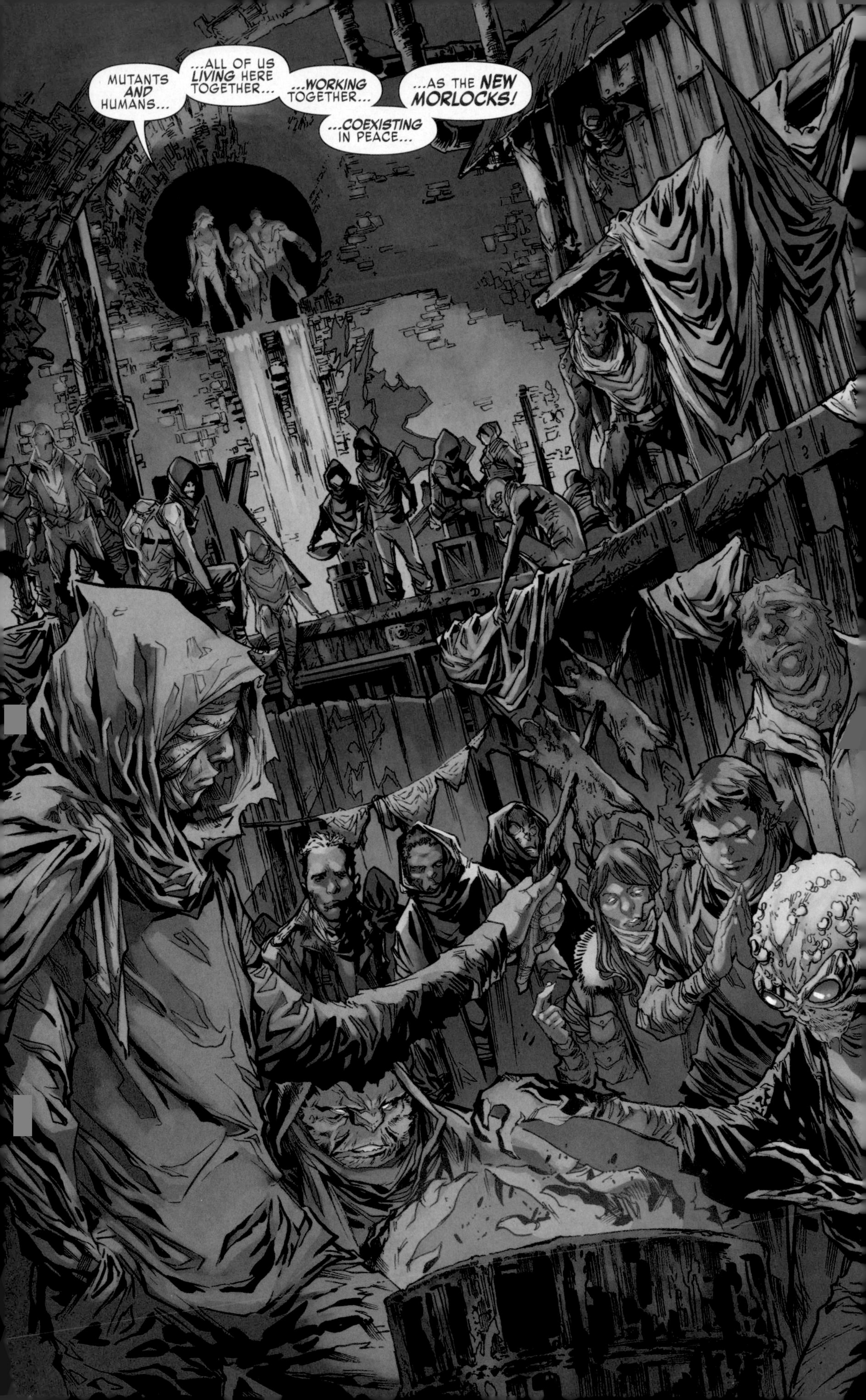
MUTANTS AND HUMANS...
...ALL OF US LIVING HERE TOGETHER...
...WORKING TOGETHER...
...COEXISTING IN PEACE...
...AS THE NEW MORLOCKS!

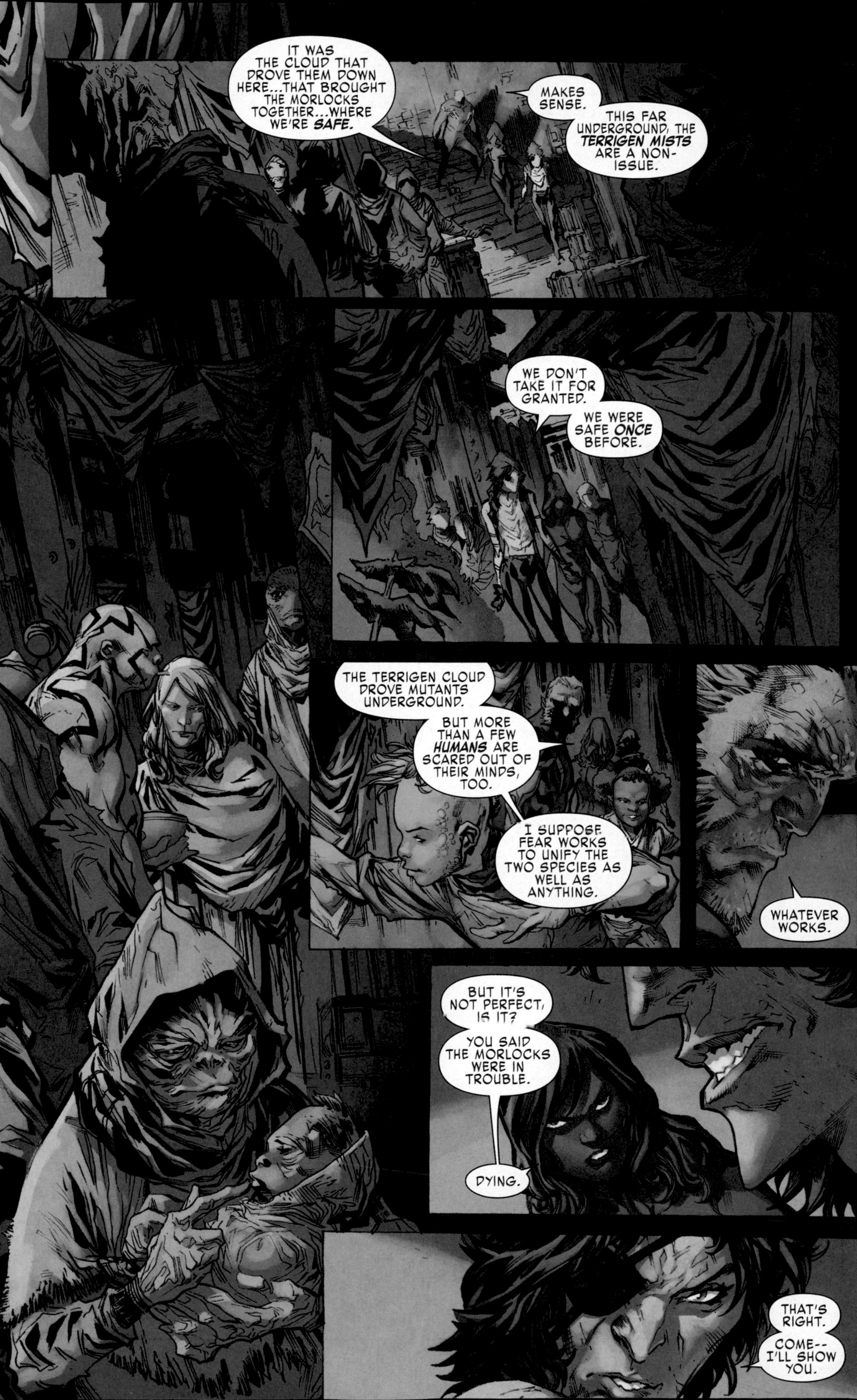

IT WAS THE CLOUD THAT DROVE THEM DOWN HERE...THAT BROUGHT THE MORLOCKS TOGETHER...WHERE WE'RE SAFE.
MAKES SENSE.
THIS FAR UNDERGROUND, THE TERRIGEN MISTS ARE A NON-ISSUE.
WE DON'T TAKE IT FOR GRANTED.
WE WERE SAFE ONCE BEFORE.
THE TERRIGEN CLOUD DROVE MUTANTS UNDERGROUND.
BUT MORE THAN A FEW HUMANS ARE SCARED OUT OF THEIR MINDS, TOO.
I SUPPOSE FEAR WORKS TO UNIFY THE TWO SPECIES AS WELL AS ANYTHING.
WHATEVER WORKS.
BUT IT'S NOT PERFECT, IS IT?
YOU SAID THE MORLOCKS WERE IN TROUBLE.
DYING.
THAT'S RIGHT.
COME-- I'LL SHOW YOU.

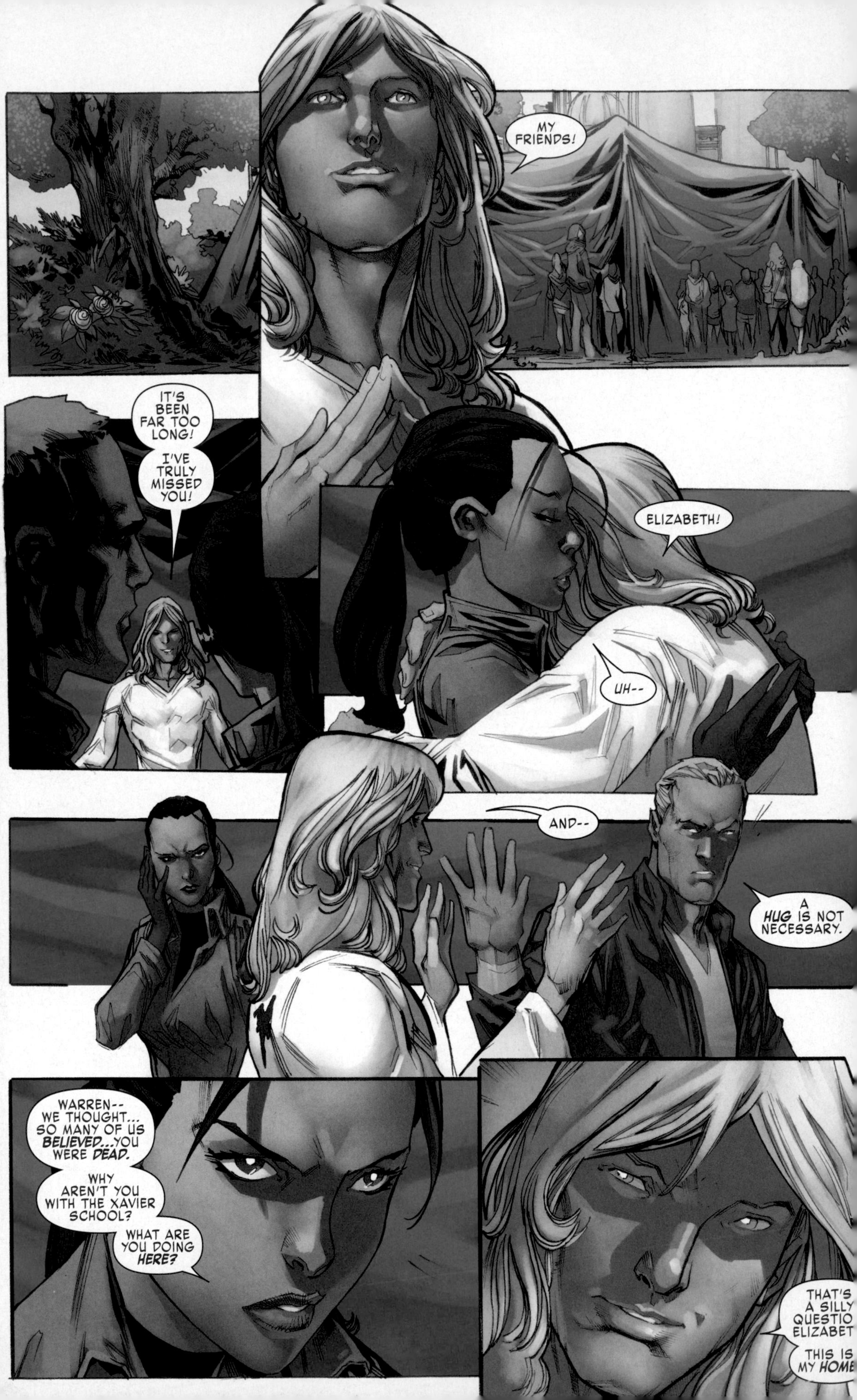
MY FRIENDS!
IT'S BEEN FAR TOO LONG!
I'VE TRULY MISSED YOU!
ELIZABETH!
UH--
AND--
A HUG IS NOT NECESSARY.
WARREN-- WE THOUGHT... SO MANY OF US BELIEVED...YOU WERE DEAD.
WHY AREN'T YOU WITH THE XAVIER SCHOOL?
WHAT ARE YOU DOING HERE?
THAT'S A SILLY QUESTIO ELIZABET
THIS IS MY HOME

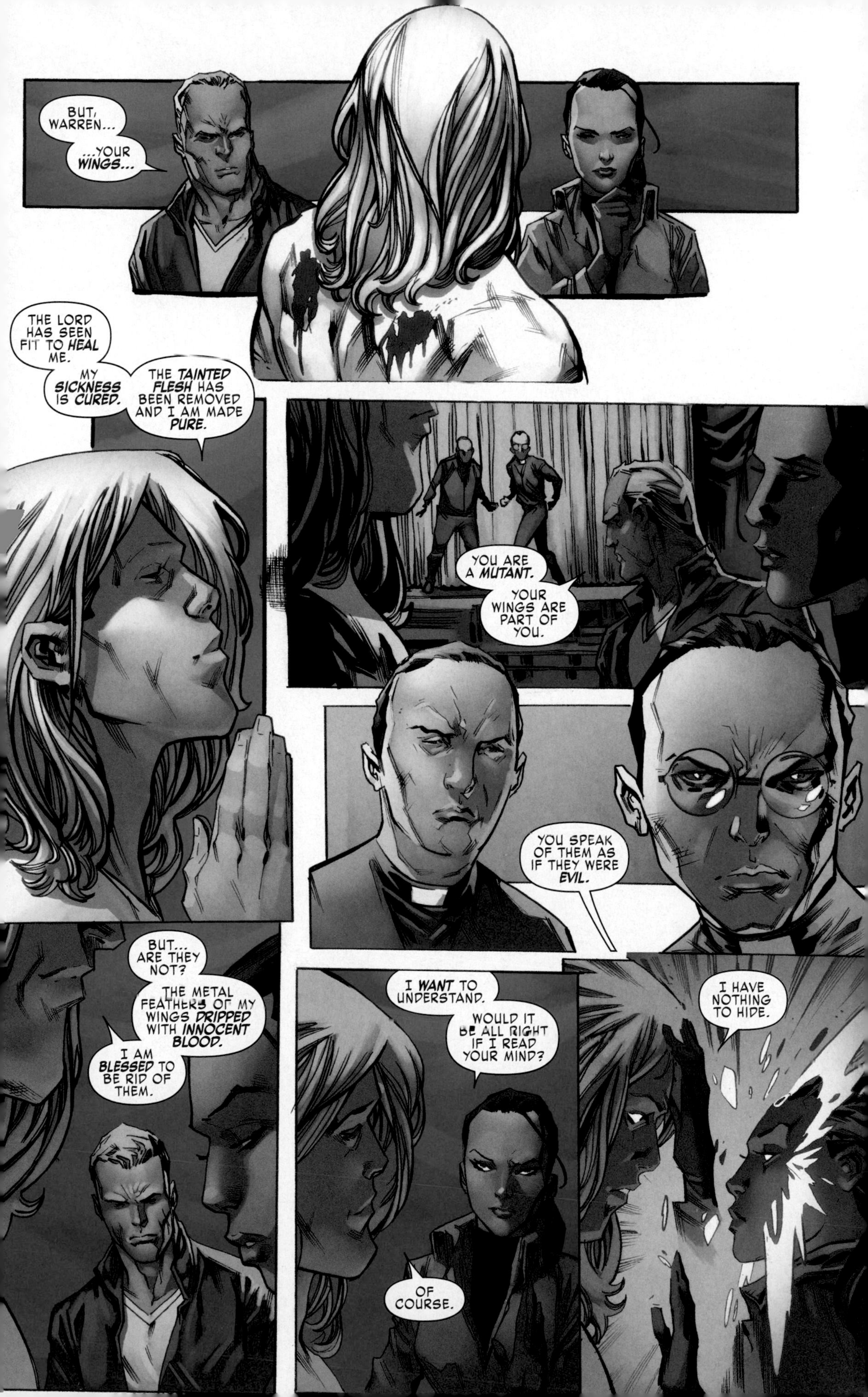
BUT, WARREN...
...YOUR WINGS...
THE LORD HAS SEEN FIT TO HEAL ME.
MY SICKNESS IS CURED.
THE TAINTED FLESH HAS BEEN REMOVED AND I AM MADE PURE.
YOU ARE A MUTANT.
YOUR WINGS ARE PART OF YOU.
YOU SPEAK OF THEM AS IF THEY WERE EVIL.
BUT... ARE THEY NOT?
THE METAL FEATHERS OF MY WINGS DRIPPED WITH INNOCENT BLOOD.
I AM BLESSED TO BE RID OF THEM.
I WANT TO UNDERSTAND.
WOULD IT BE ALL RIGHT IF I READ YOUR MIND?
OF COURSE.
I HAVE NOTHING TO HIDE.

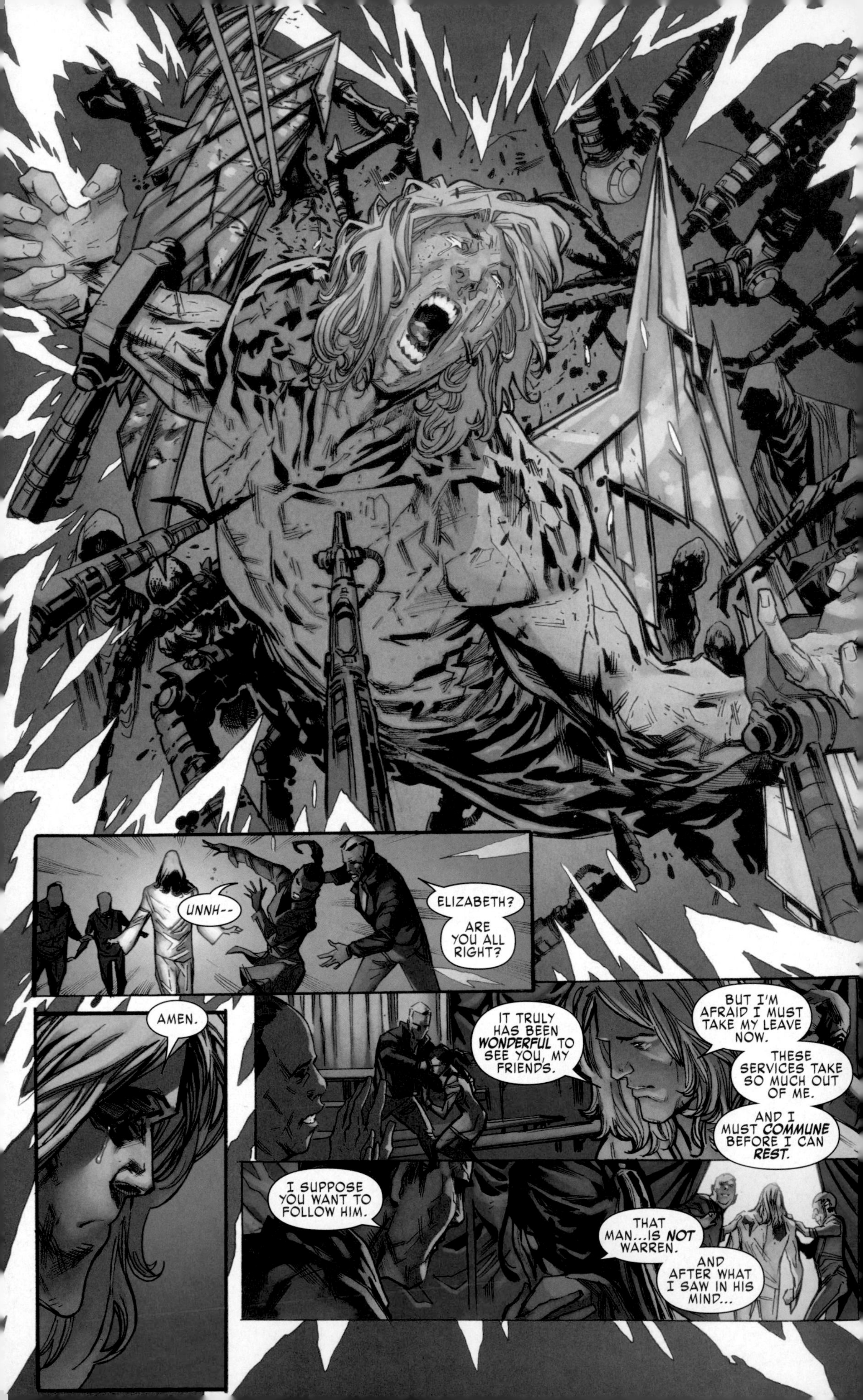
UNNH--
ELIZABETH?
ARE YOU ALL RIGHT?
AMEN.
IT TRULY HAS BEEN WONDERFUL TO SEE YOU, MY FRIENDS.
BUT I'M AFRAID I MUST TAKE MY LEAVE NOW.
THESE SERVICES TAKE SO MUCH OUT OF ME.
AND I MUST COMMUNE BEFORE I CAN REST.
I SUPPOSE YOU WANT TO FOLLOW HIM.
THAT MAN...IS NOT WARREN.
AND AFTER WHAT I SAW IN HIS MIND...

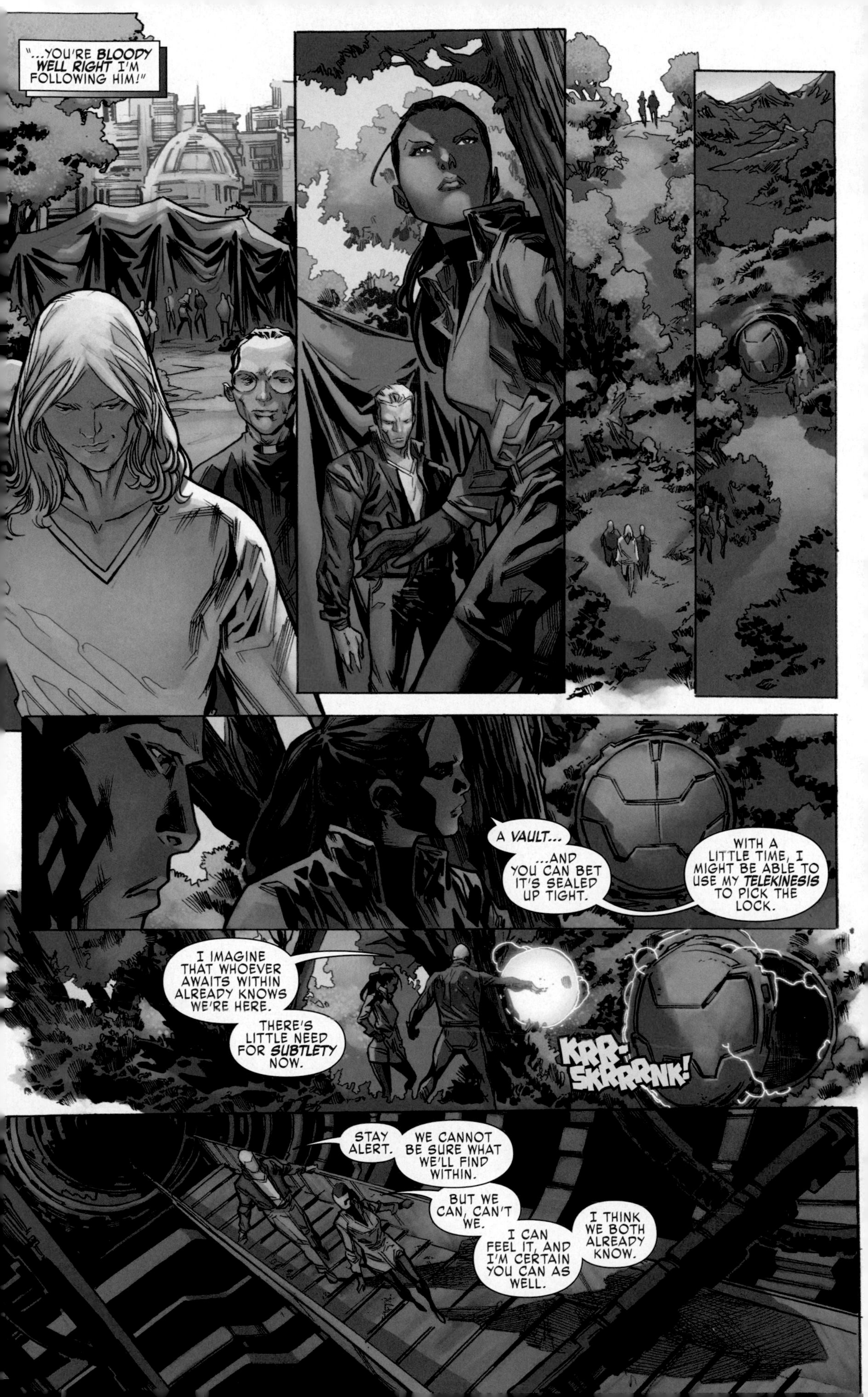
"...YOU'RE BLOODY WELL RIGHT I'M FOLLOWING HIM!"
A VAULT...
...AND YOU CAN BET IT'S SEALED UP TIGHT.
WITH A LITTLE TIME, I MIGHT BE ABLE TO USE MY TELEKINESIS TO PICK THE LOCK.
I IMAGINE THAT WHOEVER AWAITS WITHIN ALREADY KNOWS WE'RE HERE.
THERE'S LITTLE NEED FOR SUBTLETY NOW.
KRR-SKRRRNK!
STAY ALERT.
WE CANNOT BE SURE WHAT WE'LL FIND WITHIN.
BUT WE CAN, CAN'T WE.
I CAN FEEL IT, AND I'M CERTAIN YOU CAN AS WELL.
I THINK WE BOTH ALREADY KNOW.

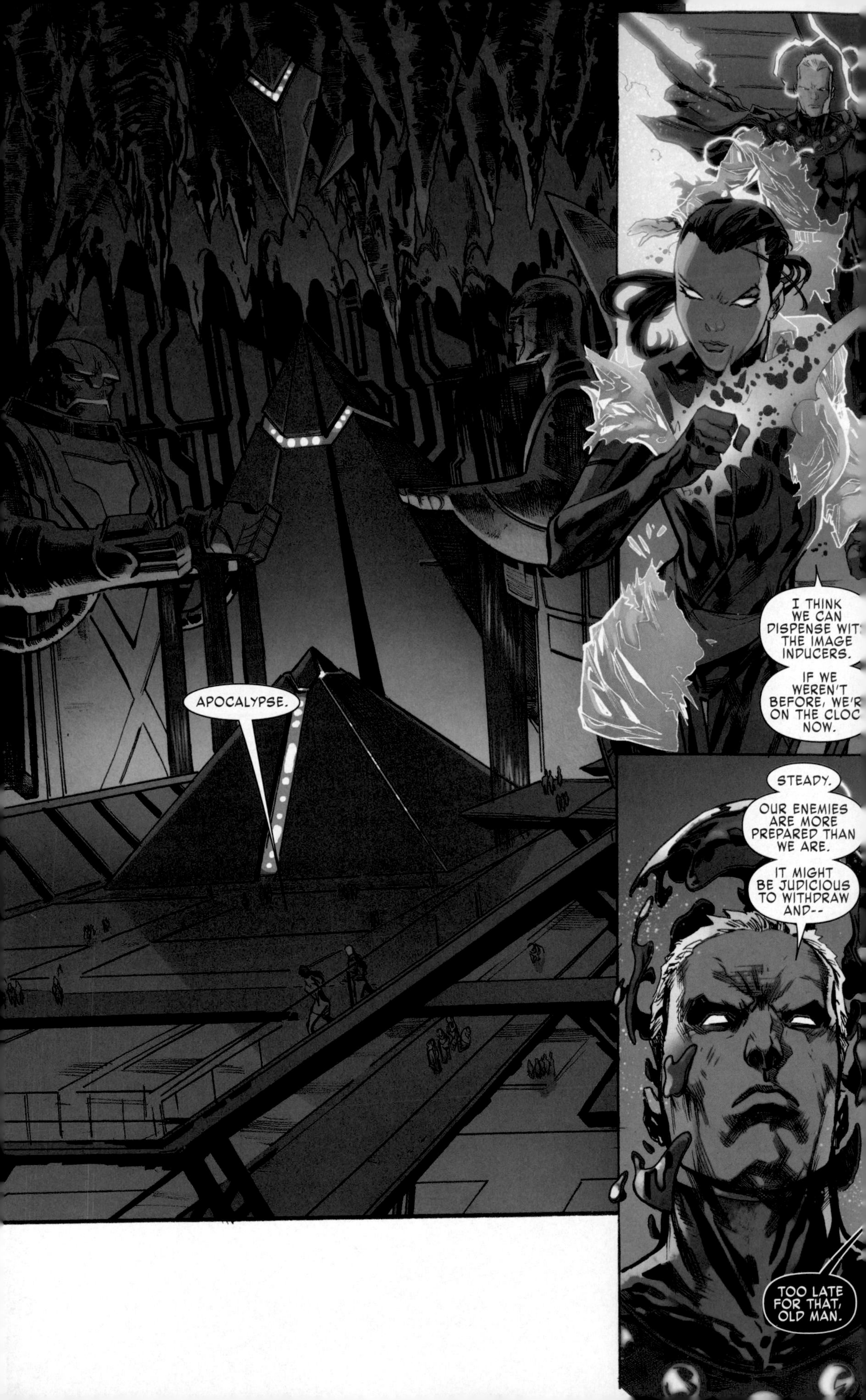
APOCALYPSE.
I THINK WE CAN DISPENSE WIT THE IMAGE INDUCERS.
IF WE WEREN'T BEFORE, WE'R ON THE CLOC NOW.
STEADY.
OUR ENEMIES ARE MORE PREPARED THAN WE ARE.
IT MIGHT BE JUDICIOUS TO WITHDRAW AND--
TOO LATE FOR THAT, OLD MAN.

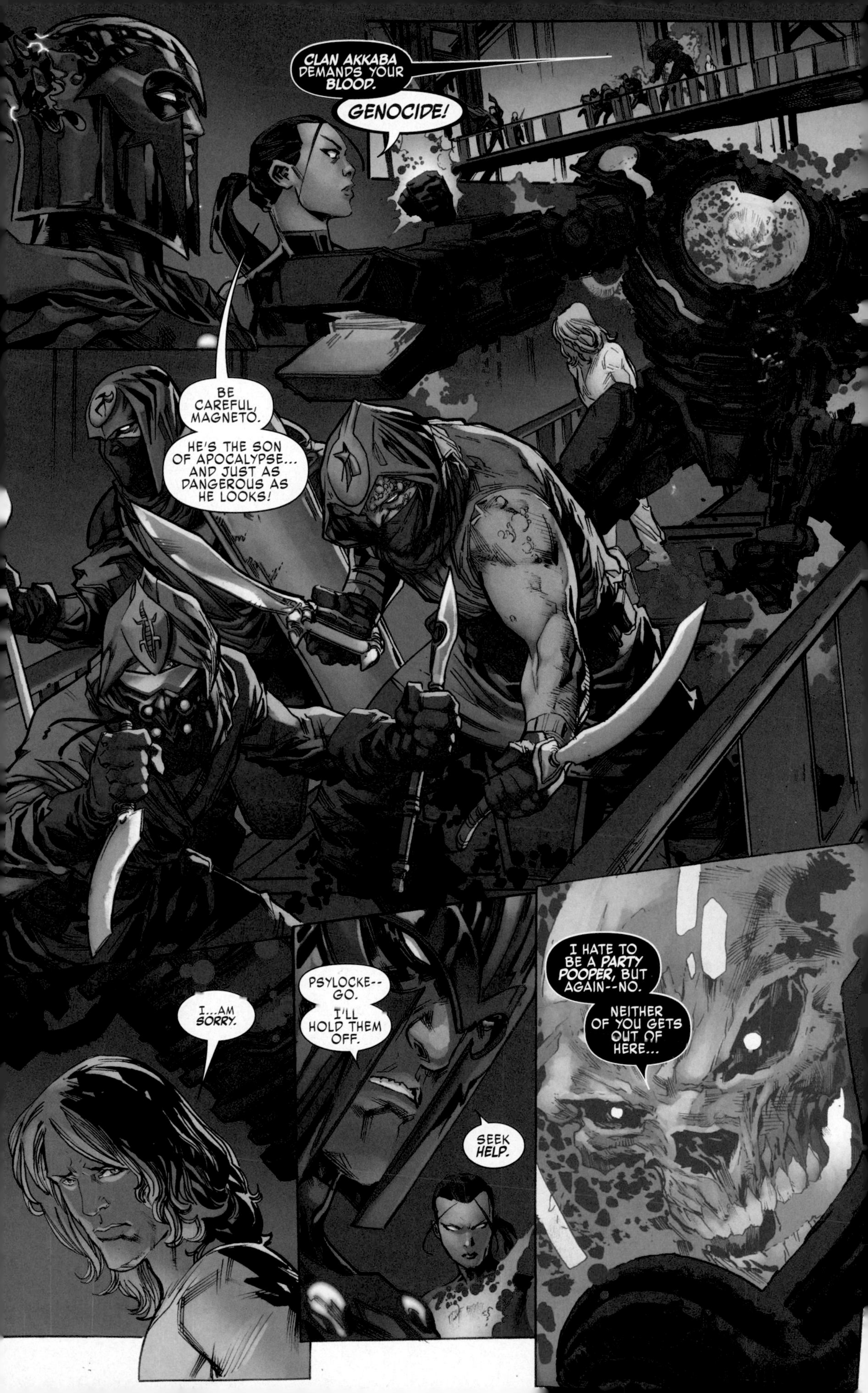

CLAN AKKABA DEMANDS YOUR BLOOD.
GENOCIDE!
BE CAREFUL, MAGNETO.
HE'S THE SON OF APOCALYPSE... AND JUST AS DANGEROUS AS HE LOOKS!
I...AM SORRY.
PSYLOCKE-- GO.
I'LL HOLD THEM OFF.
SEEK HELP.
I HATE TO BE A PARTY POOPER, BUT AGAIN--NO.
NEITHER OF YOU GETS OUT OF HERE...

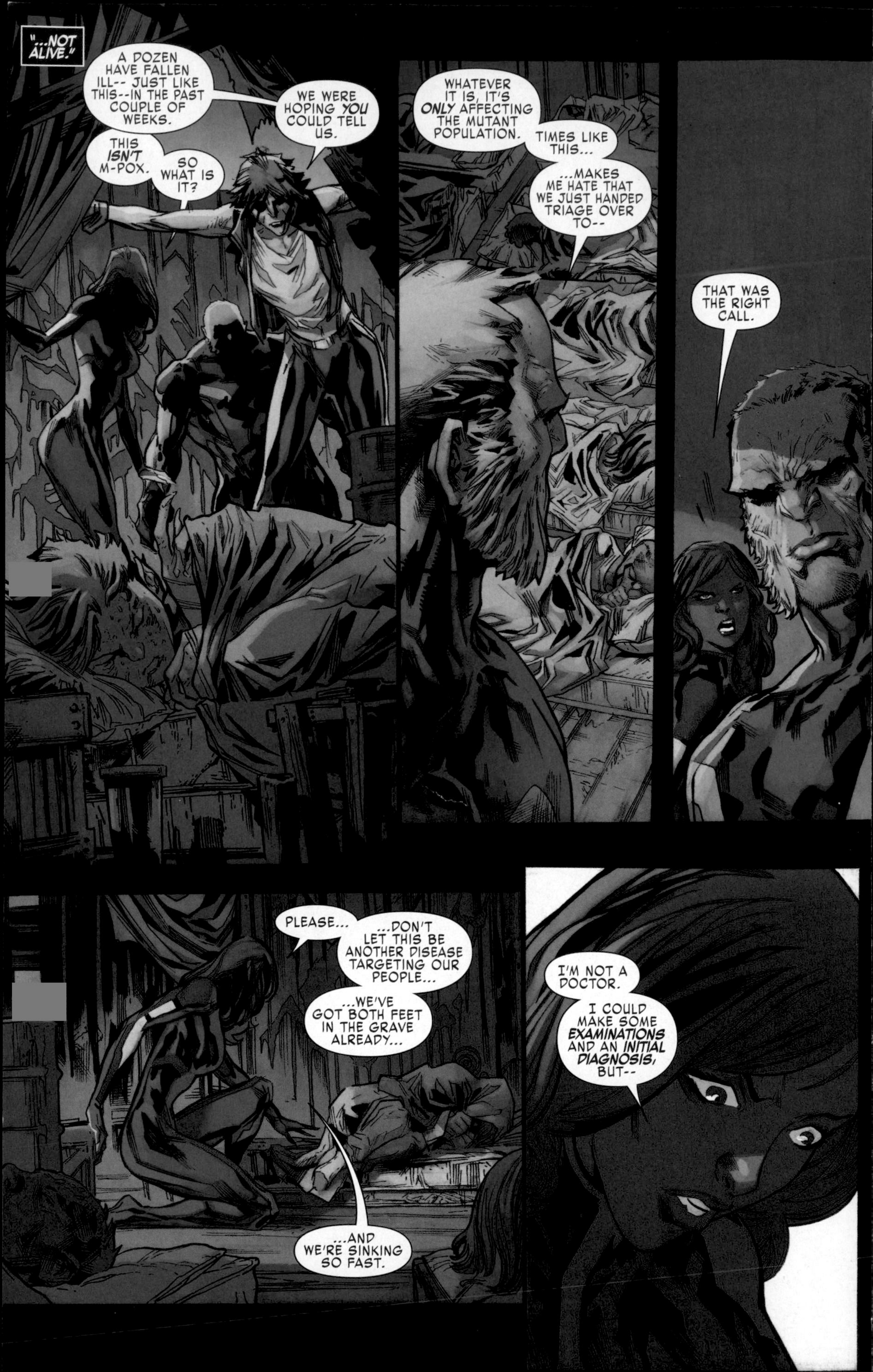
"...NOT ALIVE."
A DOZEN HAVE FALLEN ILL-- JUST LIKE THIS--IN THE PAST COUPLE OF WEEKS.
WE WERE HOPING *YOU* COULD TELL US.
THIS *ISN'T* M-POX.
SO WHAT IS IT?
WHATEVER IT IS, IT'S *ONLY* AFFECTING THE MUTANT POPULATION.
TIMES LIKE THIS...
...MAKES ME HATE THAT WE JUST HANDED TRIAGE OVER TO--
THAT WAS THE RIGHT CALL.
PLEASE...
...DON'T LET THIS BE ANOTHER DISEASE TARGETING OUR PEOPLE...
...WE'VE GOT BOTH FEET IN THE GRAVE ALREADY...
...AND WE'RE SINKING SO FAST.
I'M NOT A DOCTOR.
I COULD MAKE SOME *EXAMINATIONS* AND AN *INITIAL DIAGNOSIS,* BUT--

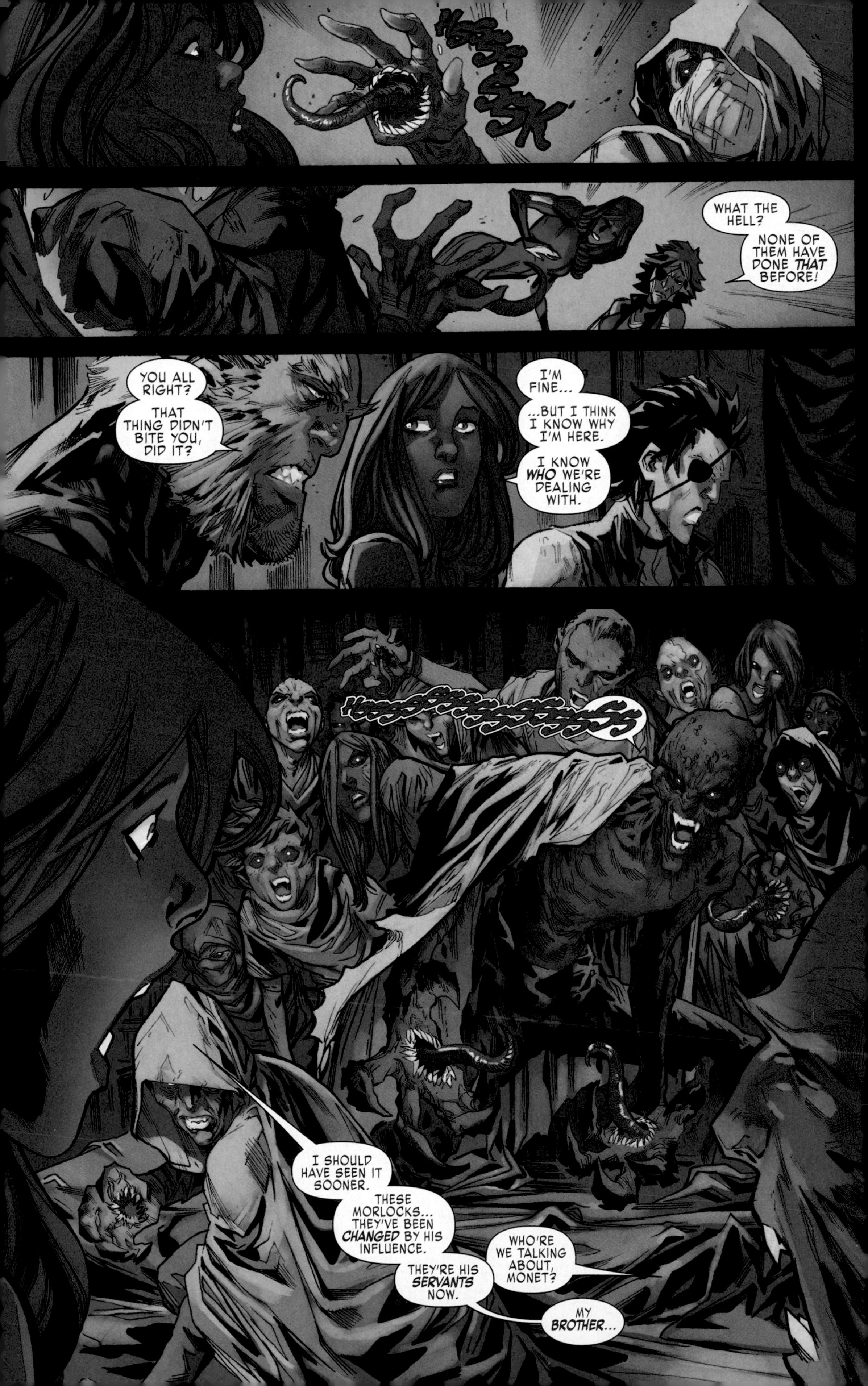
HSSSSSSSSK
WHAT THE HELL?
NONE OF THEM HAVE DONE THAT BEFORE!
YOU ALL RIGHT?
THAT THING DIDN'T BITE YOU, DID IT?
I'M FINE...
...BUT I THINK I KNOW WHY I'M HERE.
I KNOW WHO WE'RE DEALING WITH.
HSSSSSSSSSSSSSSSS
I SHOULD HAVE SEEN IT SOONER.
THESE MORLOCKS... THEY'VE BEEN CHANGED BY HIS INFLUENCE.
THEY'RE HIS SERVANTS NOW.
WHO'RE WE TALKING ABOUT, MONET?
MY BROTHER...

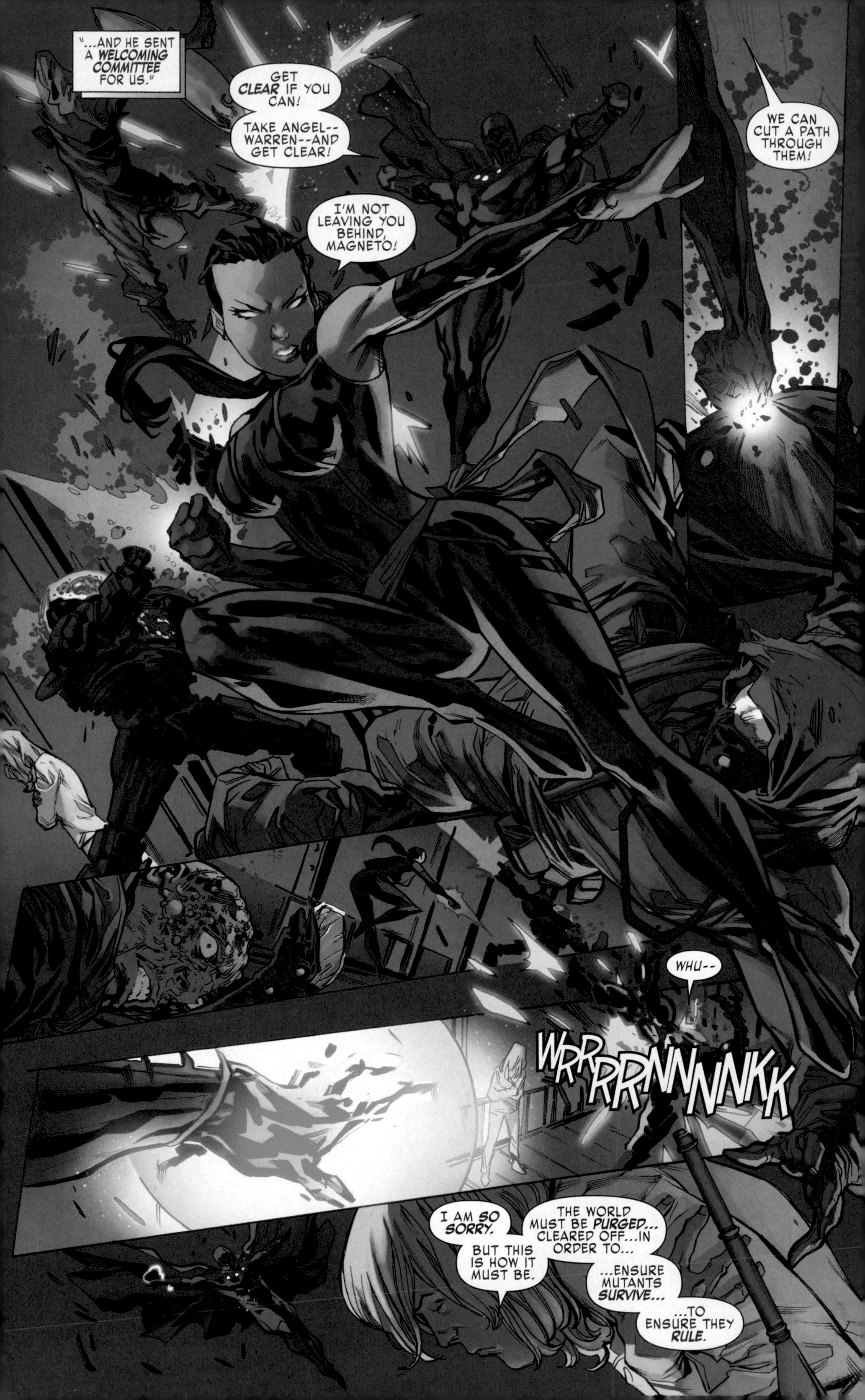
"...AND HE SENT A WELCOMING COMMITTEE FOR US."
GET CLEAR IF YOU CAN!
TAKE ANGEL--WARREN--AND GET CLEAR!
WE CAN CUT A PATH THROUGH THEM!
I'M NOT LEAVING YOU BEHIND, MAGNETO!
WHU--
WRRRRRNNNNNKK
I AM SO SORRY.
BUT THIS IS HOW IT MUST BE.
THE WORLD MUST BE PURGED... CLEARED OFF...IN ORDER TO...
...ENSURE MUTANTS SURVIVE...
...TO ENSURE THEY RULE.

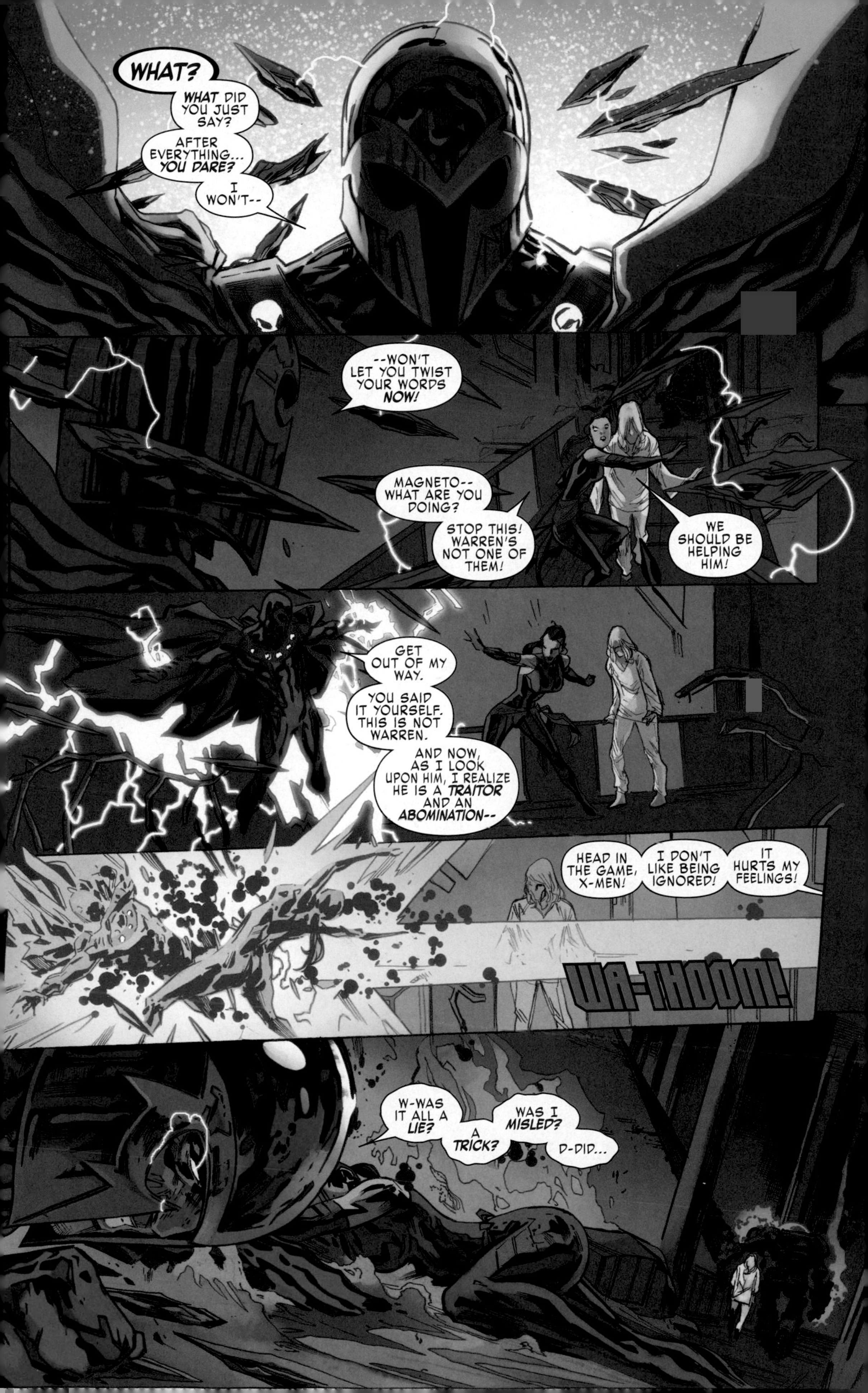
WHAT?
WHAT DID YOU JUST SAY?
AFTER EVERYTHING... YOU DARE?
I WON'T--
--WON'T LET YOU TWIST YOUR WORDS NOW!
MAGNETO-- WHAT ARE YOU DOING?
STOP THIS! WARREN'S NOT ONE OF THEM!
WE SHOULD BE HELPING HIM!
GET OUT OF MY WAY.
YOU SAID IT YOURSELF. THIS IS NOT WARREN.
AND NOW, AS I LOOK UPON HIM, I REALIZE HE IS A TRAITOR AND AN ABOMINATION--
HEAD IN THE GAME, X-MEN!
I DON'T LIKE BEING IGNORED!
IT HURTS MY FEELINGS!
WA-THOOM!
W-WAS IT ALL A LIE?
A TRICK?
WAS I MISLED?
D-DID...

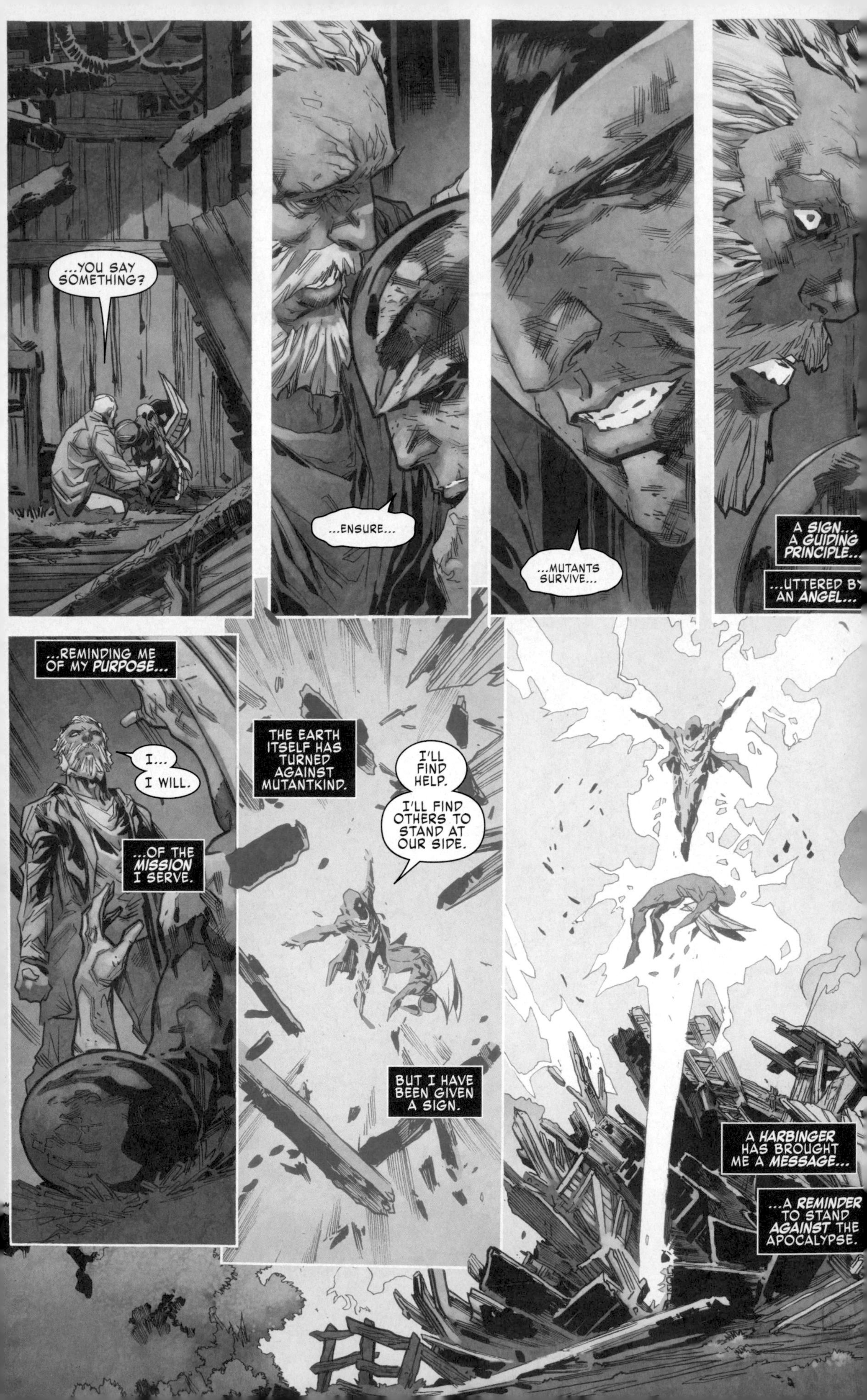
...YOU SAY SOMETHING?
...ENSURE...
...MUTANTS SURVIVE...
A SIGN... A GUIDING PRINCIPLE...
...UTTERED BY AN ANGEL...
...REMINDING ME OF MY PURPOSE...
I...
I WILL.
...OF THE MISSION I SERVE.
THE EARTH ITSELF HAS TURNED AGAINST MUTANTKIND.
I'LL FIND HELP.
I'LL FIND OTHERS TO STAND AT OUR SIDE.
BUT I HAVE BEEN GIVEN A SIGN.
A HARBINGER HAS BROUGHT ME A MESSAGE...
...A REMINDER TO STAND AGAINST THE APOCALYPSE.

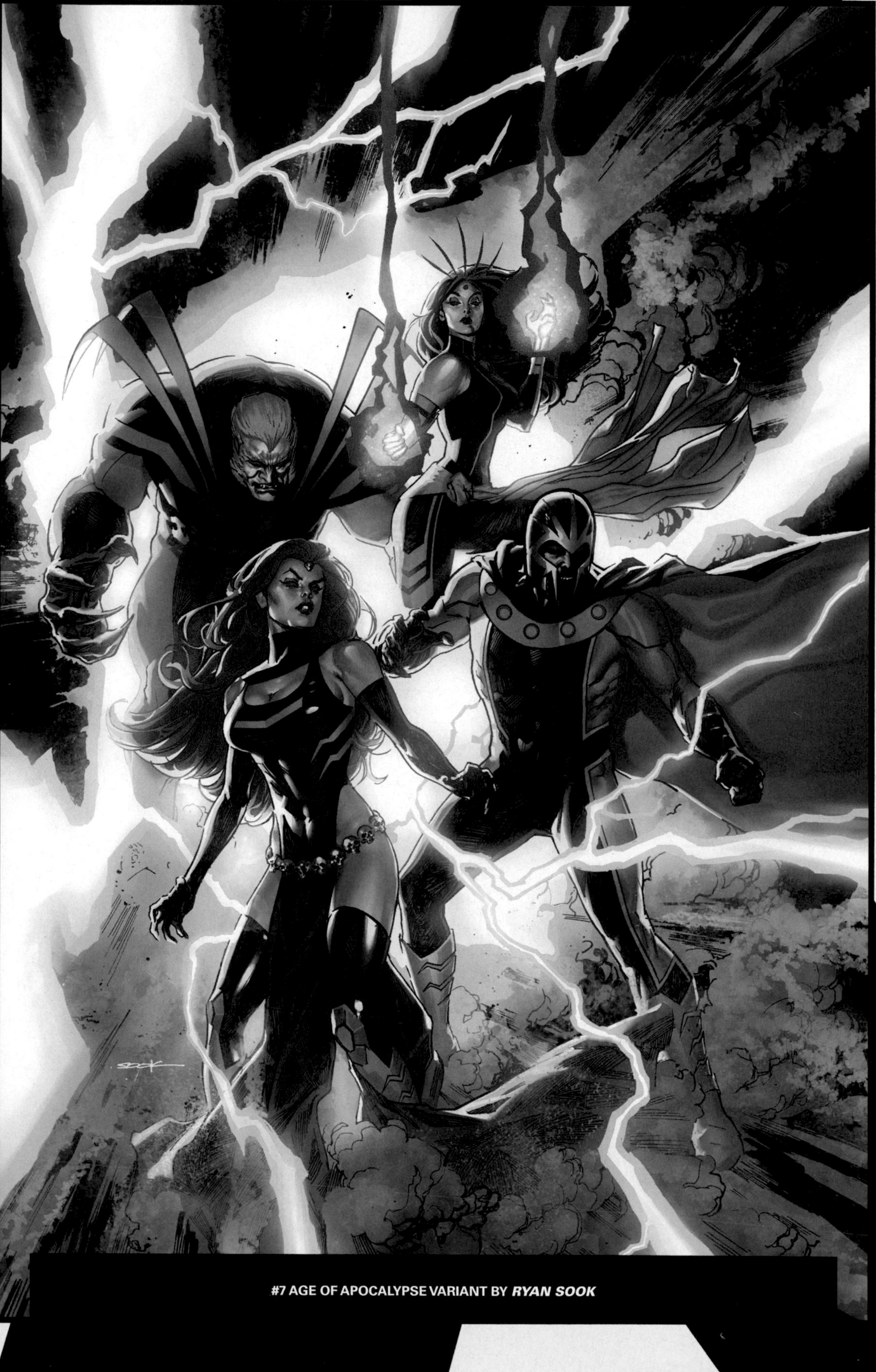

#7 AGE OF APOCALYPSE VARIANT BY ***RYAN SOOK***

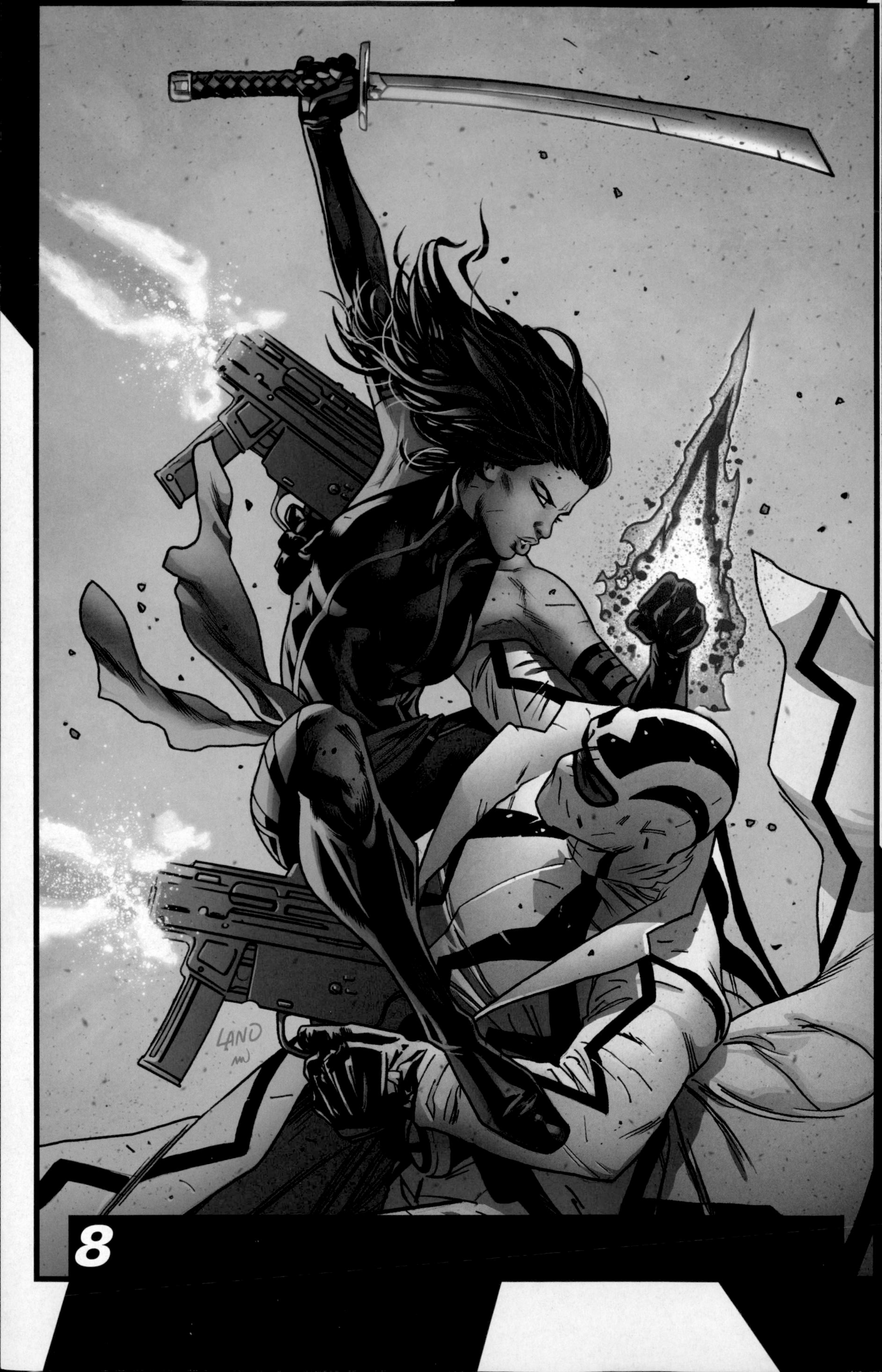
LAND

8

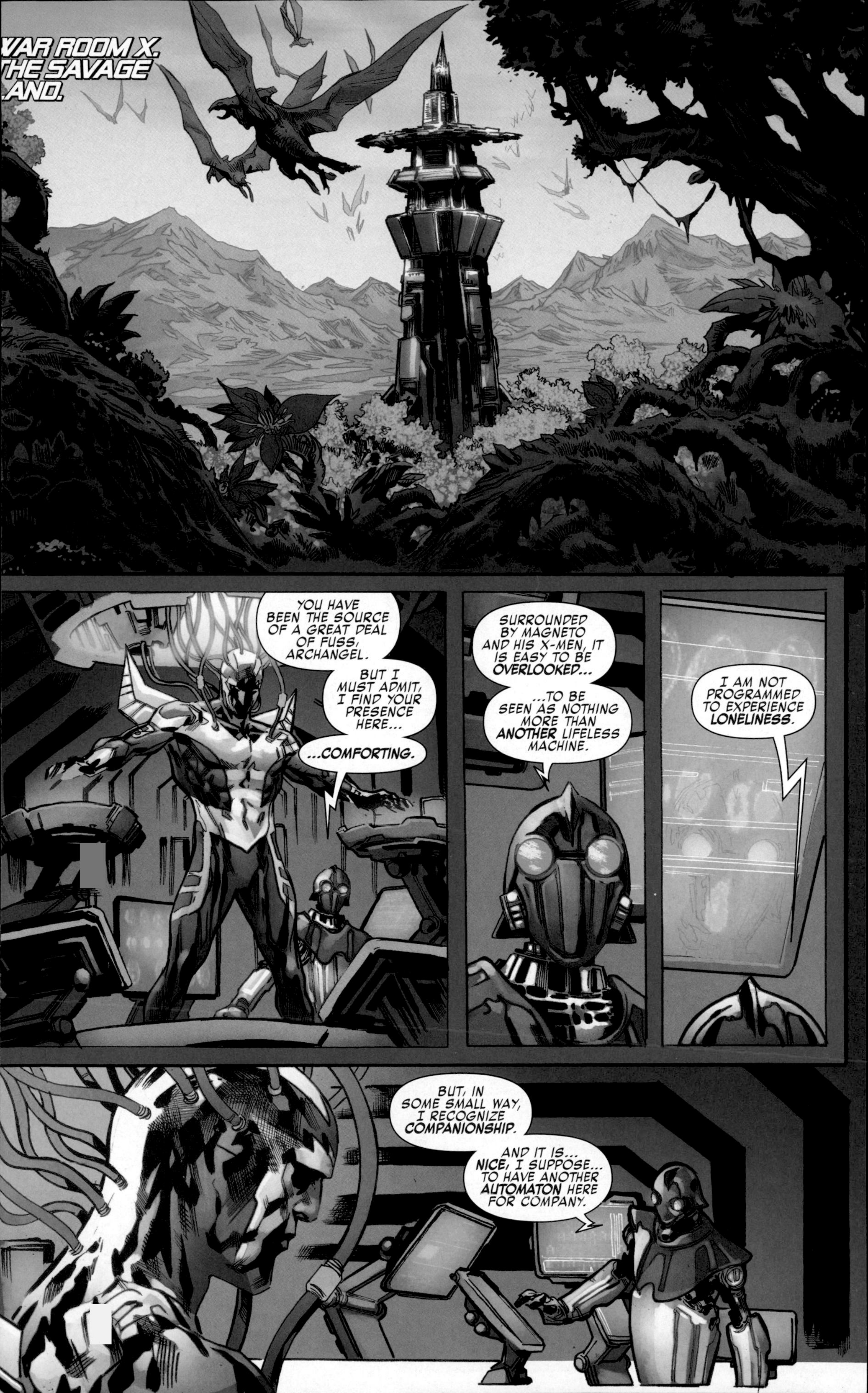
WAR ROOM X. THE SAVAGE LAND.
YOU HAVE BEEN THE SOURCE OF A GREAT DEAL OF FUSS, ARCHANGEL.
BUT I MUST ADMIT, I FIND YOUR PRESENCE HERE...
...COMFORTING.
SURROUNDED BY MAGNETO AND HIS X-MEN, IT IS EASY TO BE OVERLOOKED...
...TO BE SEEN AS NOTHING MORE THAN ANOTHER LIFELESS MACHINE.
I AM NOT PROGRAMMED TO EXPERIENCE LONELINESS.
BUT, IN SOME SMALL WAY, I RECOGNIZE COMPANIONSHIP.
AND IT IS... NICE, I SUPPOSE... TO HAVE ANOTHER AUTOMATON HERE FOR COMPANY.

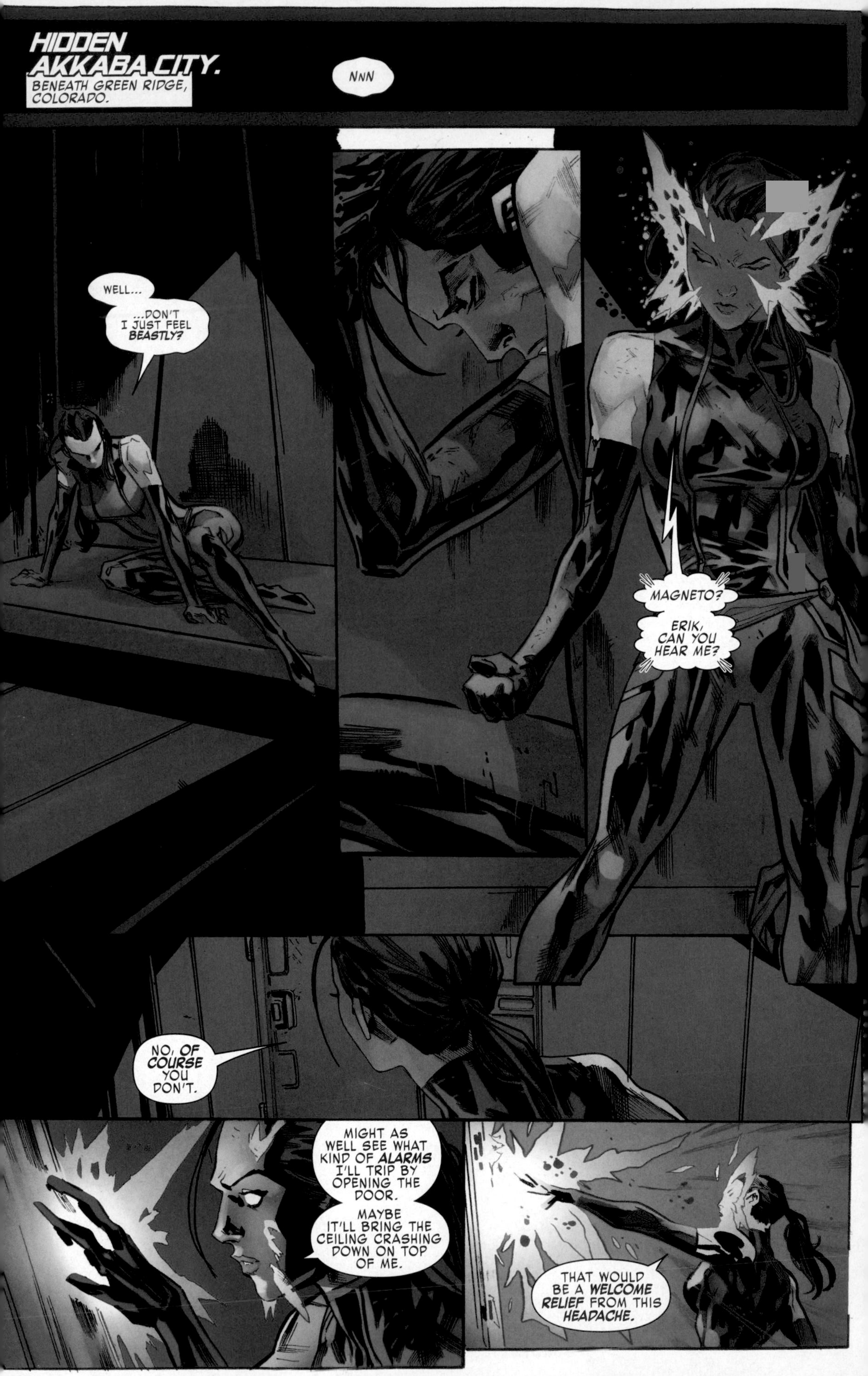
HIDDEN AKKABA CITY.
BENEATH GREEN RIDGE, COLORADO.
NNN
WELL...
...DON'T I JUST FEEL BEASTLY?
MAGNETO?
ERIK, CAN YOU HEAR ME?
NO, OF COURSE YOU DON'T.
MIGHT AS WELL SEE WHAT KIND OF ALARMS I'LL TRIP BY OPENING THE DOOR.
MAYBE IT'LL BRING THE CEILING CRASHING DOWN ON TOP OF ME.
THAT WOULD BE A WELCOME RELIEF FROM THIS HEADACHE.

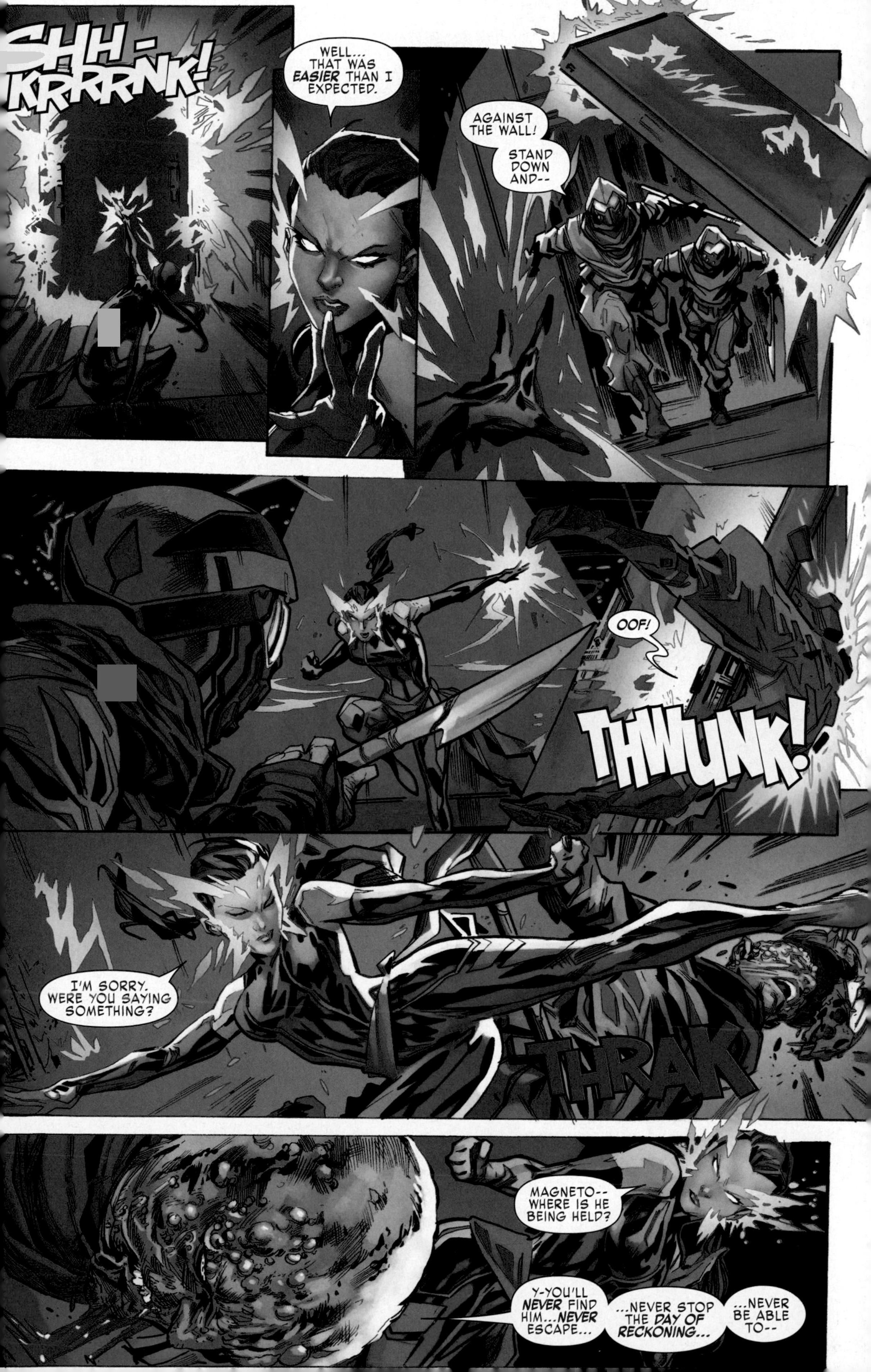
SHH-KRRRNK!
WELL... THAT WAS EASIER THAN I EXPECTED.
AGAINST THE WALL!
STAND DOWN AND--
OOF!
THWUNK!
I'M SORRY. WERE YOU SAYING SOMETHING?
THRAK
MAGNETO-- WHERE IS HE BEING HELD?
Y-YOU'LL NEVER FIND HIM...NEVER ESCAPE...
...NEVER STOP THE DAY OF RECKONING...
...NEVER BE ABLE TO--

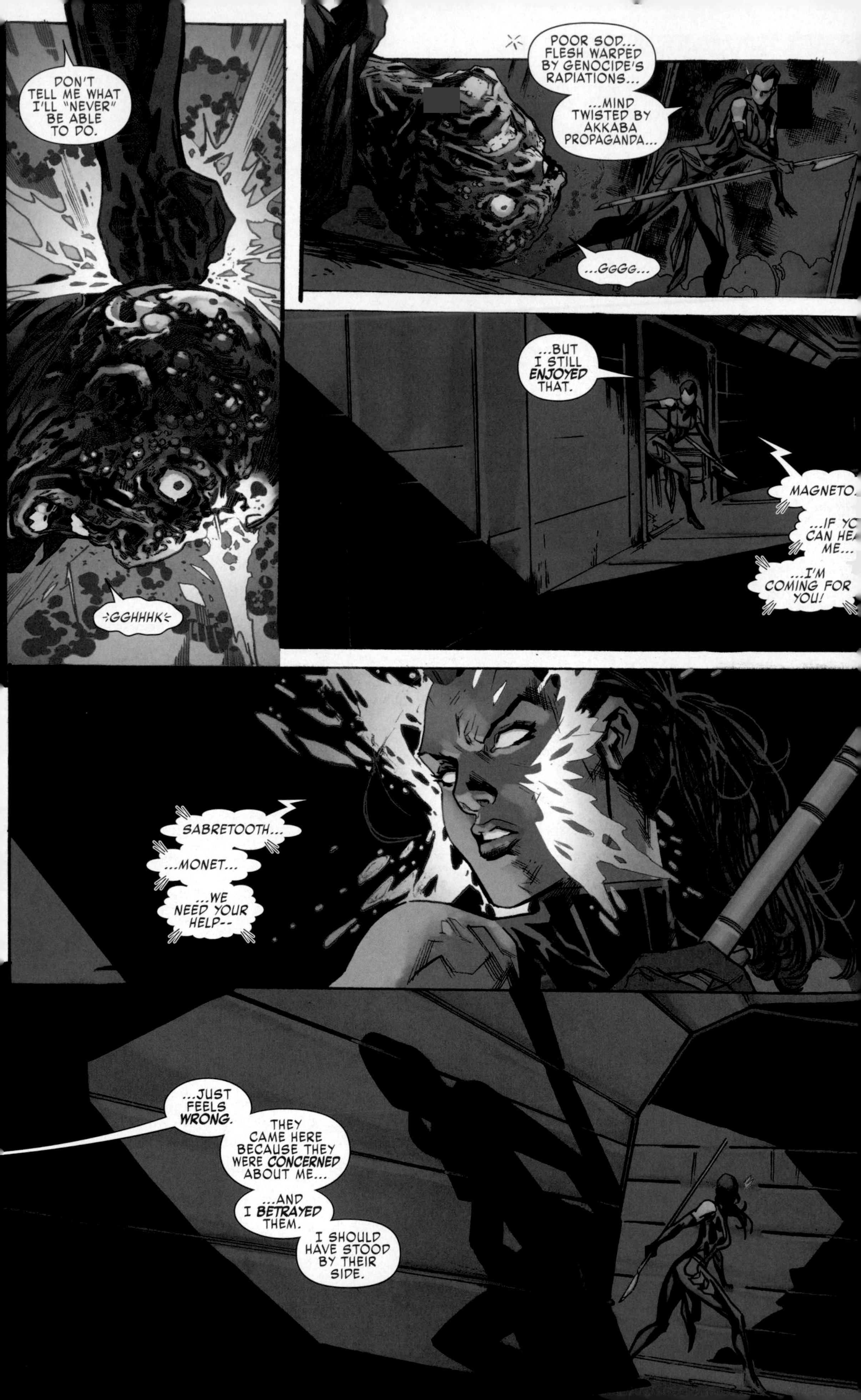
DON'T TELL ME WHAT I'LL "NEVER" BE ABLE TO DO.
GGHHHK
POOR SOD... FLESH WARPED BY GENOCIDE'S RADIATIONS...
...MIND TWISTED BY AKKABA PROPAGANDA...
...GGGG...
...BUT I STILL ENJOYED THAT.
MAGNETO
...IF YC CAN HE ME...
...I'M COMING FOR YOU!
SABRETOOTH...
...MONET...
...WE NEED YOUR HELP--
...JUST FEELS WRONG.
THEY CAME HERE BECAUSE THEY WERE CONCERNED ABOUT ME...
...AND I BETRAYED THEM.
I SHOULD HAVE STOOD BY THEIR SIDE.

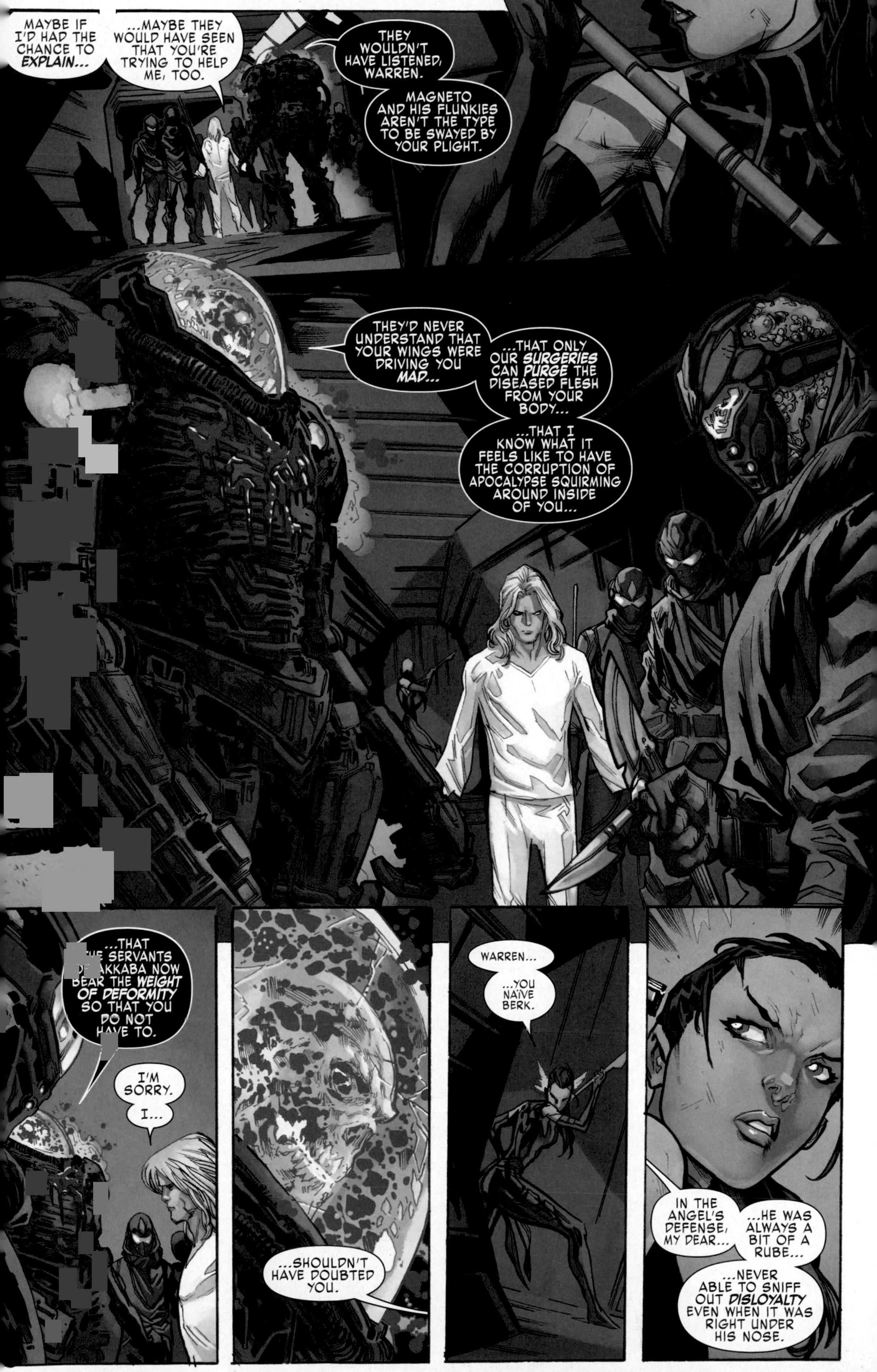

MAYBE IF I'D HAD THE CHANCE TO *EXPLAIN*...
...MAYBE THEY WOULD HAVE SEEN THAT YOU'RE TRYING TO HELP ME, TOO.
THEY WOULDN'T HAVE LISTENED, WARREN.
MAGNETO AND HIS FLUNKIES AREN'T THE TYPE TO BE SWAYED BY YOUR PLIGHT.
THEY'D NEVER UNDERSTAND THAT YOUR WINGS WERE DRIVING YOU *MAD*...
...THAT ONLY OUR *SURGERIES* CAN *PURGE* THE DISEASED FLESH FROM YOUR BODY...
...THAT I KNOW WHAT IT FEELS LIKE TO HAVE THE CORRUPTION OF APOCALYPSE SQUIRMING AROUND INSIDE OF YOU...
...THAT E SERVANTS AKKABA NOW BEAR THE *WEIGHT OF DEFORMITY* SO THAT YOU DO NOT HAVE TO.
I'M SORRY. I...
...SHOULDN'T HAVE DOUBTED YOU.
WARREN...
...YOU NAÏVE BERK.
IN THE ANGEL'S DEFENSE, MY DEAR...
...HE WAS ALWAYS A BIT OF A RUBE...
...NEVER ABLE TO SNIFF OUT *DISLOYALTY* EVEN WHEN IT WAS RIGHT UNDER HIS NOSE.

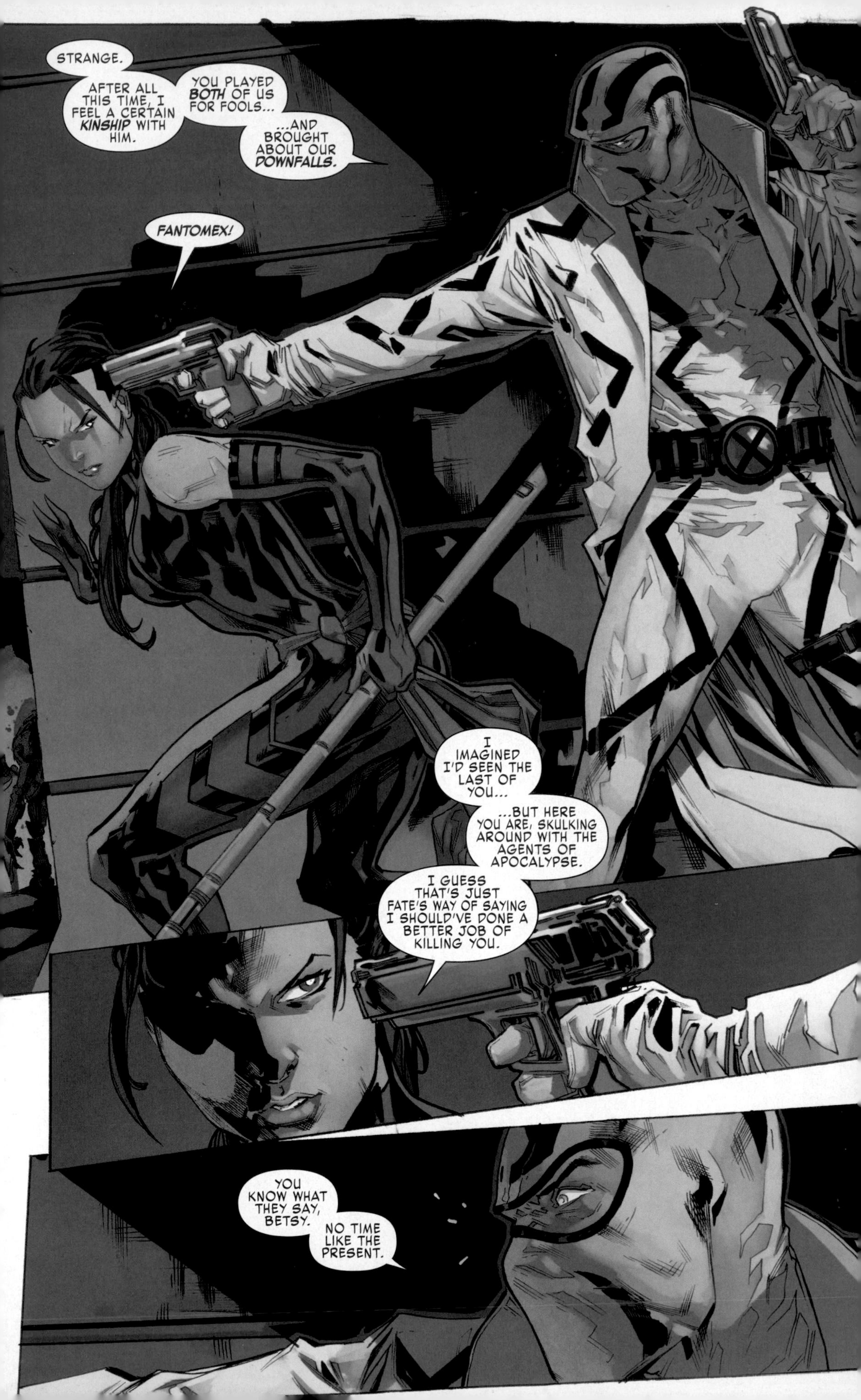
STRANGE.
AFTER ALL THIS TIME, I FEEL A CERTAIN KINSHIP WITH HIM.
YOU PLAYED BOTH OF US FOR FOOLS...
...AND BROUGHT ABOUT OUR DOWNFALLS.
FANTOMEX!
I IMAGINED I'D SEEN THE LAST OF YOU...
...BUT HERE YOU ARE, SKULKING AROUND WITH THE AGENTS OF APOCALYPSE.
I GUESS THAT'S JUST FATE'S WAY OF SAYING I SHOULD'VE DONE A BETTER JOB OF KILLING YOU.
YOU KNOW WHAT THEY SAY, BETSY.
NO TIME LIKE THE PRESENT.

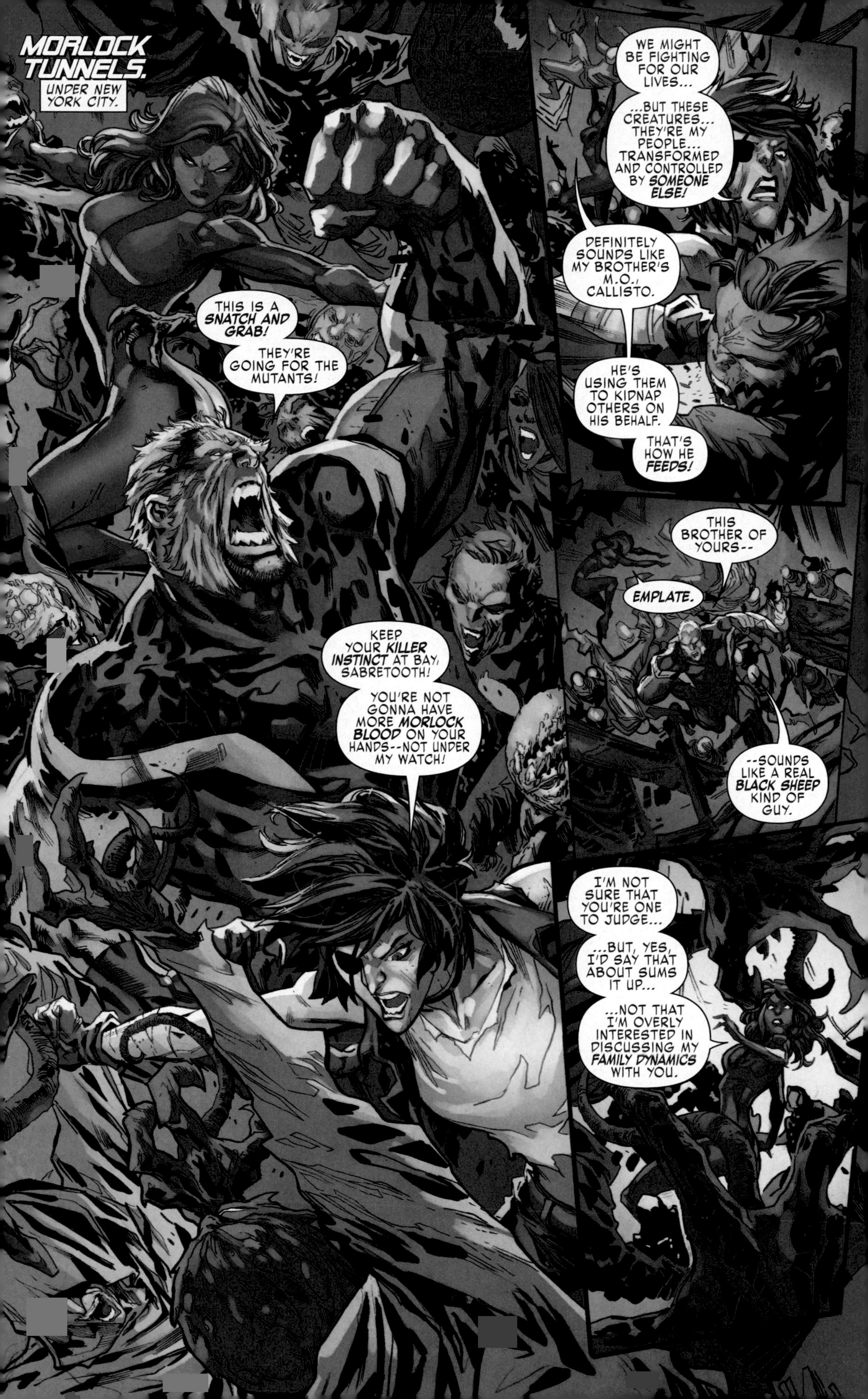
MORLOCK TUNNELS.
UNDER NEW YORK CITY.
THIS IS A SNATCH AND GRAB!
THEY'RE GOING FOR THE MUTANTS!
KEEP YOUR KILLER INSTINCT AT BAY, SABRETOOTH!
YOU'RE NOT GONNA HAVE MORE MORLOCK BLOOD ON YOUR HANDS--NOT UNDER MY WATCH!
WE MIGHT BE FIGHTING FOR OUR LIVES...
...BUT THESE CREATURES... THEY'RE MY PEOPLE... TRANSFORMED AND CONTROLLED BY SOMEONE ELSE!
DEFINITELY SOUNDS LIKE MY BROTHER'S M.O., CALLISTO.
HE'S USING THEM TO KIDNAP OTHERS ON HIS BEHALF.
THAT'S HOW HE FEEDS!
THIS BROTHER OF YOURS--
EMPLATE.
--SOUNDS LIKE A REAL BLACK SHEEP KIND OF GUY.
I'M NOT SURE THAT YOU'RE ONE TO JUDGE...
...BUT, YES, I'D SAY THAT ABOUT SUMS IT UP...
...NOT THAT I'M OVERLY INTERESTED IN DISCUSSING MY FAMILY DYNAMICS WITH YOU.

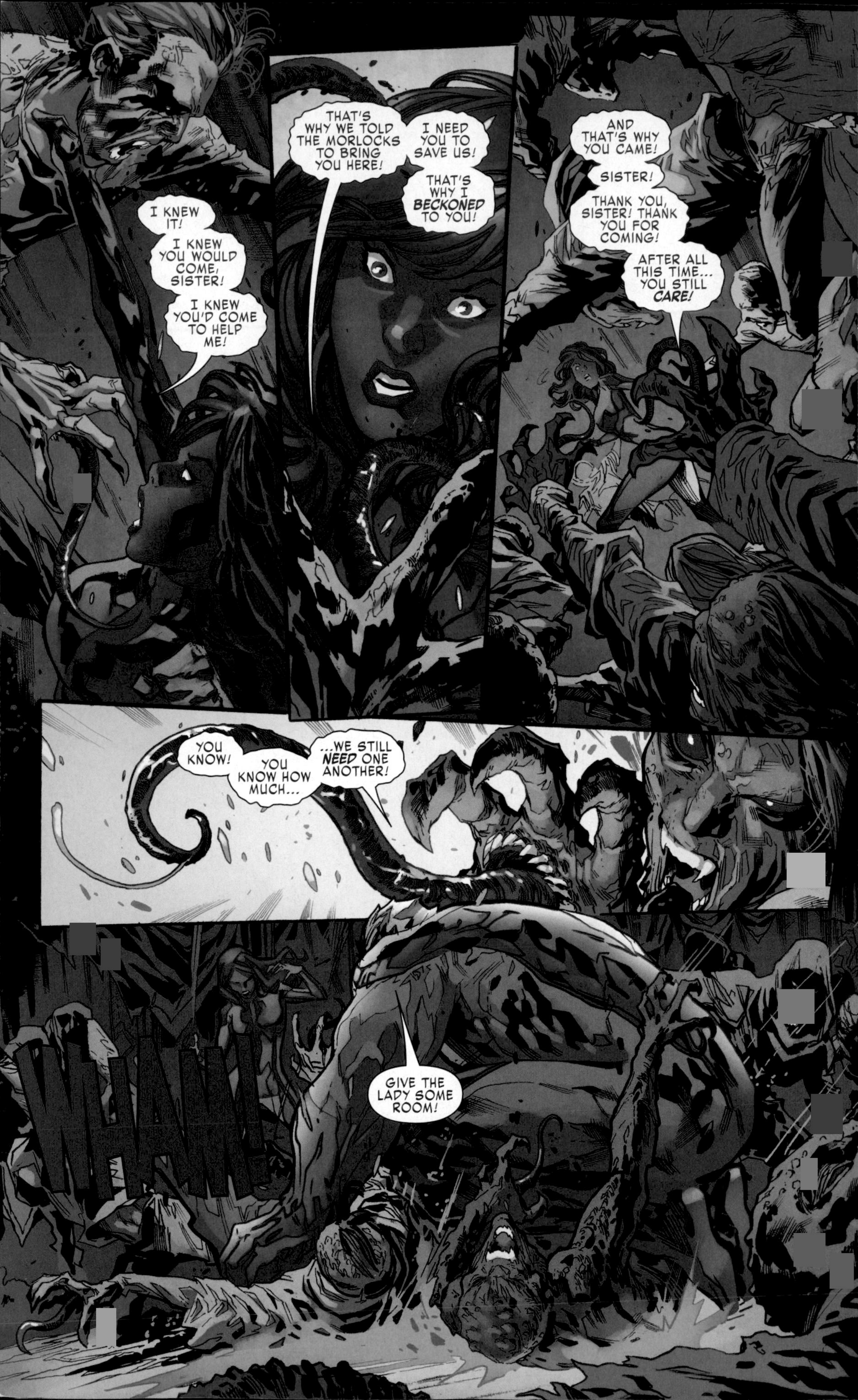
I KNEW IT!
I KNEW YOU WOULD COME, SISTER!
I KNEW YOU'D COME TO HELP ME!
THAT'S WHY WE TOLD THE MORLOCKS TO BRING YOU HERE!
I NEED YOU TO SAVE US!
THAT'S WHY I *BECKONED* TO YOU!
AND THAT'S WHY YOU CAME!
SISTER!
THANK YOU, SISTER! THANK YOU FOR COMING!
AFTER ALL THIS TIME... YOU STILL *CARE!*
YOU KNOW!
YOU KNOW HOW MUCH...
...WE STILL *NEED* ONE ANOTHER!
WHAM!
GIVE THE LADY SOME ROOM!

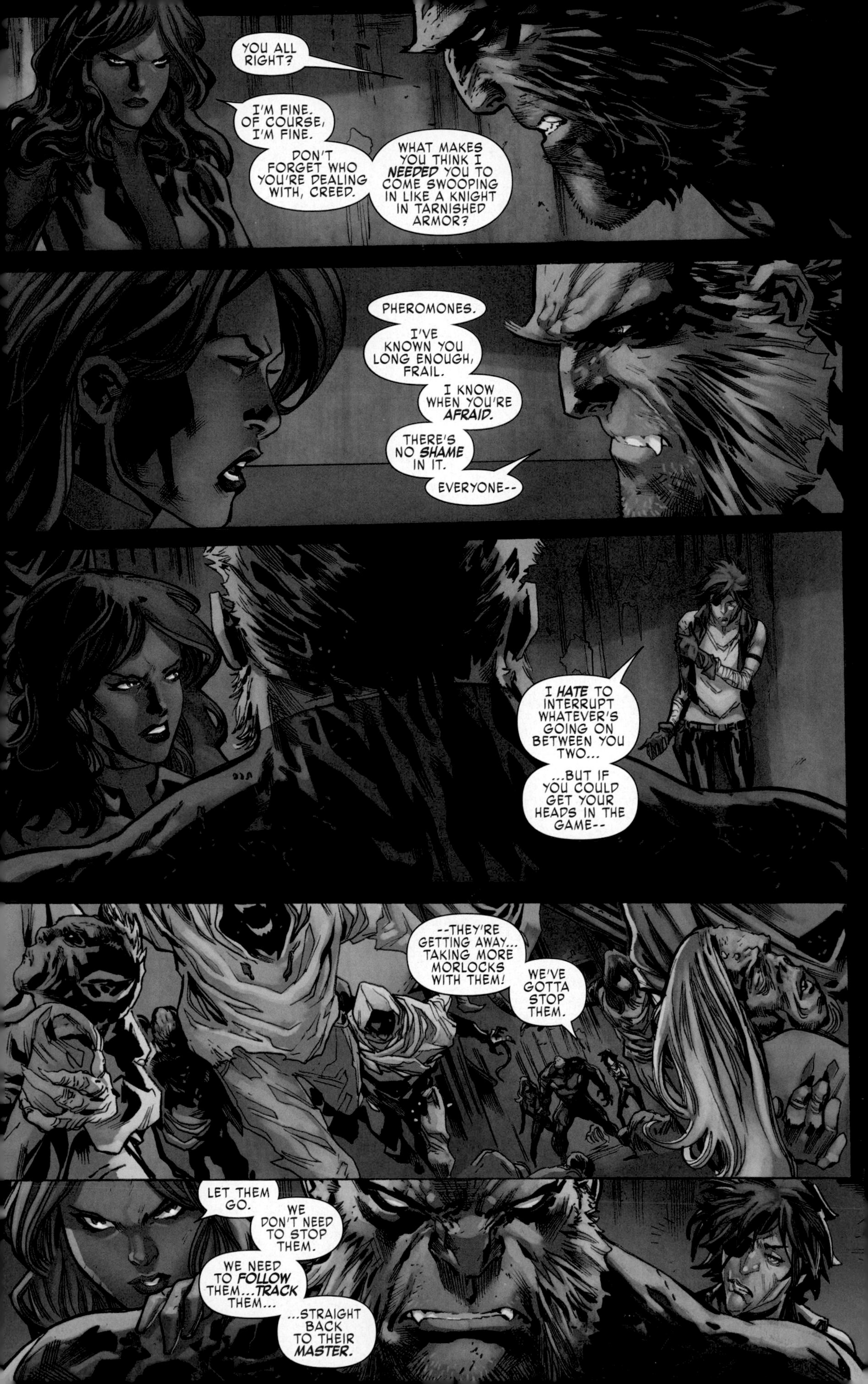
YOU ALL RIGHT?
I'M FINE. OF COURSE, I'M FINE.
DON'T FORGET WHO YOU'RE DEALING WITH, CREED.
WHAT MAKES YOU THINK I NEEDED YOU TO COME SWOOPING IN LIKE A KNIGHT IN TARNISHED ARMOR?
PHEROMONES.
I'VE KNOWN YOU LONG ENOUGH, FRAIL.
I KNOW WHEN YOU'RE AFRAID.
THERE'S NO SHAME IN IT.
EVERYONE--
I HATE TO INTERRUPT WHATEVER'S GOING ON BETWEEN YOU TWO...
...BUT IF YOU COULD GET YOUR HEADS IN THE GAME--
--THEY'RE GETTING AWAY... TAKING MORE MORLOCKS WITH THEM!
WE'VE GOTTA STOP THEM.
LET THEM GO.
WE DON'T NEED TO STOP THEM.
WE NEED TO FOLLOW THEM...TRACK THEM...
...STRAIGHT BACK TO THEIR MASTER.

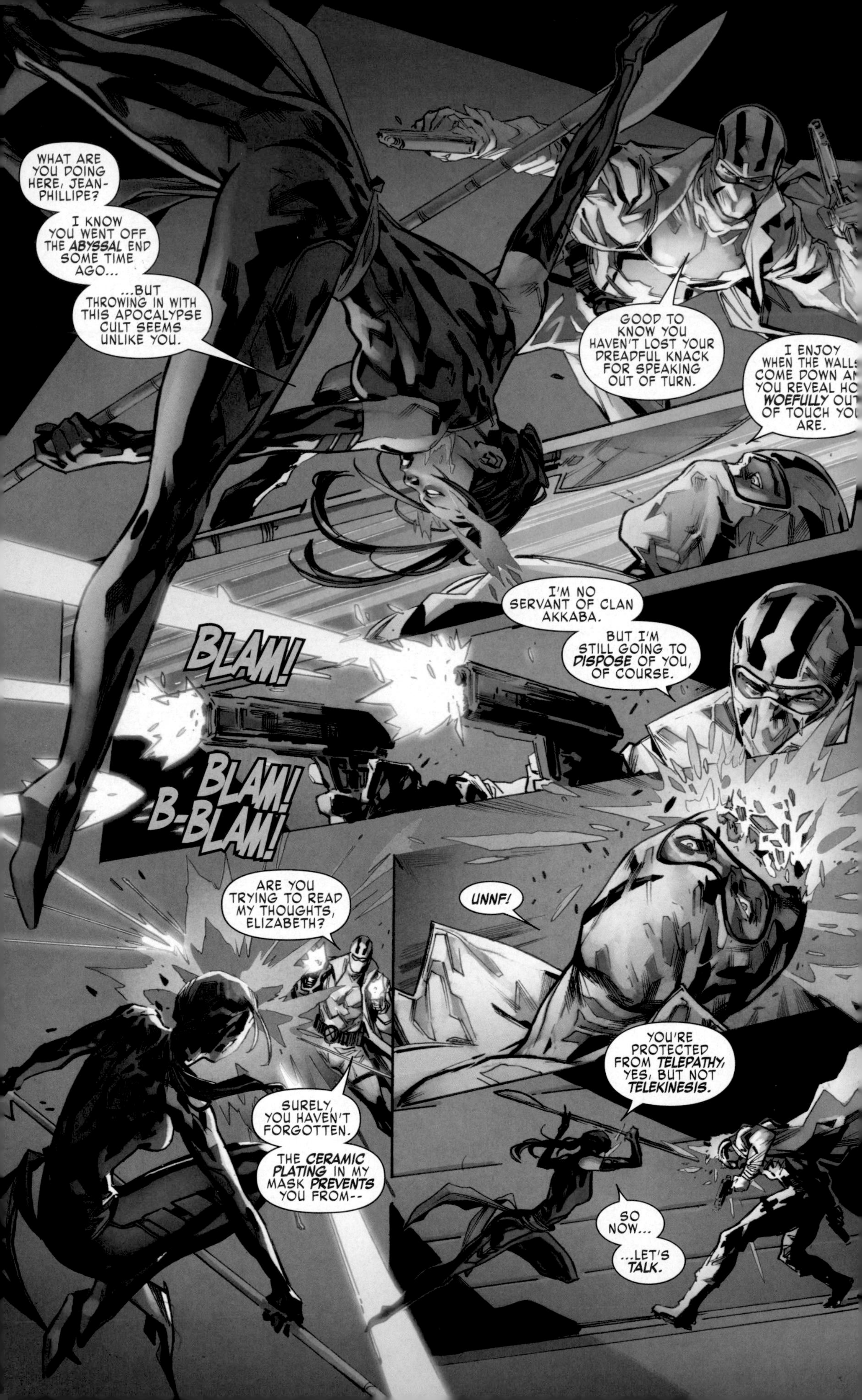

WHAT ARE YOU DOING HERE, JEAN-PHILLIPE?
I KNOW YOU WENT OFF THE ABYSSAL END SOME TIME AGO...
...BUT THROWING IN WITH THIS APOCALYPSE CULT SEEMS UNLIKE YOU.
GOOD TO KNOW YOU HAVEN'T LOST YOUR DREADFUL KNACK FOR SPEAKING OUT OF TURN.
I'M NO SERVANT OF CLAN AKKABA.
BUT I'M STILL GOING TO DISPOSE OF YOU, OF COURSE.
BLAM!
BLAM! B-BLAM!
ARE YOU TRYING TO READ MY THOUGHTS, ELIZABETH?
SURELY, YOU HAVEN'T FORGOTTEN.
THE CERAMIC PLATING IN MY MASK PREVENTS YOU FROM--
UNNF!
YOU'RE PROTECTED FROM TELEPATHY, YES, BUT NOT TELEKINESIS.
SO NOW...
...LET'S TALK.

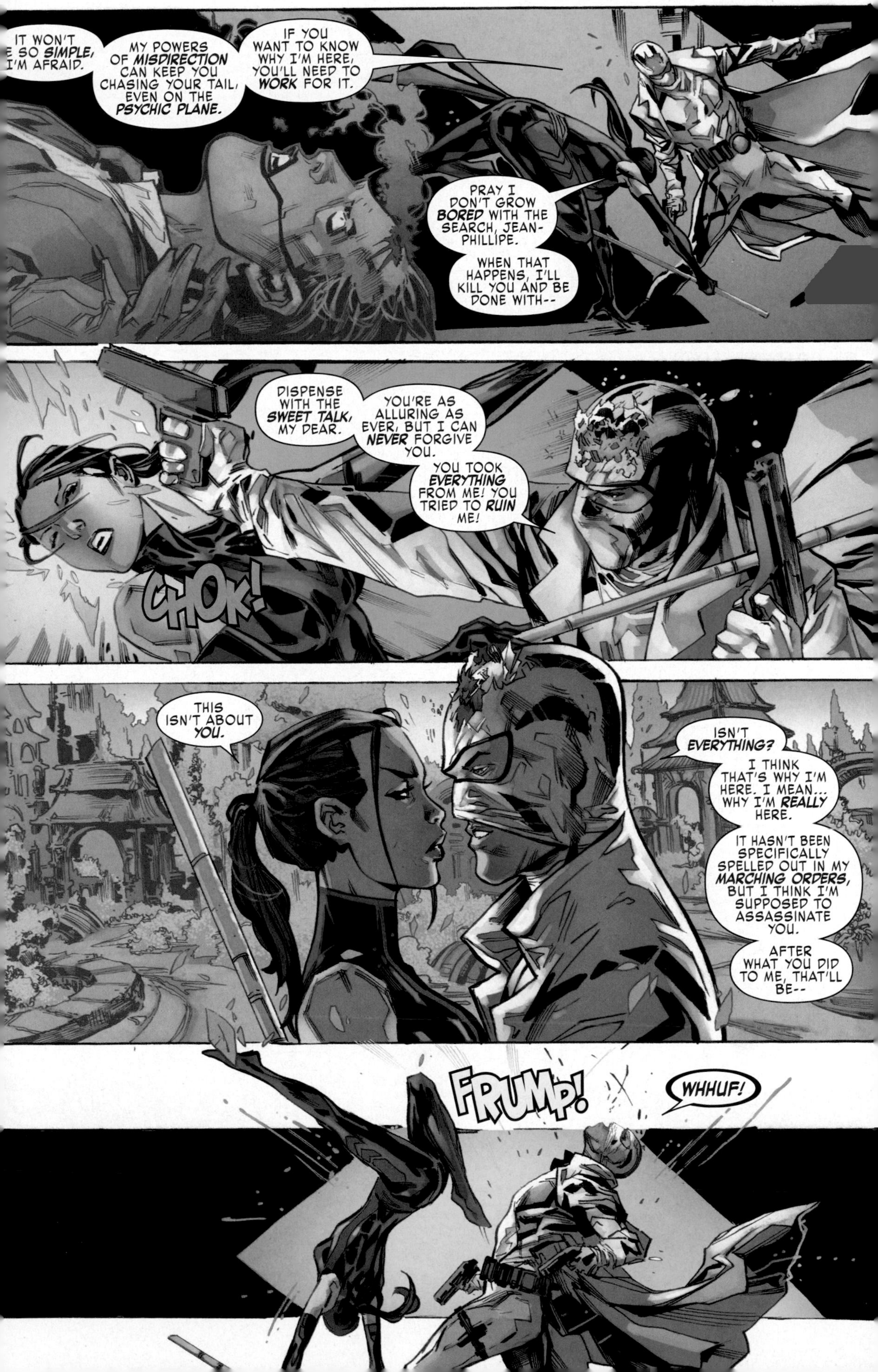

IT WON'T E SO SIMPLE, I'M AFRAID.
MY POWERS OF MISDIRECTION CAN KEEP YOU CHASING YOUR TAIL, EVEN ON THE PSYCHIC PLANE.
IF YOU WANT TO KNOW WHY I'M HERE, YOU'LL NEED TO WORK FOR IT.
PRAY I DON'T GROW BORED WITH THE SEARCH, JEAN-PHILLIPE.
WHEN THAT HAPPENS, I'LL KILL YOU AND BE DONE WITH--
DISPENSE WITH THE SWEET TALK, MY DEAR.
YOU'RE AS ALLURING AS EVER, BUT I CAN NEVER FORGIVE YOU.
YOU TOOK EVERYTHING FROM ME! YOU TRIED TO RUIN ME!
CHOK!
THIS ISN'T ABOUT YOU.
ISN'T EVERYTHING?
I THINK THAT'S WHY I'M HERE. I MEAN... WHY I'M REALLY HERE.
IT HASN'T BEEN SPECIFICALLY SPELLED OUT IN MY MARCHING ORDERS, BUT I THINK I'M SUPPOSED TO ASSASSINATE YOU.
AFTER WHAT YOU DID TO ME, THAT'LL BE--
FRUMP!
WHHUF!

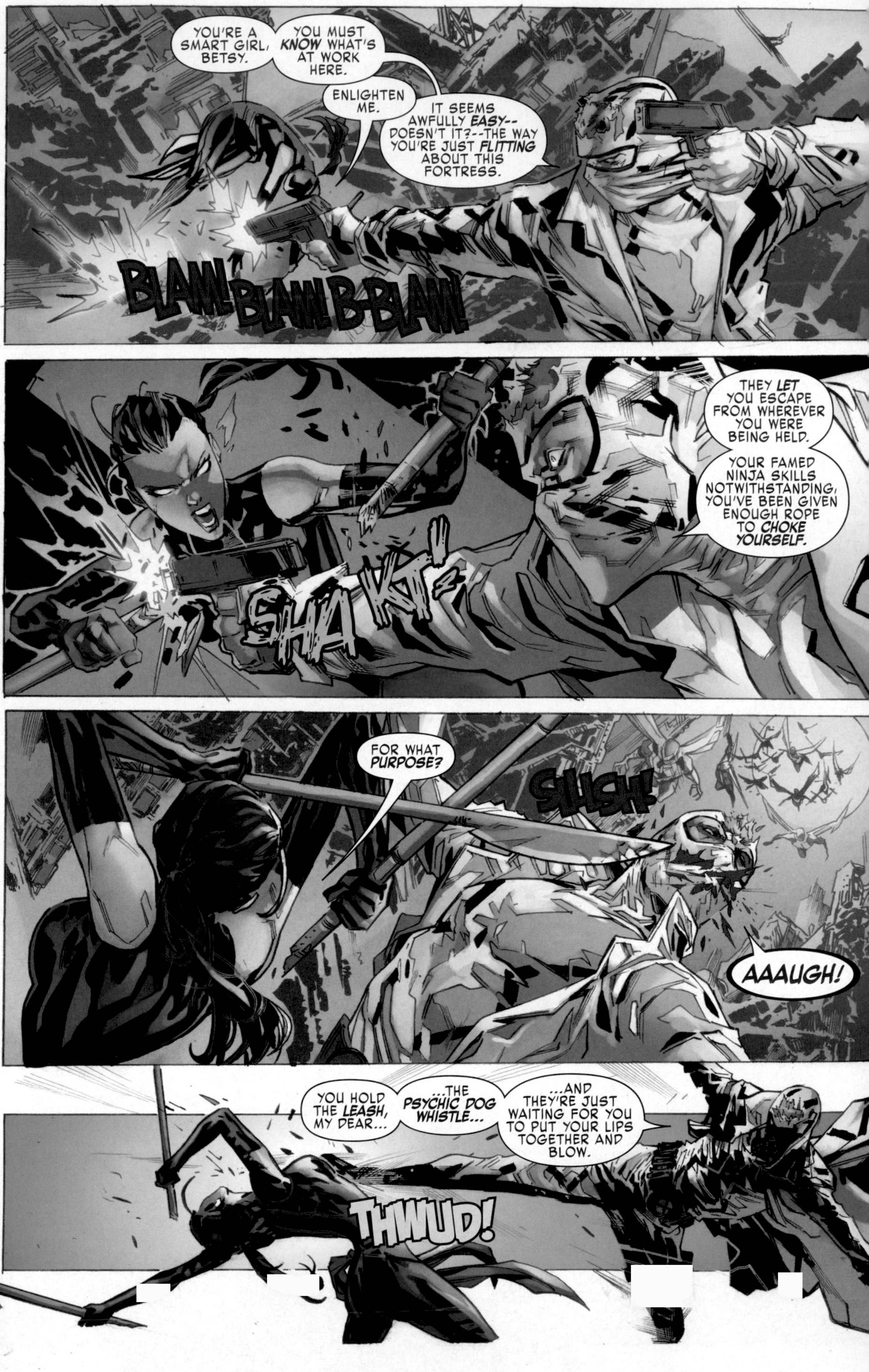
YOU'RE A SMART GIRL, BETSY.
YOU MUST KNOW WHAT'S AT WORK HERE.
ENLIGHTEN ME.
IT SEEMS AWFULLY EASY--DOESN'T IT?--THE WAY YOU'RE JUST FLITTING ABOUT THIS FORTRESS.
BLAM! BLAM! B-BLAM!
THEY LET YOU ESCAPE FROM WHEREVER YOU WERE BEING HELD.
YOUR FAMED NINJA SKILLS NOTWITHSTANDING, YOU'VE BEEN GIVEN ENOUGH ROPE TO CHOKE YOURSELF.
SHAKT!
FOR WHAT PURPOSE?
SHLSH!
AAAUGH!
YOU HOLD THE LEASH, MY DEAR...
...THE PSYCHIC DOG WHISTLE...
...AND THEY'RE JUST WAITING FOR YOU TO PUT YOUR LIPS TOGETHER AND BLOW.
THWUD!

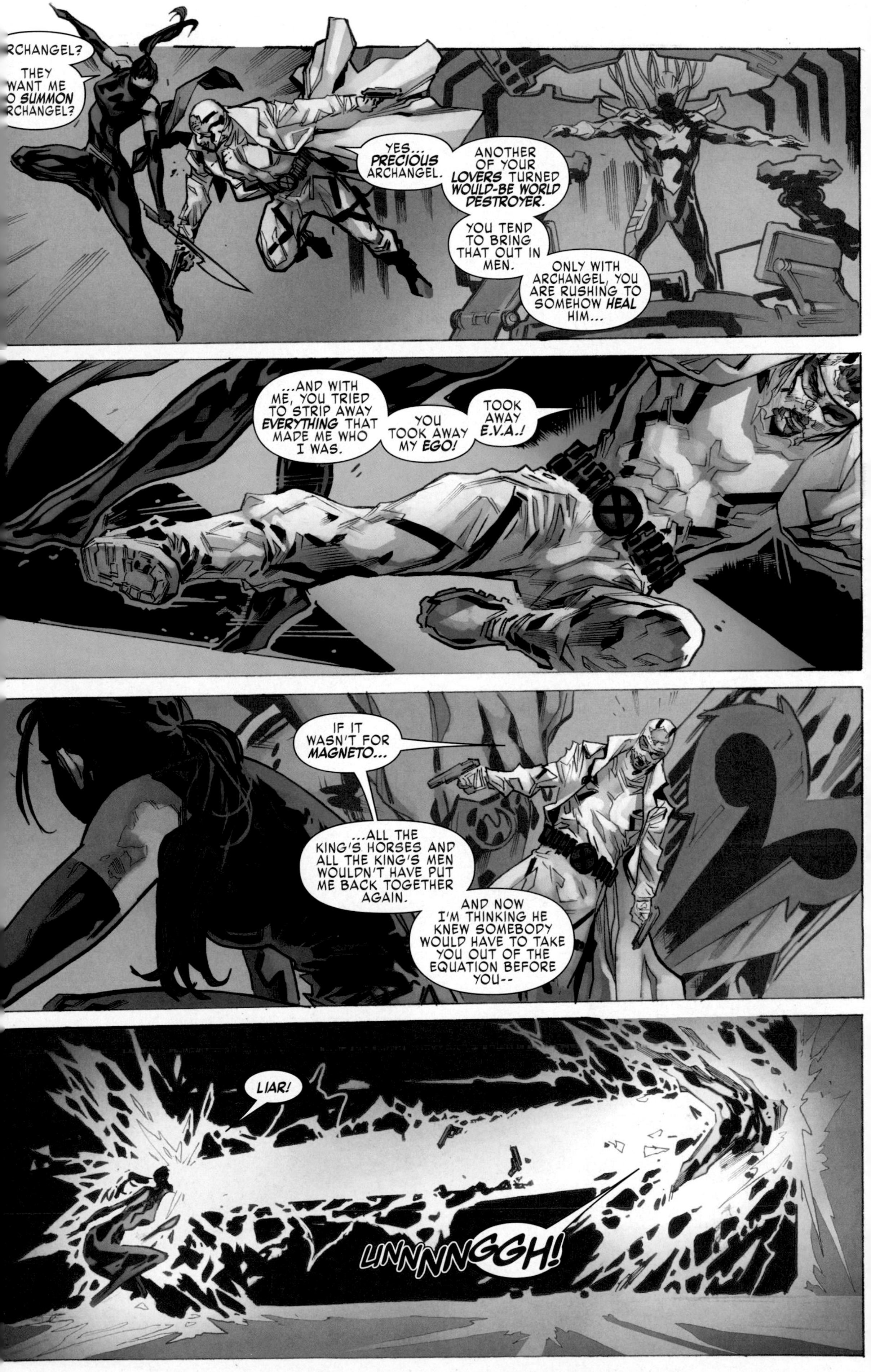

RCHANGEL?
THEY WANT ME O SUMMON RCHANGEL?
YES... PRECIOUS ARCHANGEL.
ANOTHER OF YOUR LOVERS TURNED WOULD-BE WORLD DESTROYER.
YOU TEND TO BRING THAT OUT IN MEN.
ONLY WITH ARCHANGEL, YOU ARE RUSHING TO SOMEHOW HEAL HIM...
...AND WITH ME, YOU TRIED TO STRIP AWAY EVERYTHING THAT MADE ME WHO I WAS.
YOU TOOK AWAY MY EGO!
TOOK AWAY E.V.A.!
IF IT WASN'T FOR MAGNETO...
...ALL THE KING'S HORSES AND ALL THE KING'S MEN WOULDN'T HAVE PUT ME BACK TOGETHER AGAIN.
AND NOW I'M THINKING HE KNEW SOMEBODY WOULD HAVE TO TAKE YOU OUT OF THE EQUATION BEFORE YOU--
LIAR!
UNNNNGGH!

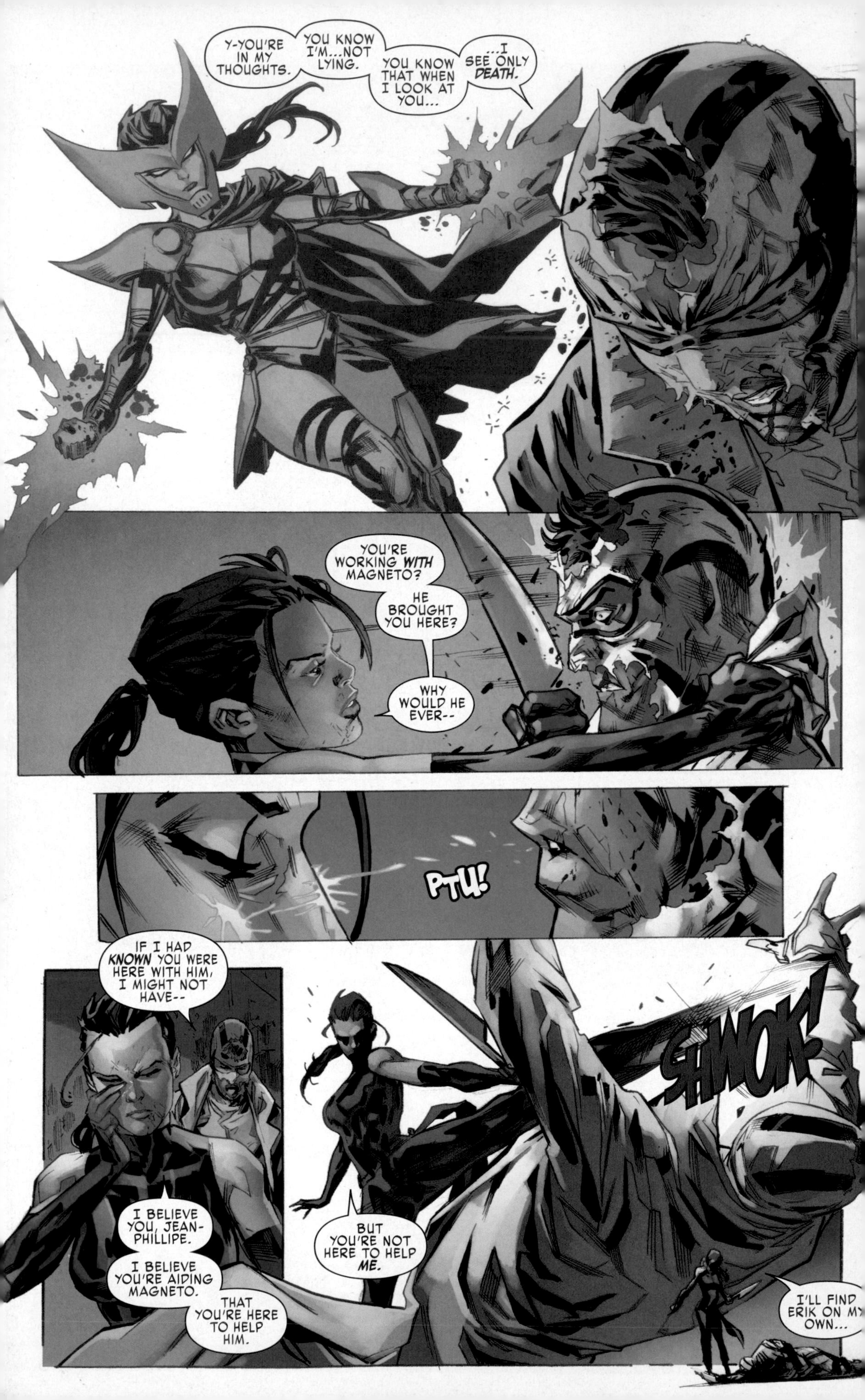

Y-YOU'RE IN MY THOUGHTS.
YOU KNOW I'M...NOT LYING.
YOU KNOW THAT WHEN I LOOK AT YOU...
...I SEE ONLY *DEATH.*
YOU'RE WORKING *WITH* MAGNETO?
HE BROUGHT YOU HERE?
WHY WOULD HE EVER--
PTU!
IF I HAD *KNOWN* YOU WERE HERE WITH HIM, I MIGHT NOT HAVE--
SHWOK!
I BELIEVE YOU, JEAN-PHILLIPE.
I BELIEVE YOU'RE AIDING MAGNETO.
THAT YOU'RE HERE TO HELP HIM.
BUT YOU'RE NOT HERE TO HELP *ME.*
I'LL FIND ERIK ON MY OWN...

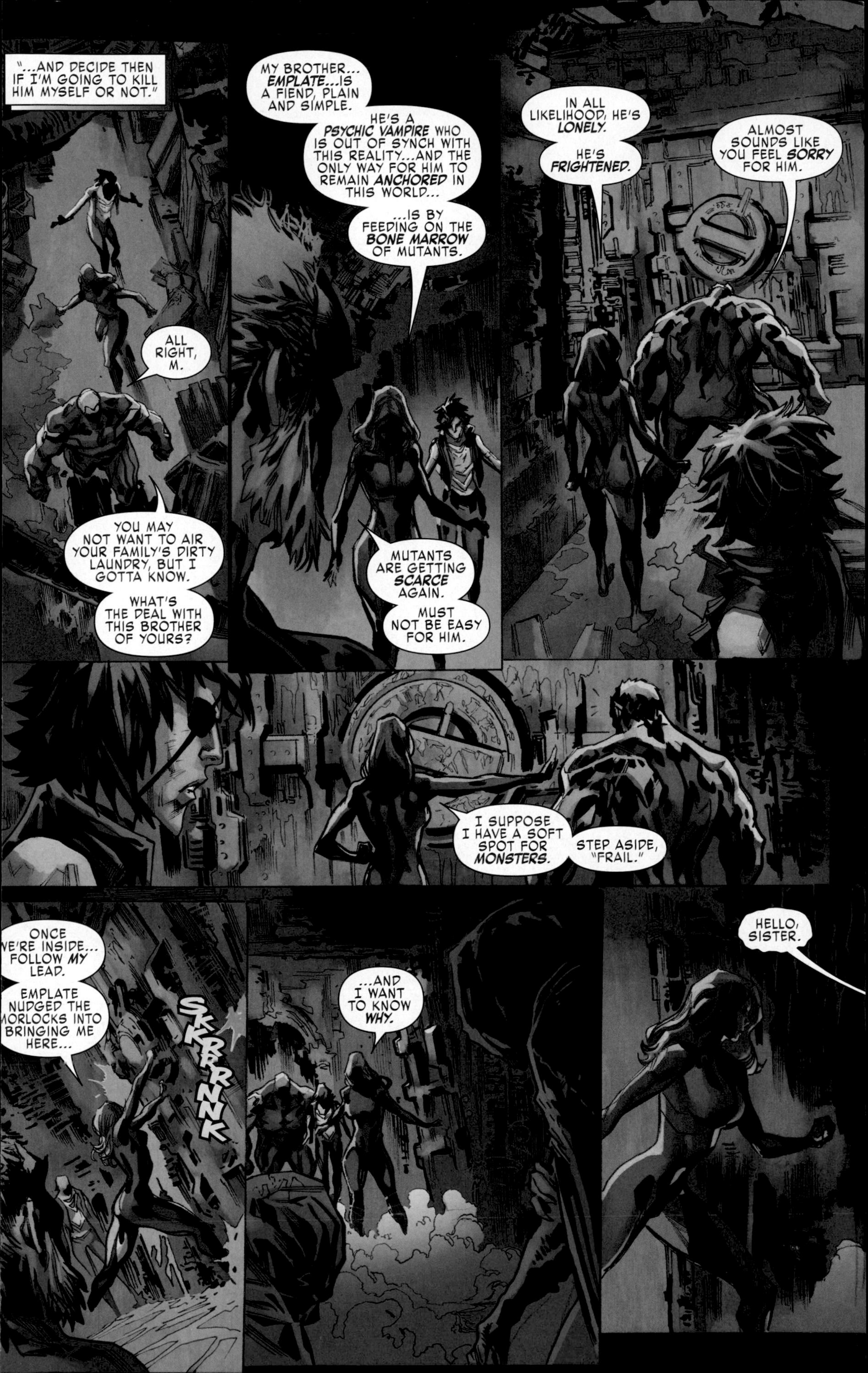
"...AND DECIDE THEN IF I'M GOING TO KILL HIM MYSELF OR NOT."
ALL RIGHT, M.
YOU MAY NOT WANT TO AIR YOUR FAMILY'S DIRTY LAUNDRY, BUT I GOTTA KNOW.
WHAT'S THE DEAL WITH THIS BROTHER OF YOURS?
MY BROTHER... EMPLATE... IS A FIEND, PLAIN AND SIMPLE.
HE'S A PSYCHIC VAMPIRE WHO IS OUT OF SYNCH WITH THIS REALITY...AND THE ONLY WAY FOR HIM TO REMAIN ANCHORED IN THIS WORLD...
...IS BY FEEDING ON THE BONE MARROW OF MUTANTS.
MUTANTS ARE GETTING SCARCE AGAIN.
MUST NOT BE EASY FOR HIM.
IN ALL LIKELIHOOD, HE'S LONELY.
HE'S FRIGHTENED.
ALMOST SOUNDS LIKE YOU FEEL SORRY FOR HIM.
I SUPPOSE I HAVE A SOFT SPOT FOR MONSTERS.
STEP ASIDE, "FRAIL."
ONCE WE'RE INSIDE... FOLLOW MY LEAD.
EMPLATE NUDGED THE MORLOCKS INTO BRINGING ME HERE...
SKRRRNK
...AND I WANT TO KNOW WHY.
HELLO, SISTER.

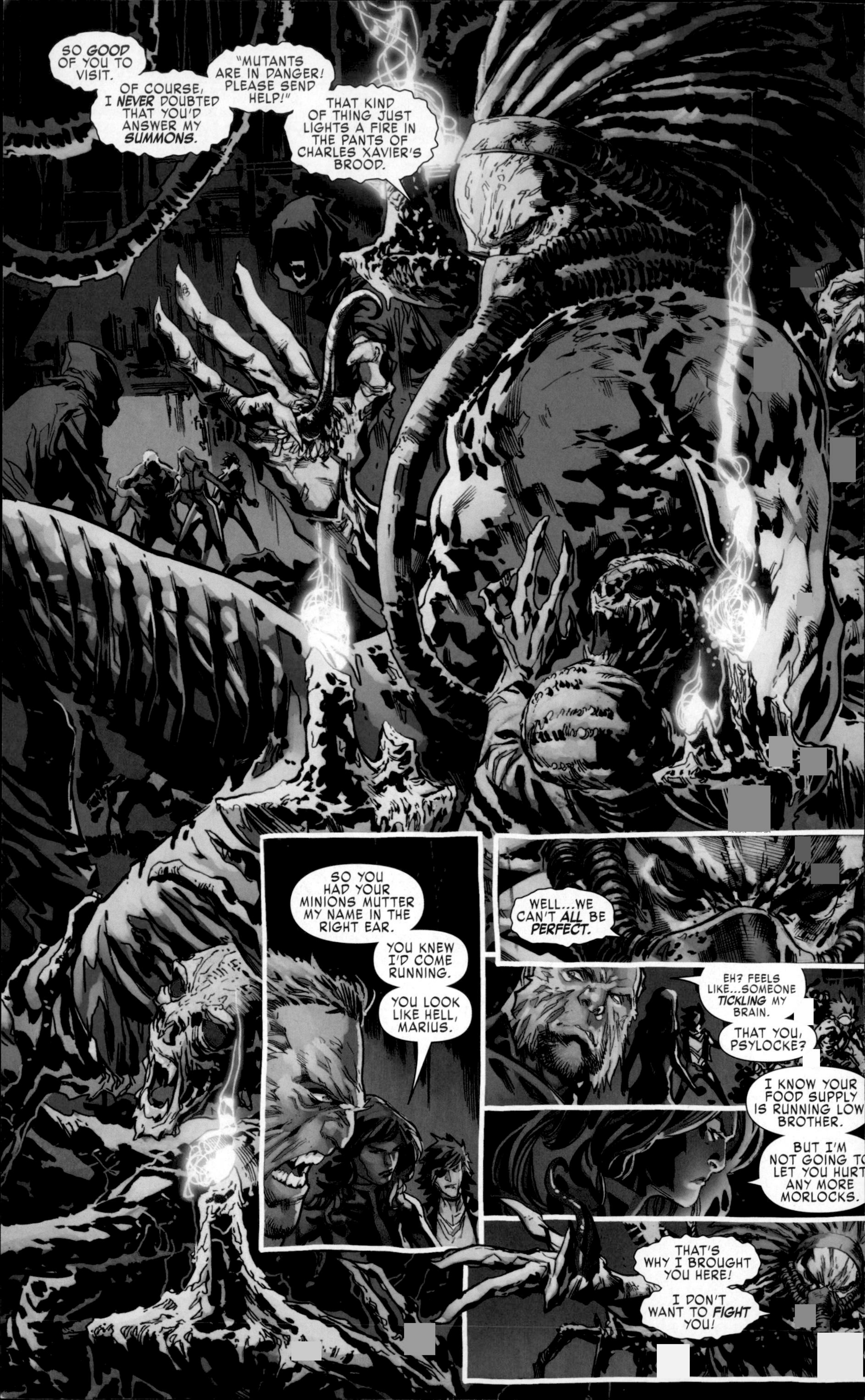
SO GOOD OF YOU TO VISIT.
OF COURSE, I NEVER DOUBTED THAT YOU'D ANSWER MY SUMMONS.
"MUTANTS ARE IN DANGER! PLEASE SEND HELP!"
THAT KIND OF THING JUST LIGHTS A FIRE IN THE PANTS OF CHARLES XAVIER'S BROOD.
SO YOU HAD YOUR MINIONS MUTTER MY NAME IN THE RIGHT EAR.
YOU KNEW I'D COME RUNNING.
YOU LOOK LIKE HELL, MARIUS.
WELL...WE CAN'T ALL BE PERFECT.
EH? FEELS LIKE...SOMEONE TICKLING MY BRAIN.
THAT YOU, PSYLOCKE?
I KNOW YOUR FOOD SUPPLY IS RUNNING LOW, BROTHER.
BUT I'M NOT GOING TO LET YOU HURT ANY MORE MORLOCKS.
THAT'S WHY I BROUGHT YOU HERE!
I DON'T WANT TO FIGHT YOU!

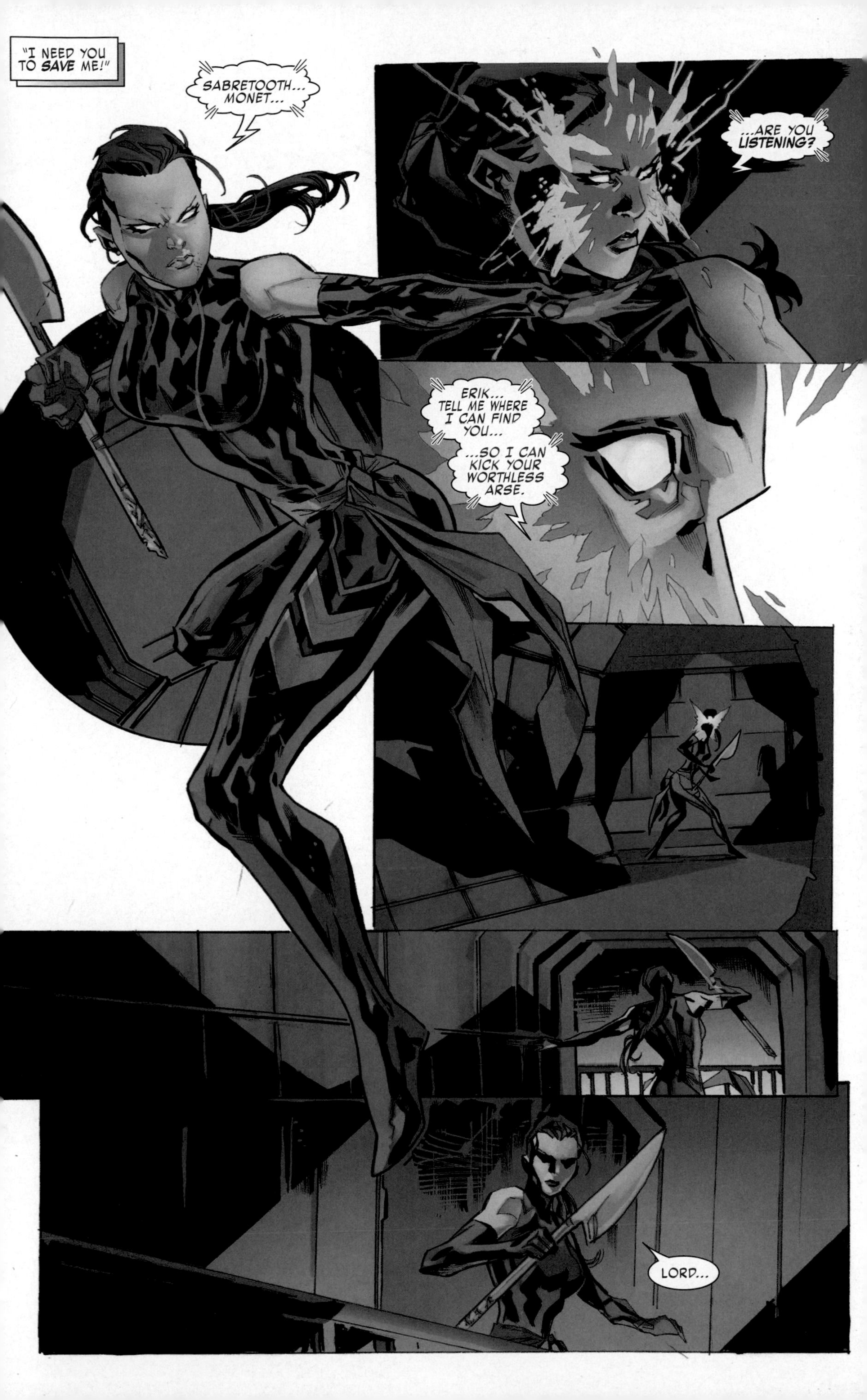
"I NEED YOU TO SAVE ME!"
SABRETOOTH... MONET...
...ARE YOU LISTENING?
ERIK... TELL ME WHERE I CAN FIND YOU...
...SO I CAN KICK YOUR WORTHLESS ARSE.
LORD...

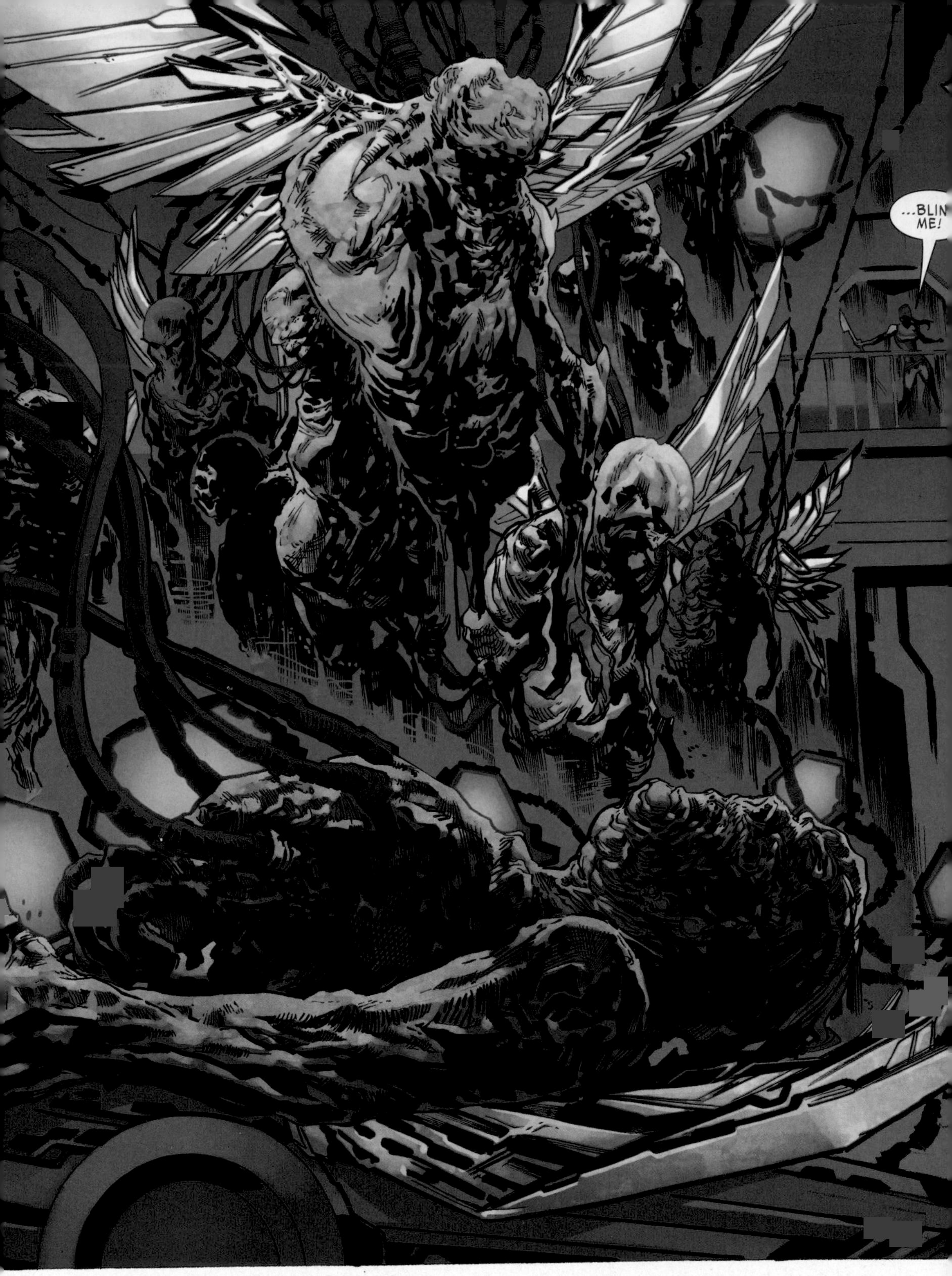
...BLIN
ME!

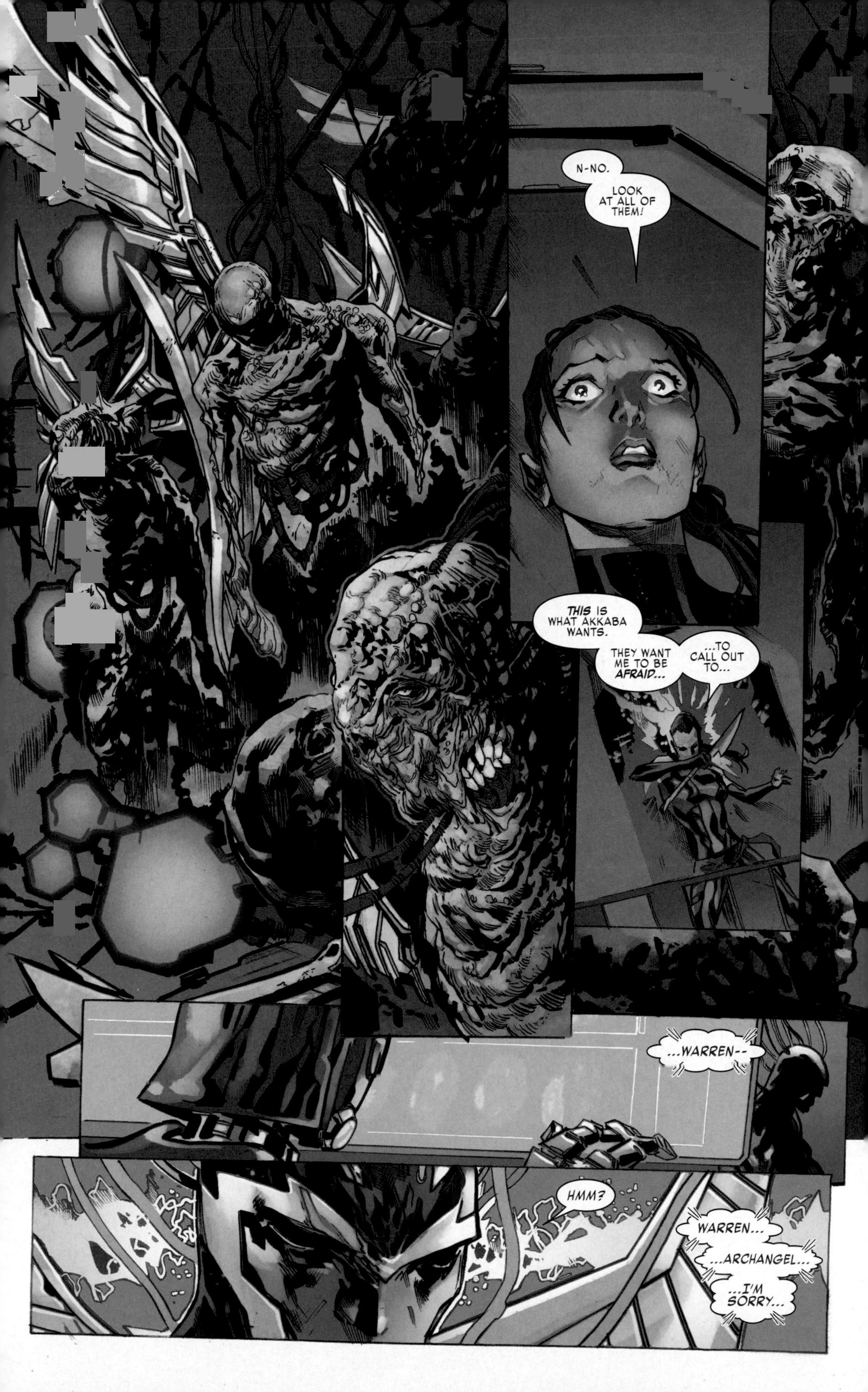
N-NO.
LOOK AT ALL OF THEM!
THIS IS WHAT AKKABA WANTS.
THEY WANT ME TO BE AFRAID...
...TO CALL OUT TO...
...WARREN--
HMM?
WARREN...
...ARCHANGEL...
...I'M SORRY...

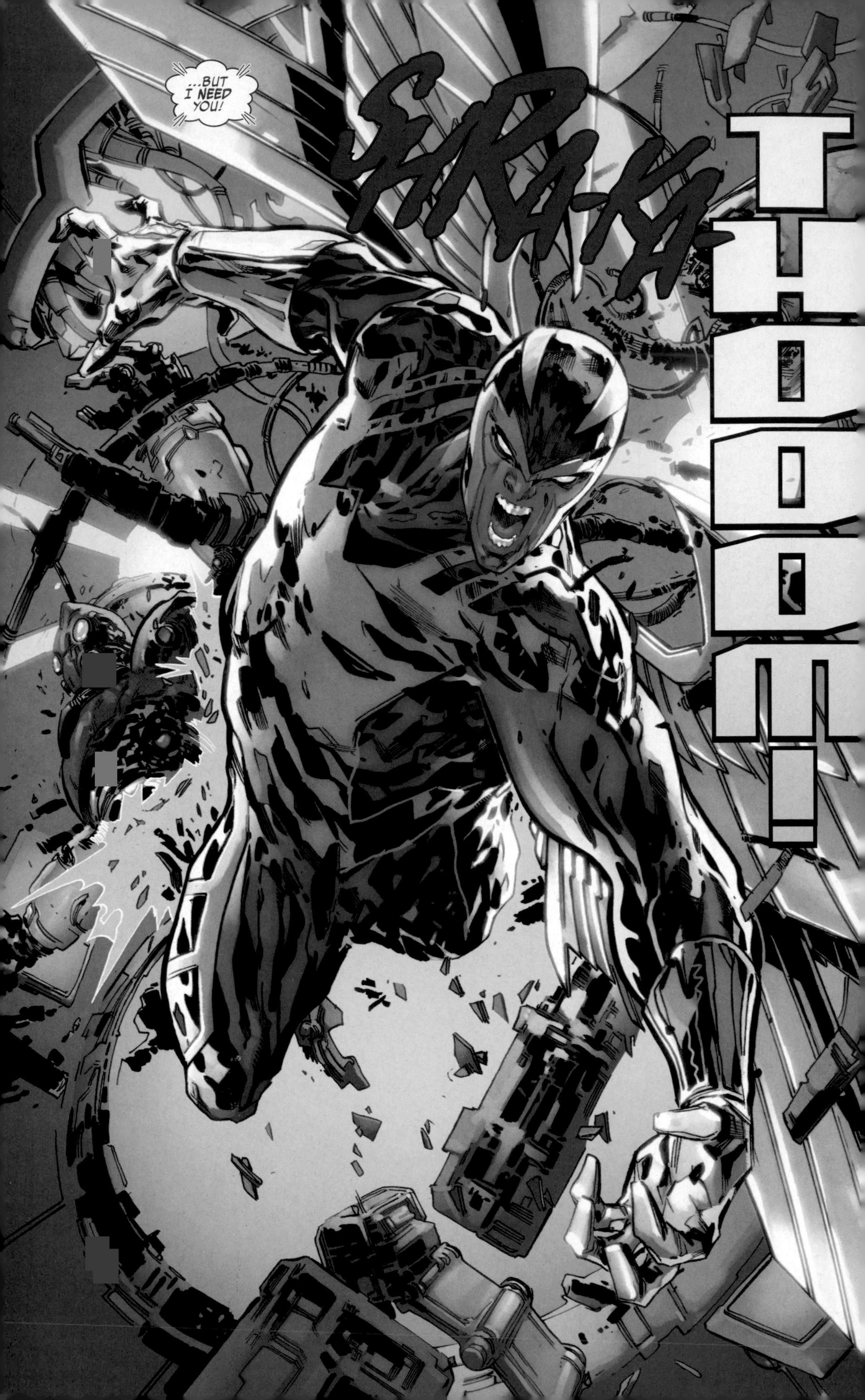
...BUT I NEED YOU!
SKRA-KA-
THOOM!

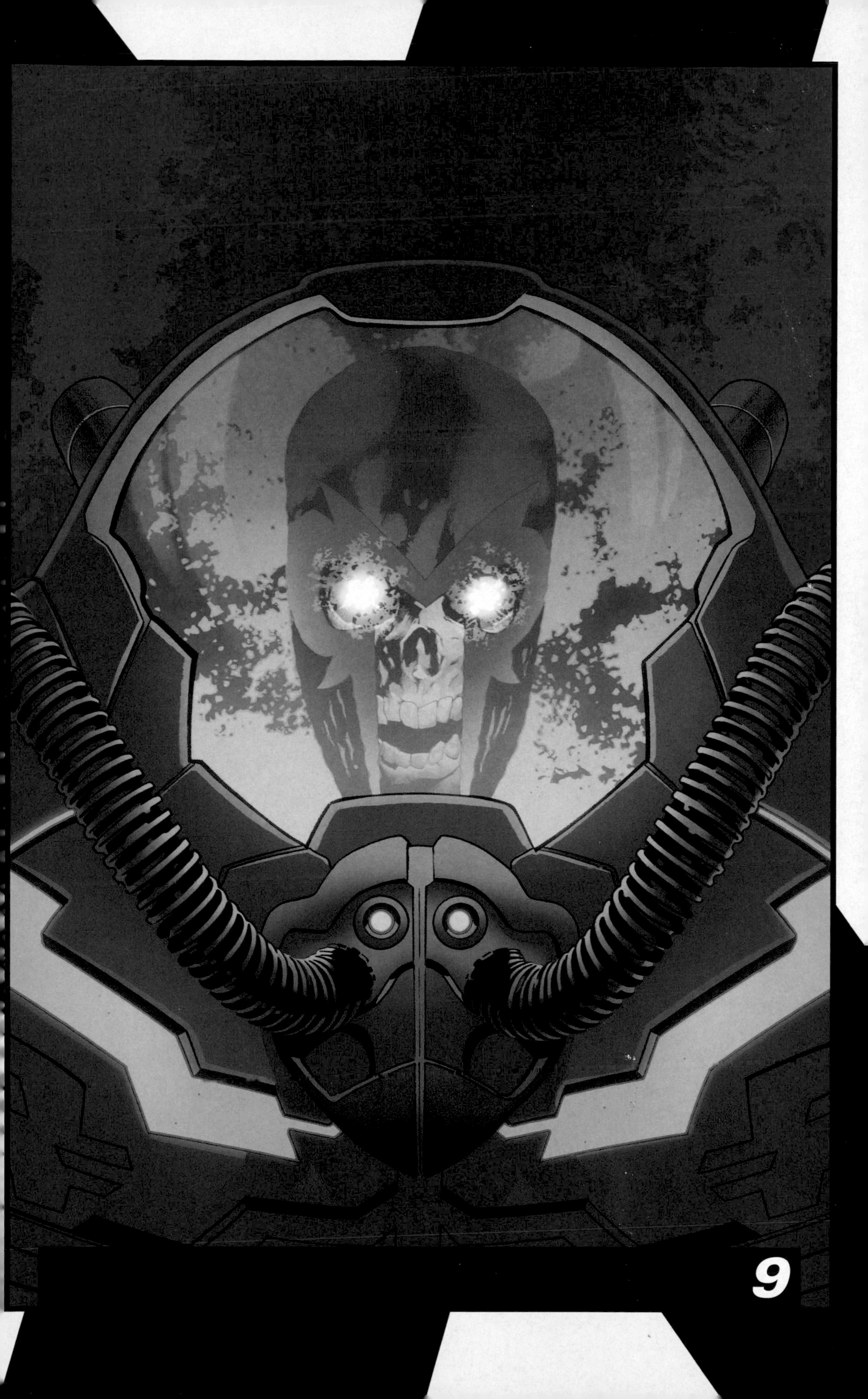
9

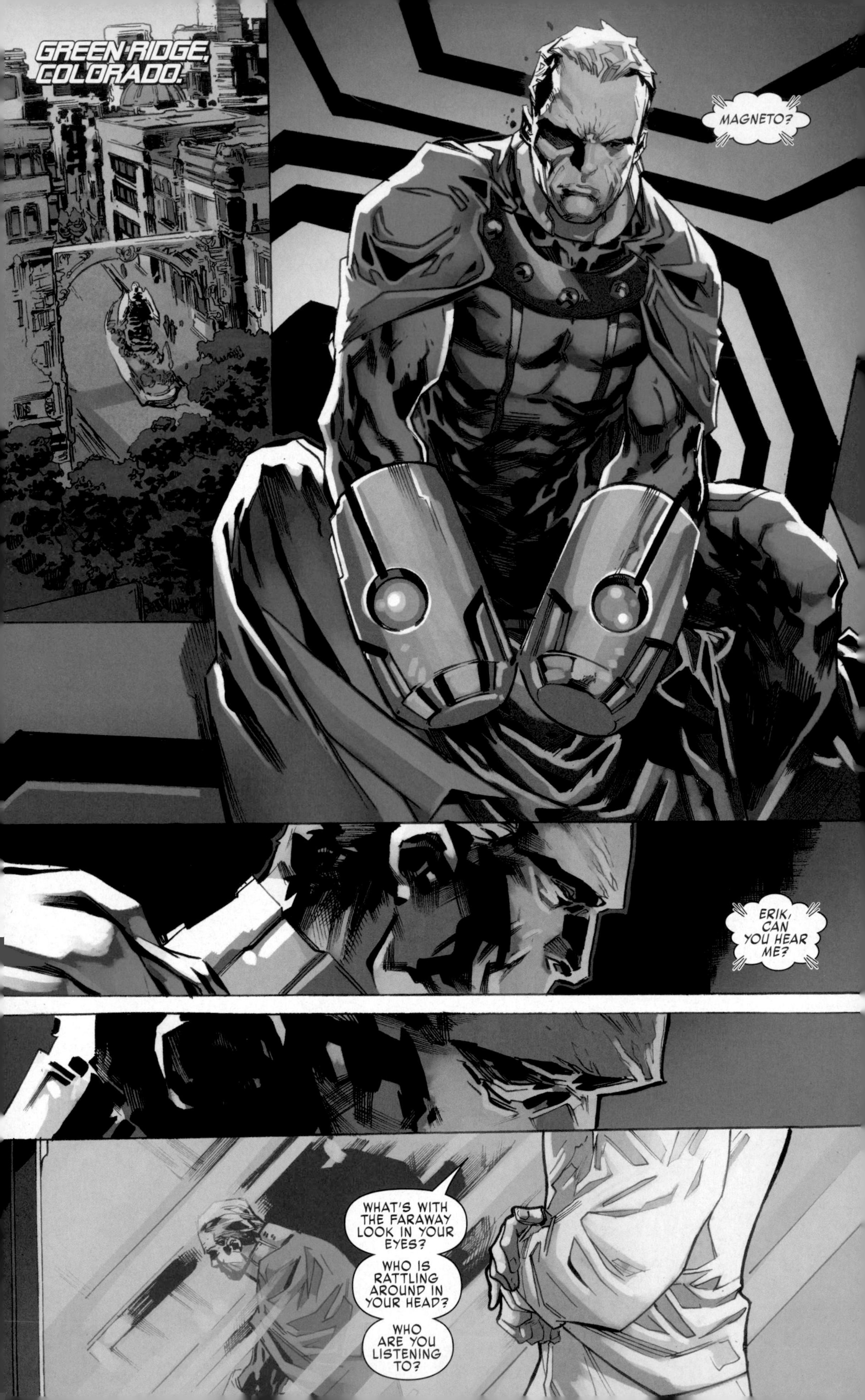
GREEN RIDGE, COLORADO.
MAGNETO?
ERIK, CAN YOU HEAR ME?
WHAT'S WITH THE FARAWAY LOOK IN YOUR EYES?
WHO IS RATTLING AROUND IN YOUR HEAD?
WHO ARE YOU LISTENING TO?

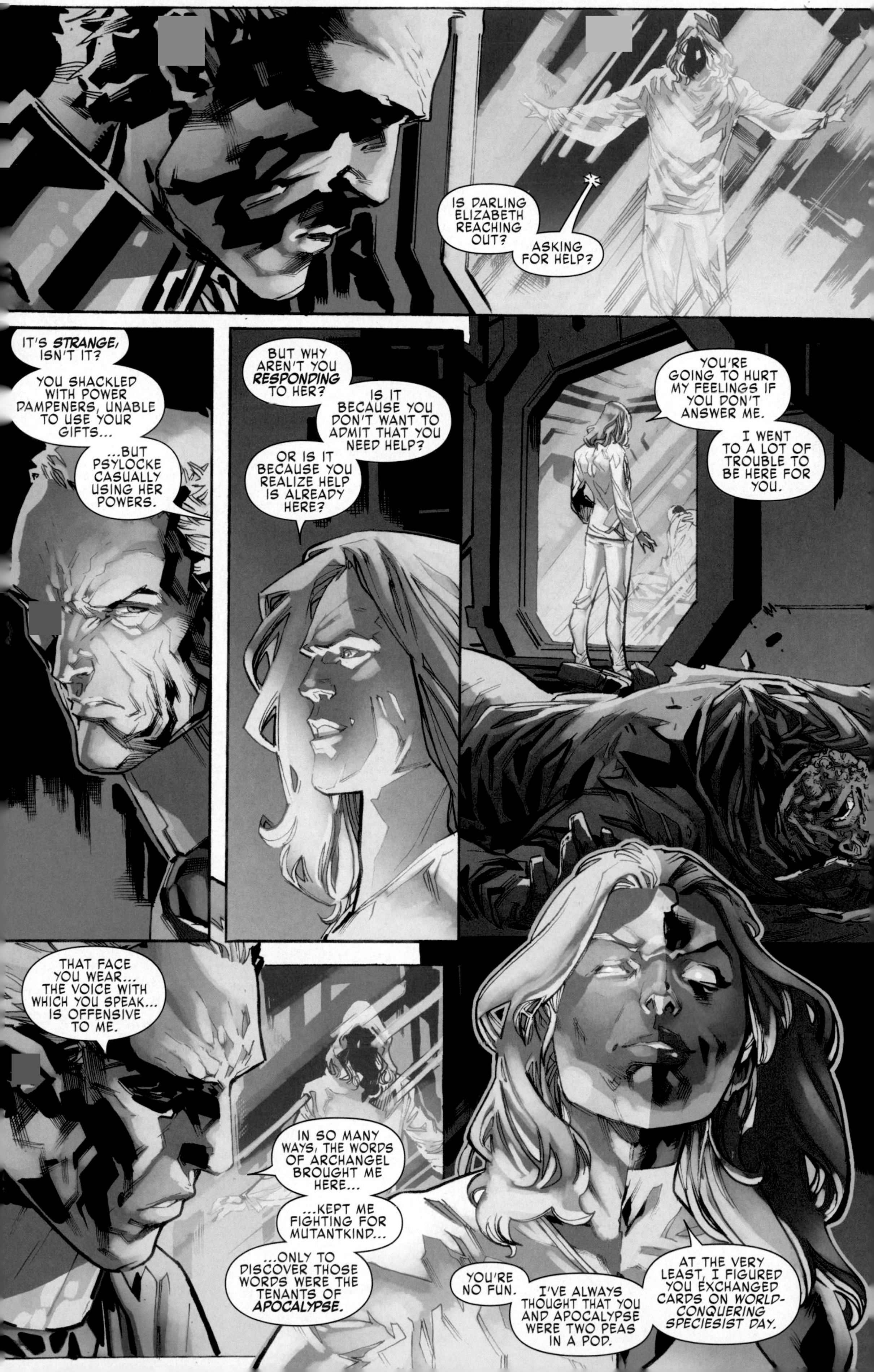
IS DARLING ELIZABETH REACHING OUT?
ASKING FOR HELP?
IT'S STRANGE, ISN'T IT?
YOU SHACKLED WITH POWER DAMPENERS, UNABLE TO USE YOUR GIFTS...
...BUT PSYLOCKE CASUALLY USING HER POWERS.
BUT WHY AREN'T YOU RESPONDING TO HER?
IS IT BECAUSE YOU DON'T WANT TO ADMIT THAT YOU NEED HELP?
OR IS IT BECAUSE YOU REALIZE HELP IS ALREADY HERE?
YOU'RE GOING TO HURT MY FEELINGS IF YOU DON'T ANSWER ME.
I WENT TO A LOT OF TROUBLE TO BE HERE FOR YOU.
THAT FACE YOU WEAR... THE VOICE WITH WHICH YOU SPEAK... IS OFFENSIVE TO ME.
IN SO MANY WAYS, THE WORDS OF ARCHANGEL BROUGHT ME HERE...
...KEPT ME FIGHTING FOR MUTANTKIND...
...ONLY TO DISCOVER THOSE WORDS WERE THE TENANTS OF APOCALYPSE.
YOU'RE NO FUN.
I'VE ALWAYS THOUGHT THAT YOU AND APOCALYPSE WERE TWO PEAS IN A POD.
AT THE VERY LEAST, I FIGURED YOU EXCHANGED CARDS ON WORLD-CONQUERING SPECIESIST DAY.

I'D CAUTION YOU AGAINST MAKING SUCH COMPARISONS LIGHTLY, MYSTIQUE.

WHY? ARE YOU GOING TO GLARE EVEN MORE INTENTLY AT ME FROM THE OTHER SIDE OF THE CELL DOOR?

RELAX, ERIK. TRY NOT TO GET BENT OUT OF SHAPE.

YOU'RE NOT DEALING WITH APOCALYPSE ANYHOW, BUT HIS SON, *GENOCIDE...*

...WHO'S JUST DESPERATE TO TAKE OVER THE FAMILY BUSINESS.

STILL, HE'S A TOUGH CUSTOMER.

LUCKY FOR YOU, YOU HAD THE FORESIGHT TO BRING FANTOMEX AND MYSELF HERE AS BACKUP.

I'M NOT SURE WHERE JEAN-PHILLIPE RAN OFF TO.

DID YOU EVER BOTHER TO TELL HIM THAT PSYLOCKE WOULD BE WITH YOU?

THERE'S BLOOD BETWEEN THOSE TWO, MOST OF IT BAD.

I'VE CHANGED SHAPE HUNDREDS OF TIMES SINCE THEN...

...AND WITH EVERY SHIFT, MY BRAIN CHANGES SUBTLY...

...PERSONALITY AND MEMORIES WITH IT.

I ONLY HOLD ONTO THE MOST IMPORTANT GRUDGES.

IF YOU SAY SO.

THE SAME COULD BE SAID FOR MOST OF US.

THE SAME COULD BE SAID FOR YOU AND I.

EVERYTHING I'VE BASED MY LIFE UPON FOR THE LAST SEVERAL MONTHS...

...IT WAS ALL BECAUSE OF AN UNTRUTH.

AND DOESN'T THAT JUST MAKE YOU WANT TO PUNISH THOSE WHO DARED LIE TO YOU?

YES.

YES, I DOES

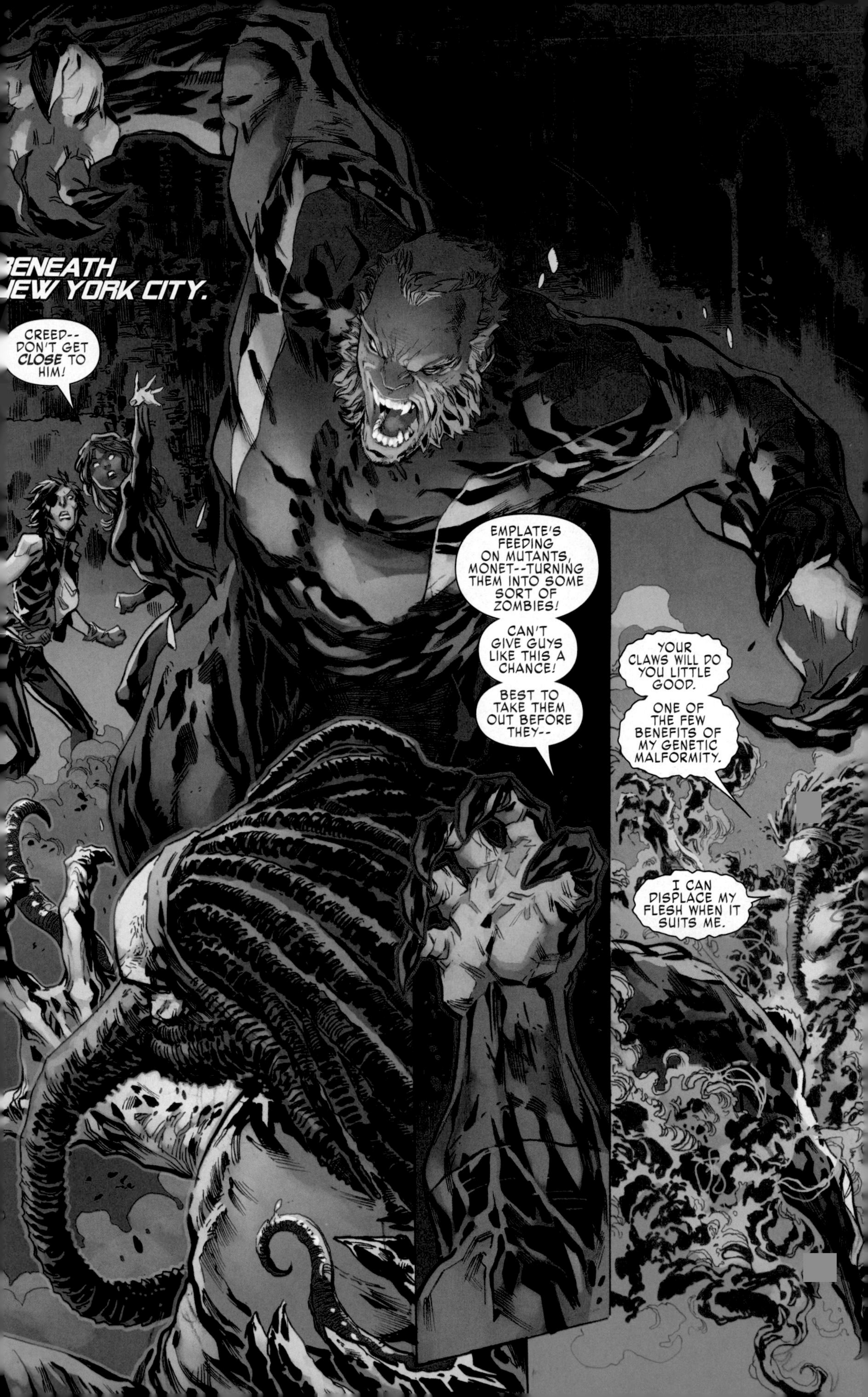
BENEATH NEW YORK CITY.
CREED-- DON'T GET CLOSE TO HIM!
EMPLATE'S FEEDING ON MUTANTS, MONET--TURNING THEM INTO SOME SORT OF ZOMBIES!
CAN'T GIVE GUYS LIKE THIS A CHANCE!
BEST TO TAKE THEM OUT BEFORE THEY--
YOUR CLAWS WILL DO YOU LITTLE GOOD.
ONE OF THE FEW BENEFITS OF MY GENETIC MALFORMITY.
I CAN DISPLACE MY FLESH WHEN IT SUITS ME.

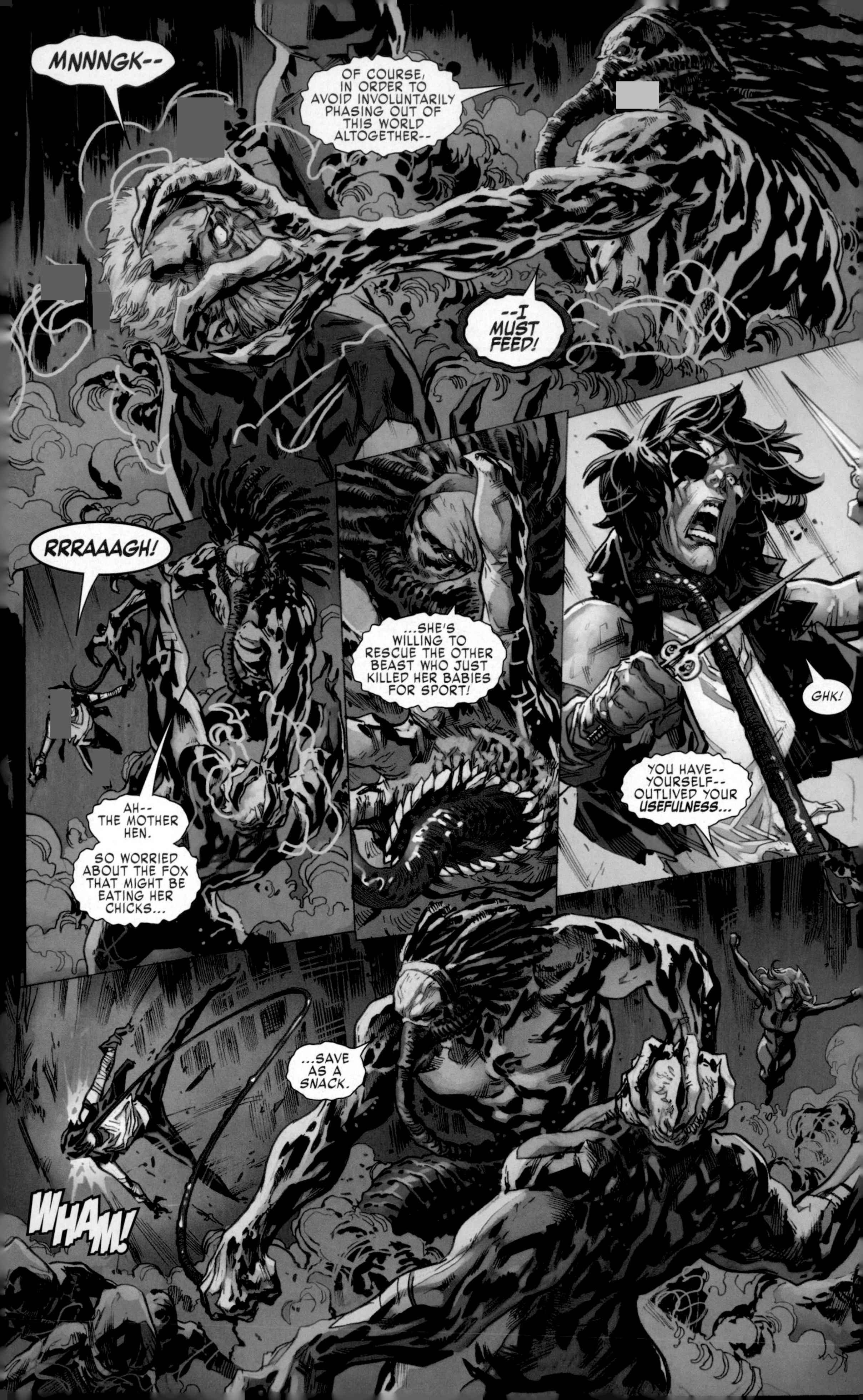
MNNNGK--
OF COURSE, IN ORDER TO AVOID INVOLUNTARILY PHASING OUT OF THIS WORLD ALTOGETHER--
--I MUST FEED!
RRRAAAGH!
AH-- THE MOTHER HEN.
SO WORRIED ABOUT THE FOX THAT MIGHT BE EATING HER CHICKS...
...SHE'S WILLING TO RESCUE THE OTHER BEAST WHO JUST KILLED HER BABIES FOR SPORT!
GHK!
YOU HAVE-- YOURSELF-- OUTLIVED YOUR USEFULNESS...
...SAVE AS A SNACK.
WHAM!

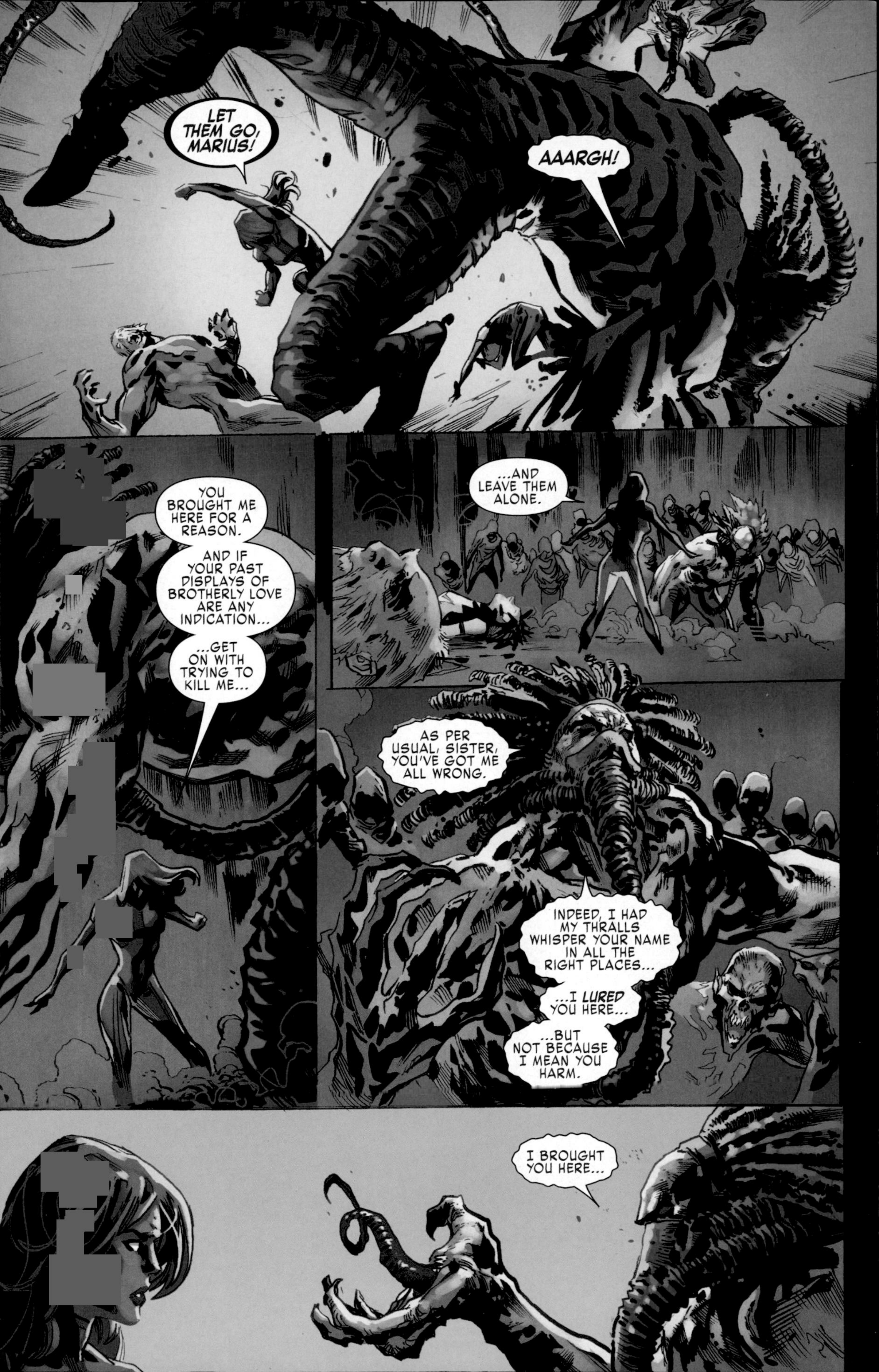
LET THEM GO, MARIUS!
AAARGH!
YOU BROUGHT ME HERE FOR A REASON.
AND IF YOUR PAST DISPLAYS OF BROTHERLY LOVE ARE ANY INDICATION...
...GET ON WITH TRYING TO KILL ME...
...AND LEAVE THEM ALONE.
AS PER USUAL, SISTER, YOU'VE GOT ME ALL WRONG.
INDEED, I HAD MY THRALLS WHISPER YOUR NAME IN ALL THE RIGHT PLACES...
...I *LURED* YOU HERE...
...BUT NOT BECAUSE I MEAN YOU HARM.
I BROUGHT YOU HERE...

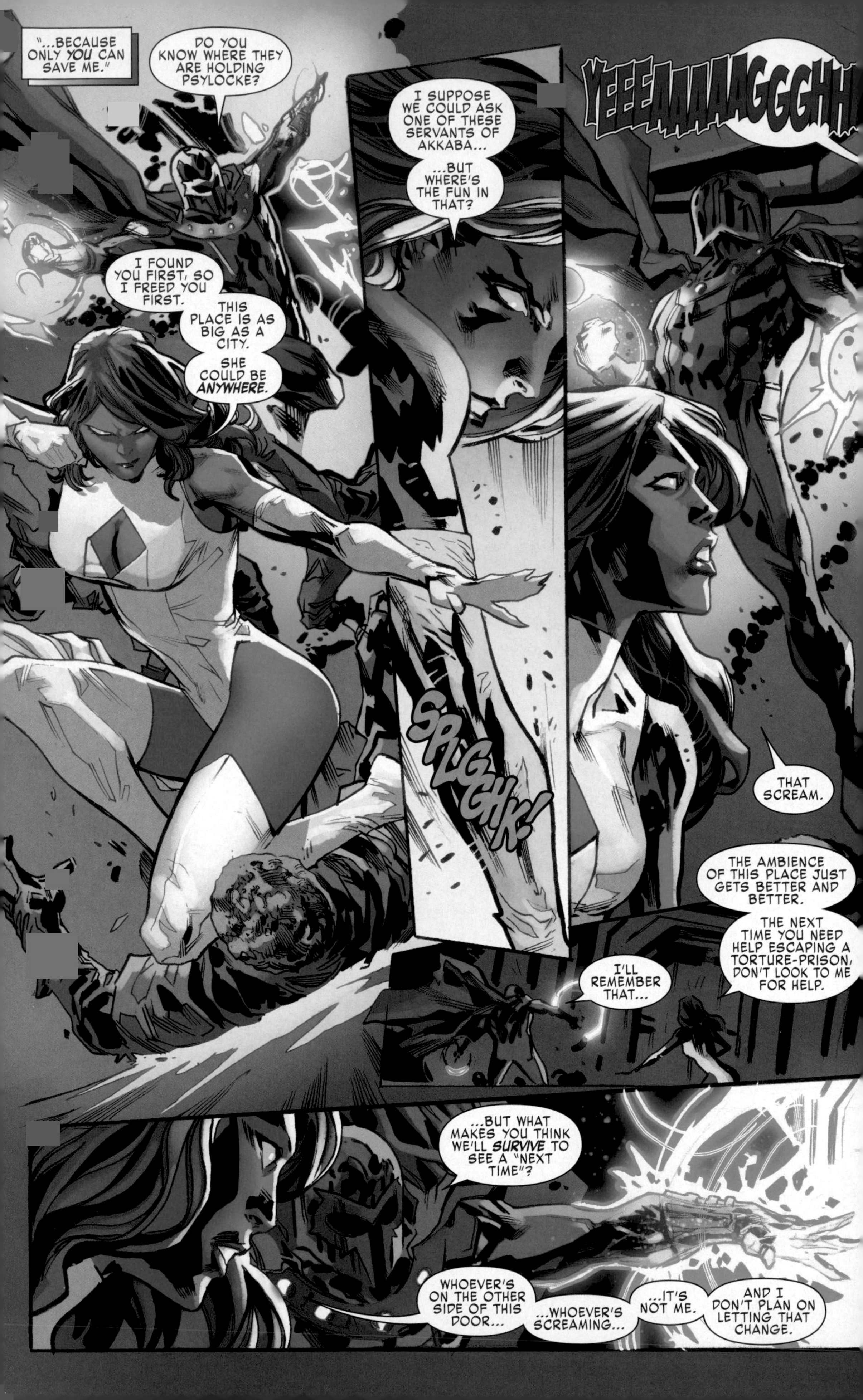

"...BECAUSE ONLY *YOU* CAN SAVE ME."
DO YOU KNOW WHERE THEY ARE HOLDING PSYLOCKE?
I FOUND YOU FIRST, SO I FREED YOU FIRST.
THIS PLACE IS AS BIG AS A CITY.
SHE COULD BE *ANYWHERE*.
I SUPPOSE WE COULD ASK ONE OF THESE SERVANTS OF AKKABA...
...BUT WHERE'S THE FUN IN THAT?
SPLGHK!
YEEEAAAAAGGGHH
THAT SCREAM.
THE AMBIENCE OF THIS PLACE JUST GETS BETTER AND BETTER.
THE NEXT TIME YOU NEED HELP ESCAPING A TORTURE-PRISON, DON'T LOOK TO ME FOR HELP.
I'LL REMEMBER THAT...
...BUT WHAT MAKES YOU THINK WE'LL *SURVIVE* TO SEE A "NEXT TIME"?
WHOEVER'S ON THE OTHER SIDE OF THIS DOOR...
...WHOEVER'S SCREAMING...
...IT'S NOT ME.
AND I DON'T PLAN ON LETTING THAT CHANGE.

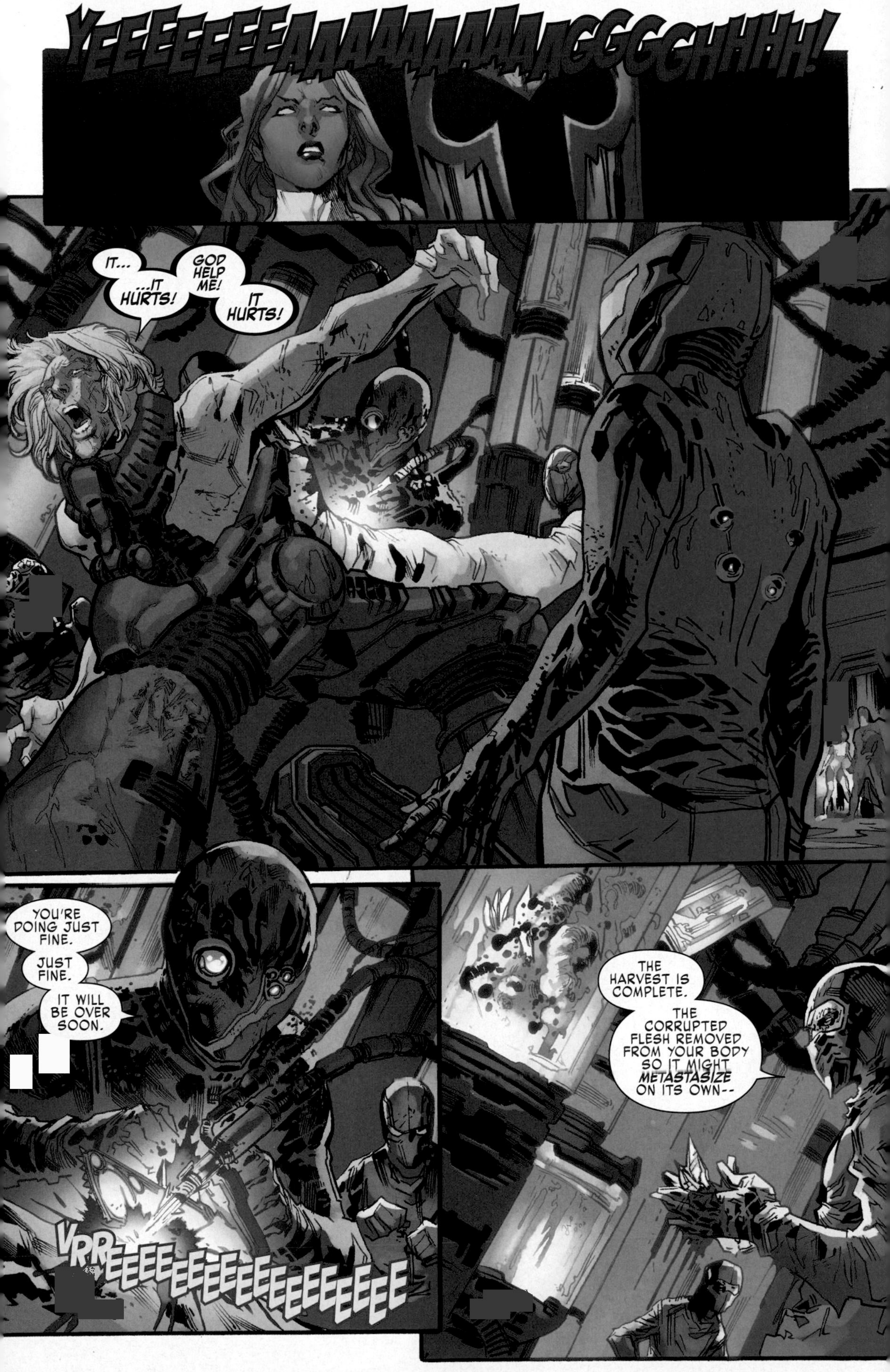
YEEEEEEEAAAAAAAAAAGGGGHHHH!
IT...
...IT HURTS!
GOD HELP ME!
IT HURTS!
YOU'RE DOING JUST FINE.
JUST FINE.
IT WILL BE OVER SOON.
VRREEEEEEEEEEEEEEEEEE
THE HARVEST IS COMPLETE.
THE CORRUPTED FLESH REMOVED FROM YOUR BODY SO IT MIGHT *METASTASIZE* ON ITS OWN--

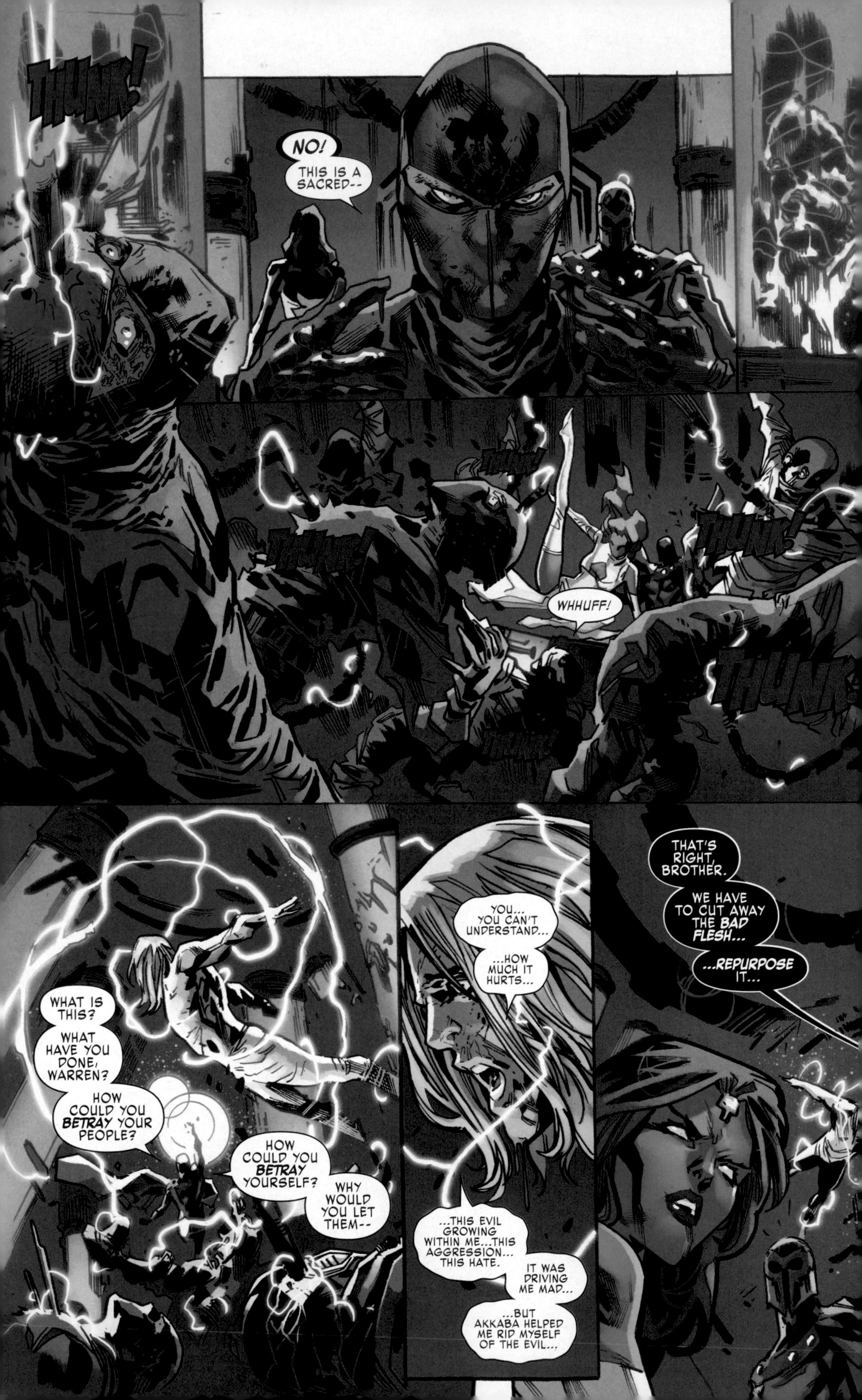
THUNK!
NO!
THIS IS A SACRED--
THUNK!
THUNK!
THUNK!
WHHUFF!
THUNK!
THUNK!
WHAT IS THIS?
WHAT HAVE YOU DONE, WARREN?
HOW COULD YOU BETRAY YOUR PEOPLE?
HOW COULD YOU BETRAY YOURSELF?
WHY WOULD YOU LET THEM--
YOU... YOU CAN'T UNDERSTAND...
...HOW MUCH IT HURTS...
...THIS EVIL GROWING WITHIN ME...THIS AGGRESSION... THIS HATE.
IT WAS DRIVING ME MAD...
...BUT AKKABA HELPED ME RID MYSELF OF THE EVIL...
THAT'S RIGHT, BROTHER.
WE HAVE TO CUT AWAY THE BAD FLESH...
...REPURPOSE IT...

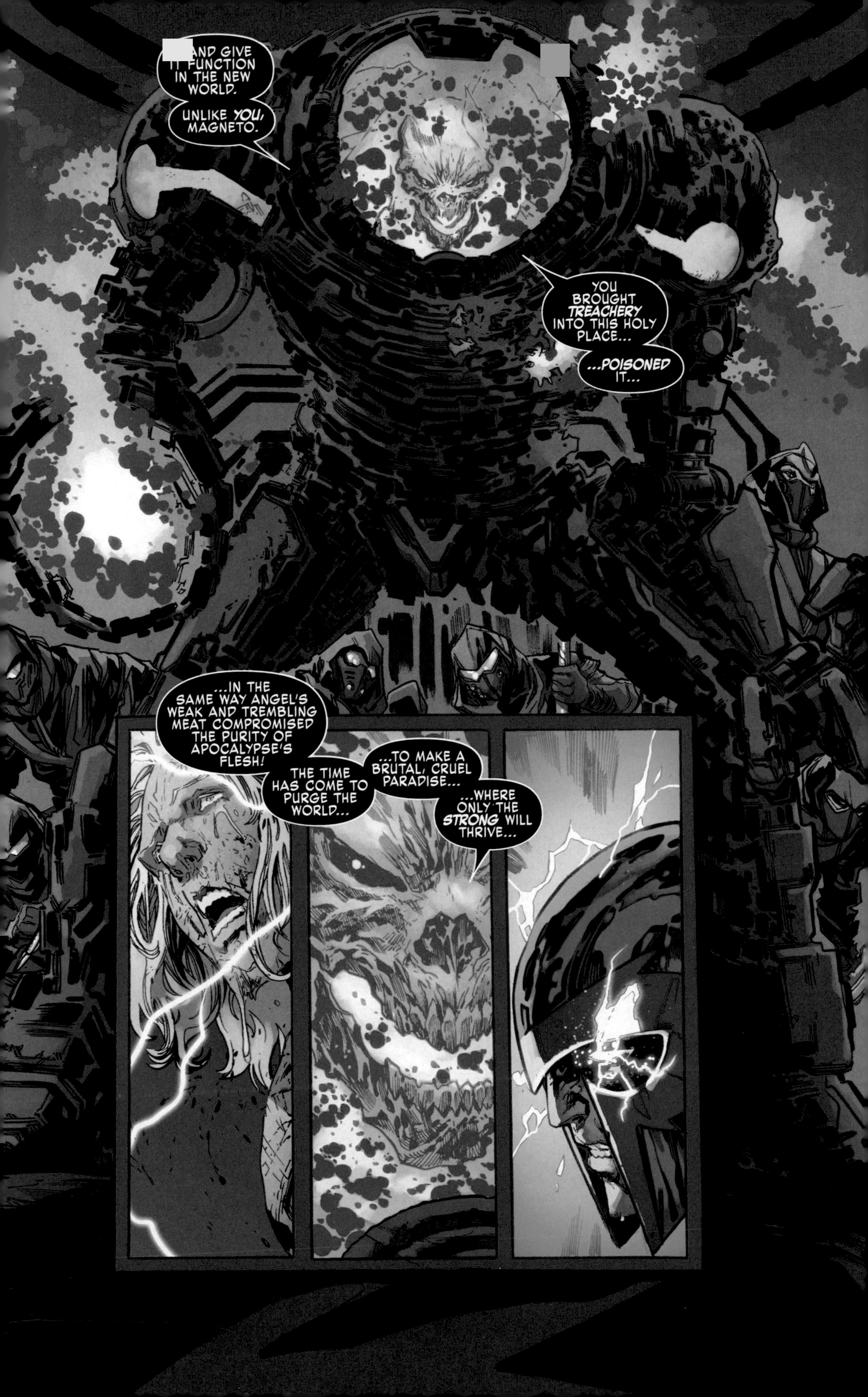
AND GIVE IT FUNCTION IN THE NEW WORLD.
UNLIKE YOU, MAGNETO.
YOU BROUGHT TREACHERY INTO THIS HOLY PLACE...
...POISONED IT...
...IN THE SAME WAY ANGEL'S WEAK AND TREMBLING MEAT COMPROMISED THE PURITY OF APOCALYPSE'S FLESH!
THE TIME HAS COME TO PURGE THE WORLD...
...TO MAKE A BRUTAL, CRUEL PARADISE...
...WHERE ONLY THE STRONG WILL THRIVE...

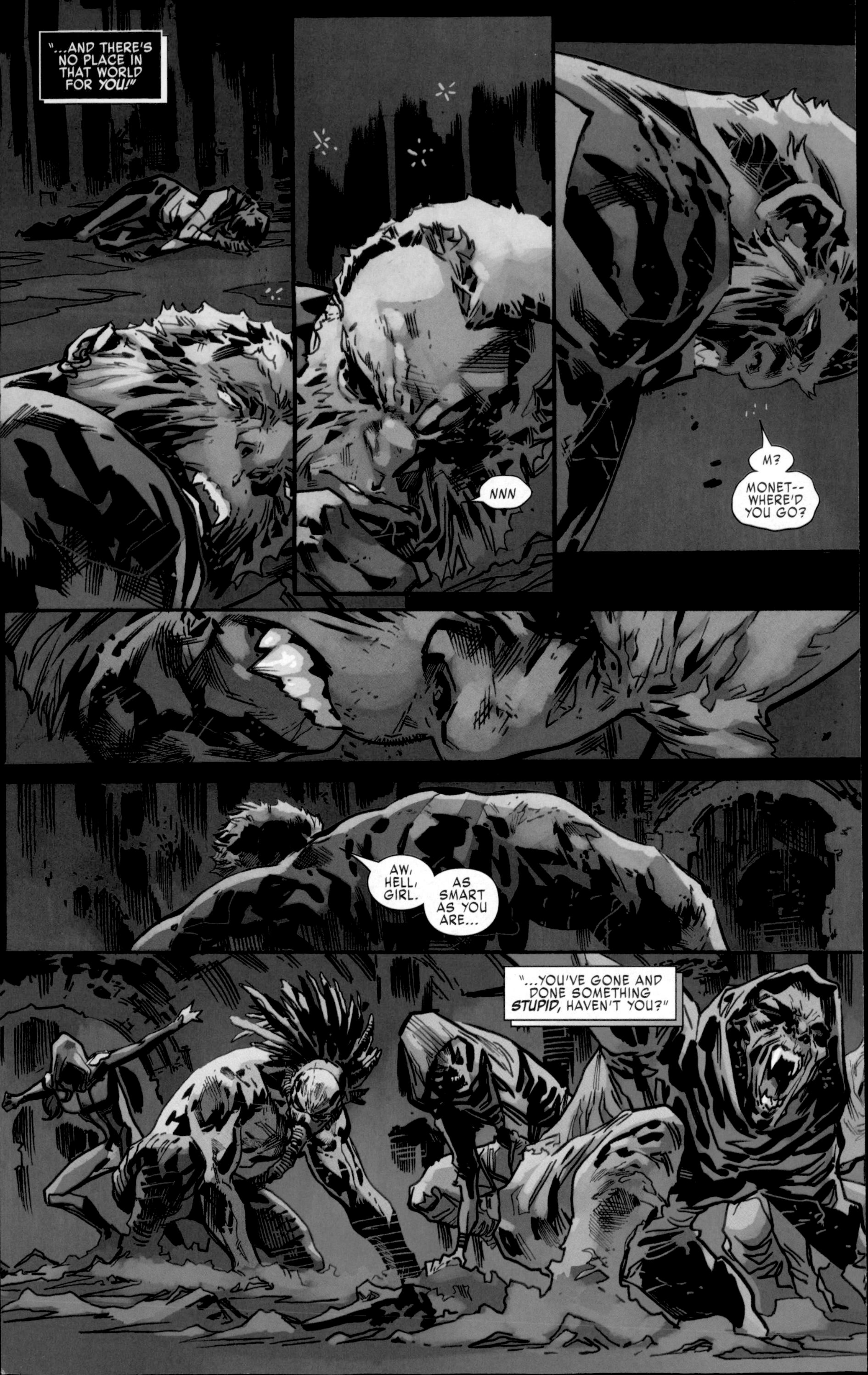
"...AND THERE'S NO PLACE IN THAT WORLD FOR YOU!"
NNN
M?
MONET-- WHERE'D YOU GO?
AW, HELL, GIRL.
AS SMART AS YOU ARE...
"...YOU'VE GONE AND DONE SOMETHING STUPID, HAVEN'T YOU?"

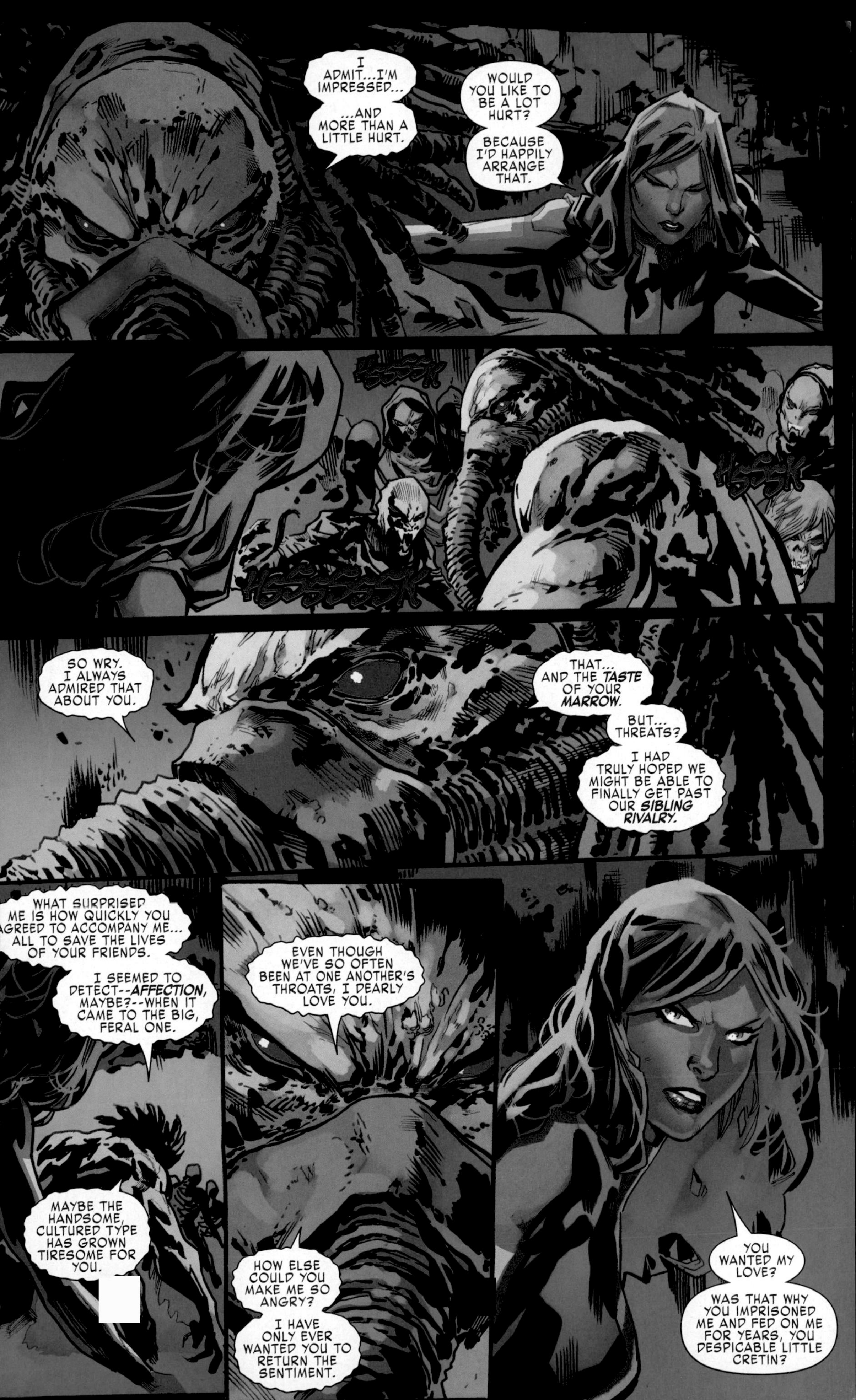
I ADMIT...I'M IMPRESSED...
...AND MORE THAN A LITTLE HURT.
WOULD YOU LIKE TO BE A LOT HURT?
BECAUSE I'D HAPPILY ARRANGE THAT.
HSSSK
HSSSK
HSSSSSSK
SO WRY. I ALWAYS ADMIRED THAT ABOUT YOU.
THAT... AND THE TASTE OF YOUR MARROW.
BUT... THREATS?
I HAD TRULY HOPED WE MIGHT BE ABLE TO FINALLY GET PAST OUR SIBLING RIVALRY.
WHAT SURPRISED ME IS HOW QUICKLY YOU AGREED TO ACCOMPANY ME... ALL TO SAVE THE LIVES OF YOUR FRIENDS.
I SEEMED TO DETECT--AFFECTION, MAYBE?--WHEN IT CAME TO THE BIG, FERAL ONE.
MAYBE THE HANDSOME, CULTURED TYPE HAS GROWN TIRESOME FOR YOU.
EVEN THOUGH WE'VE SO OFTEN BEEN AT ONE ANOTHER'S THROATS, I DEARLY LOVE YOU.
HOW ELSE COULD YOU MAKE ME SO ANGRY?
I HAVE ONLY EVER WANTED YOU TO RETURN THE SENTIMENT.
YOU WANTED MY LOVE?
WAS THAT WHY YOU IMPRISONED ME AND FED ON ME FOR YEARS, YOU DESPICABLE LITTLE CRETIN?

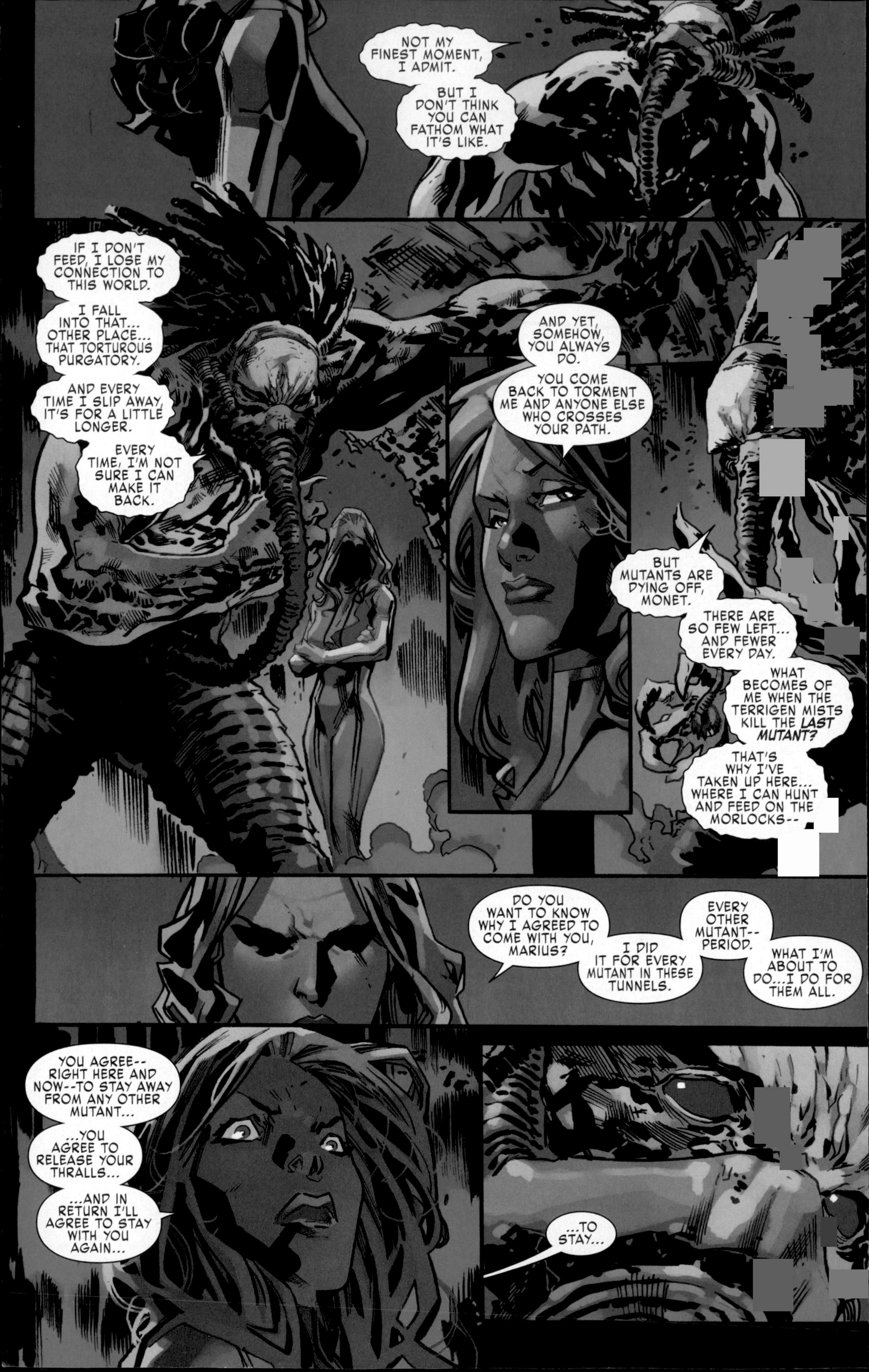
NOT MY FINEST MOMENT, I ADMIT.
BUT I DON'T THINK YOU CAN FATHOM WHAT IT'S LIKE.
IF I DON'T FEED, I LOSE MY CONNECTION TO THIS WORLD.
I FALL INTO THAT... OTHER PLACE... THAT TORTUROUS PURGATORY.
AND EVERY TIME I SLIP AWAY, IT'S FOR A LITTLE LONGER.
EVERY TIME, I'M NOT SURE I CAN MAKE IT BACK.
AND YET, SOMEHOW, YOU ALWAYS DO.
YOU COME BACK TO TORMENT ME AND ANYONE ELSE WHO CROSSES YOUR PATH.
BUT MUTANTS ARE DYING OFF, MONET.
THERE ARE SO FEW LEFT... AND FEWER EVERY DAY.
WHAT BECOMES OF ME WHEN THE TERRIGEN MISTS KILL THE *LAST MUTANT?*
THAT'S WHY I'VE TAKEN UP HERE... WHERE I CAN HUNT AND FEED ON THE MORLOCKS--
DO YOU WANT TO KNOW WHY I AGREED TO COME WITH YOU, MARIUS?
I DID IT FOR EVERY MUTANT IN THESE TUNNELS.
EVERY OTHER MUTANT--PERIOD.
WHAT I'M ABOUT TO DO...I DO FOR THEM ALL.
YOU AGREE--RIGHT HERE AND NOW--TO STAY AWAY FROM ANY OTHER MUTANT...
...YOU AGREE TO RELEASE YOUR THRALLS...
...AND IN RETURN I'LL AGREE TO STAY WITH YOU AGAIN...
...TO STAY...

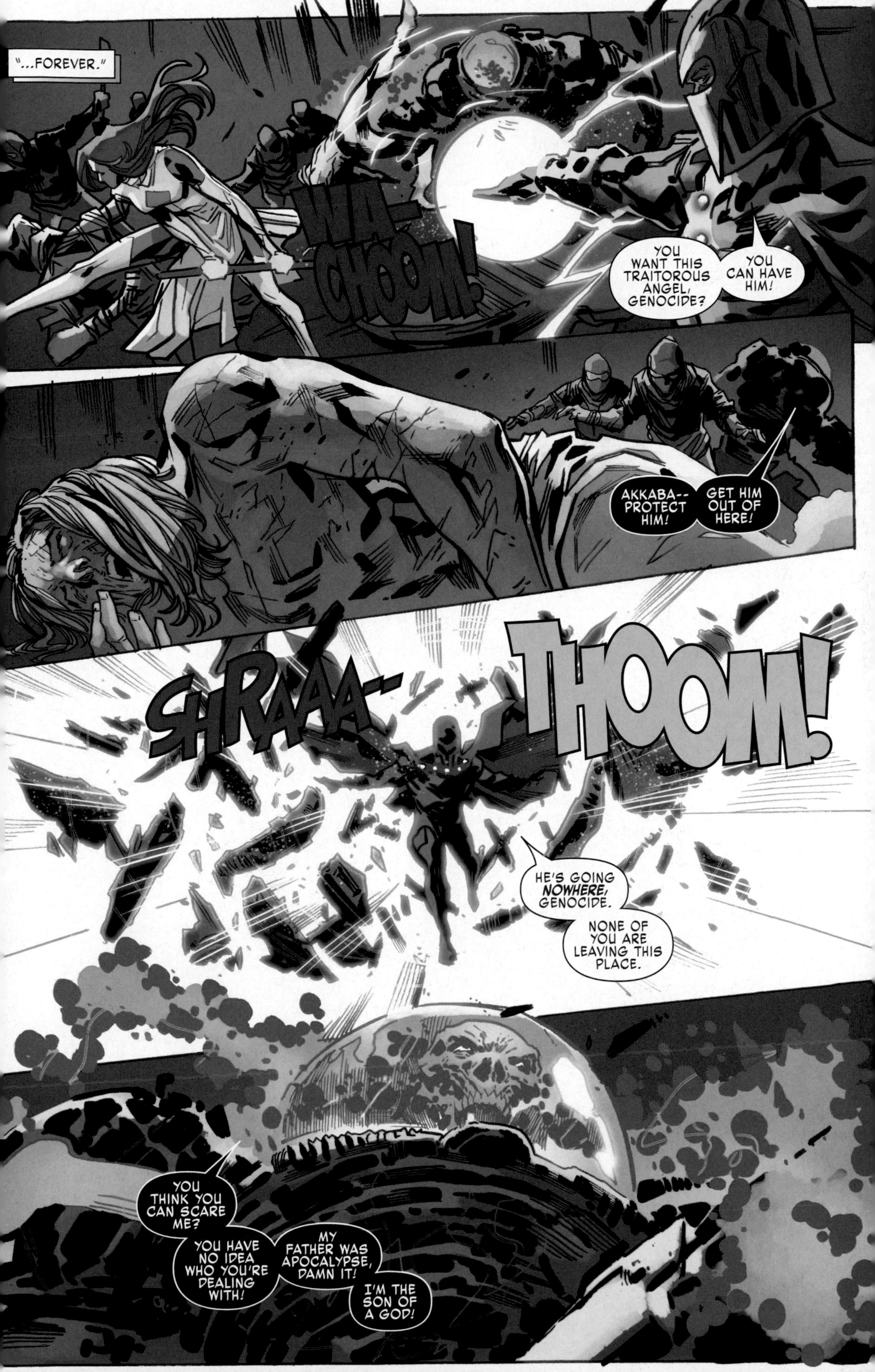
"...FOREVER."
WA-CHOOM!
YOU WANT THIS TRAITOROUS ANGEL, GENOCIDE?
YOU CAN HAVE HIM!
AKKABA-- PROTECT HIM!
GET HIM OUT OF HERE!
SHRAAA--
THOOM!
HE'S GOING NOWHERE, GENOCIDE.
NONE OF YOU ARE LEAVING THIS PLACE.
YOU THINK YOU CAN SCARE ME?
YOU HAVE NO IDEA WHO YOU'RE DEALING WITH!
MY FATHER WAS APOCALYPSE, DAMN IT!
I'M THE SON OF A GOD!

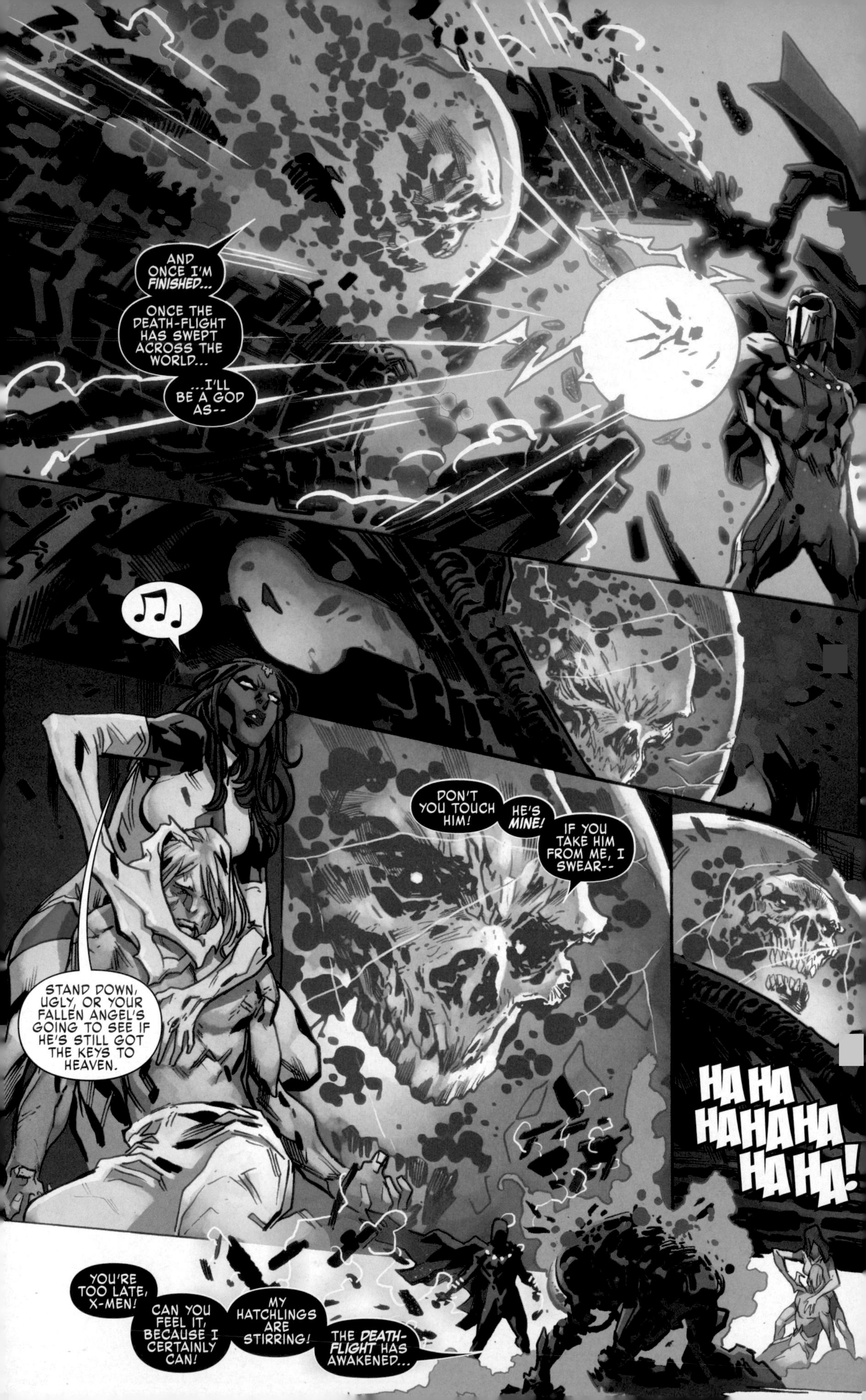
AND ONCE I'M FINISHED...
ONCE THE DEATH-FLIGHT HAS SWEPT ACROSS THE WORLD...
...I'LL BE A GOD AS--
♫♩
DON'T YOU TOUCH HIM!
HE'S MINE!
IF YOU TAKE HIM FROM ME, I SWEAR--
STAND DOWN, UGLY, OR YOUR FALLEN ANGEL'S GOING TO SEE IF HE'S STILL GOT THE KEYS TO HEAVEN.
HA HA HAHAHA HA HA!
YOU'RE TOO LATE, X-MEN!
CAN YOU FEEL IT, BECAUSE I CERTAINLY CAN!
MY HATCHLINGS ARE STIRRING!
THE DEATH-FLIGHT HAS AWAKENED...

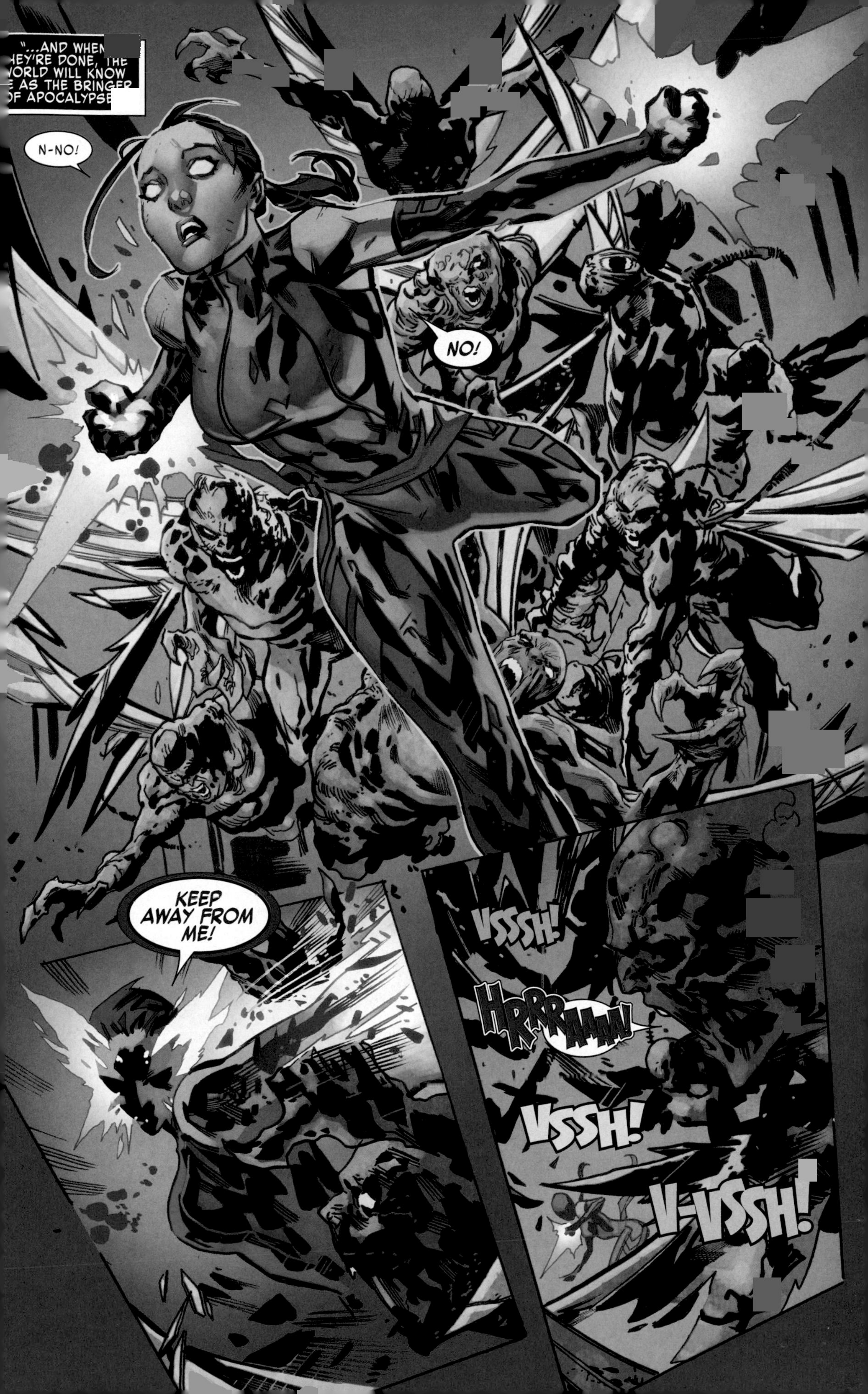
"...AND WHEN
HEY'RE DONE, THE
WORLD WILL KNOW
E AS THE BRINGER
OF APOCALYPSE
N-NO!
NO!
KEEP AWAY FROM ME!
VSSSH!
HRRRAAAAA!
VSSH!
V-VSSH!

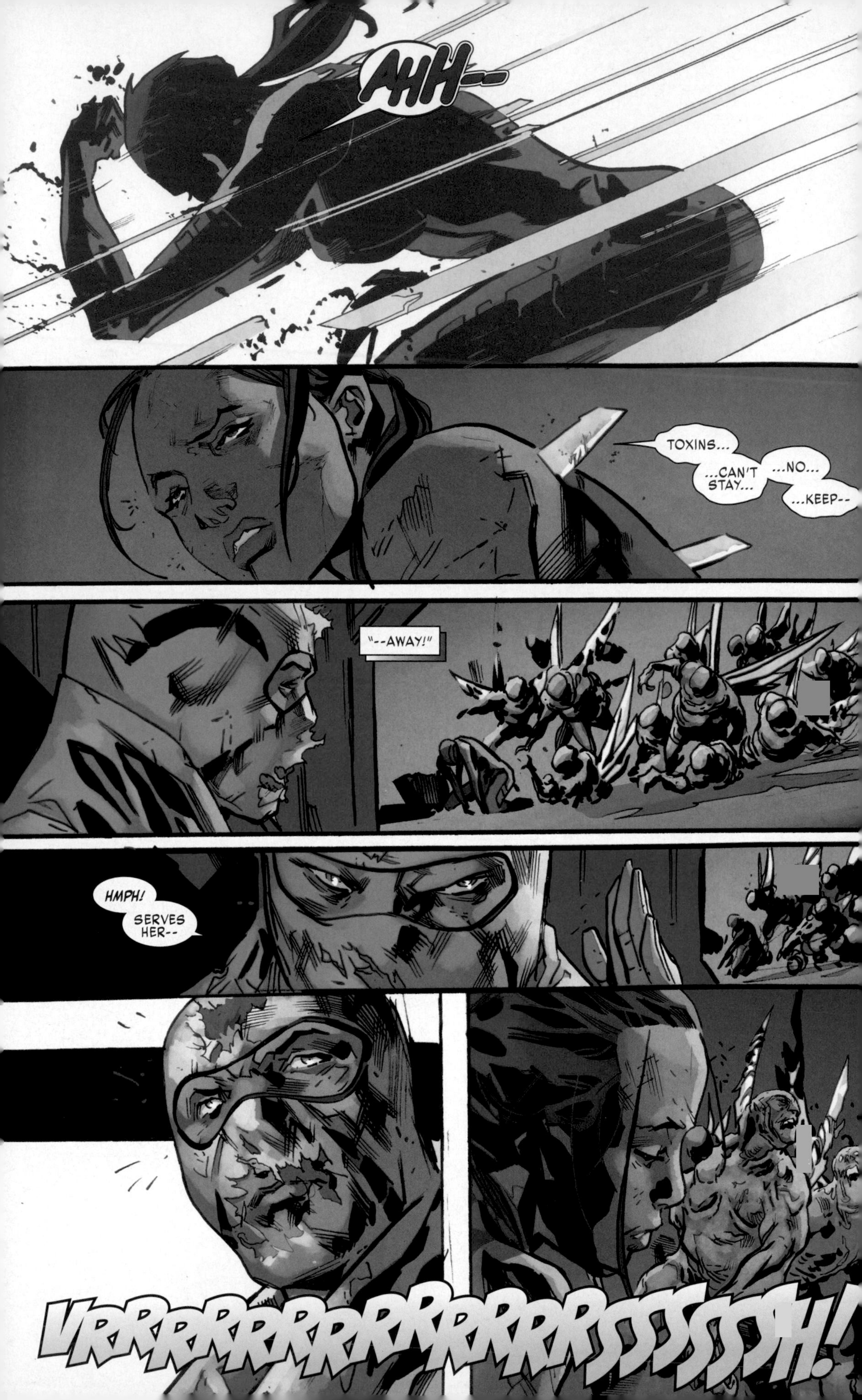
AHH--
TOXINS...
...CAN'T STAY...
...NO...
...KEEP--
"--AWAY!"
HMPH! SERVES HER--
VRRRRRRRRRRRRRRRSSSSSSSH!

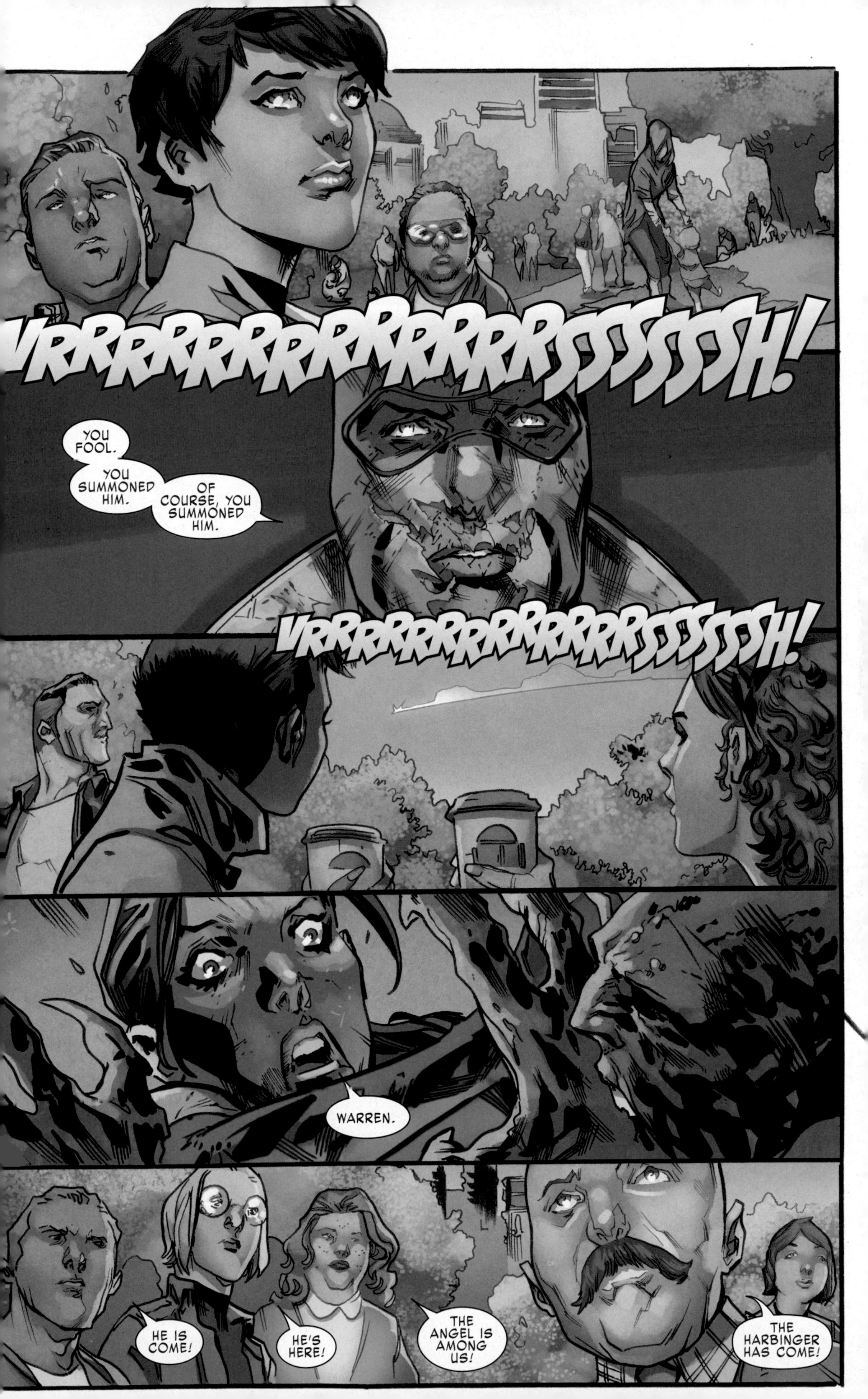
VRRRRRRRRRRRRRRRSSSSSSSH!
YOU FOOL.
YOU SUMMONED HIM.
OF COURSE, YOU SUMMONED HIM.
VRRRRRRRRRRRRRRRSSSSSSSH!
WARREN.
HE IS COME!
HE'S HERE!
THE ANGEL IS AMONG US!
THE HARBINGER HAS COME!

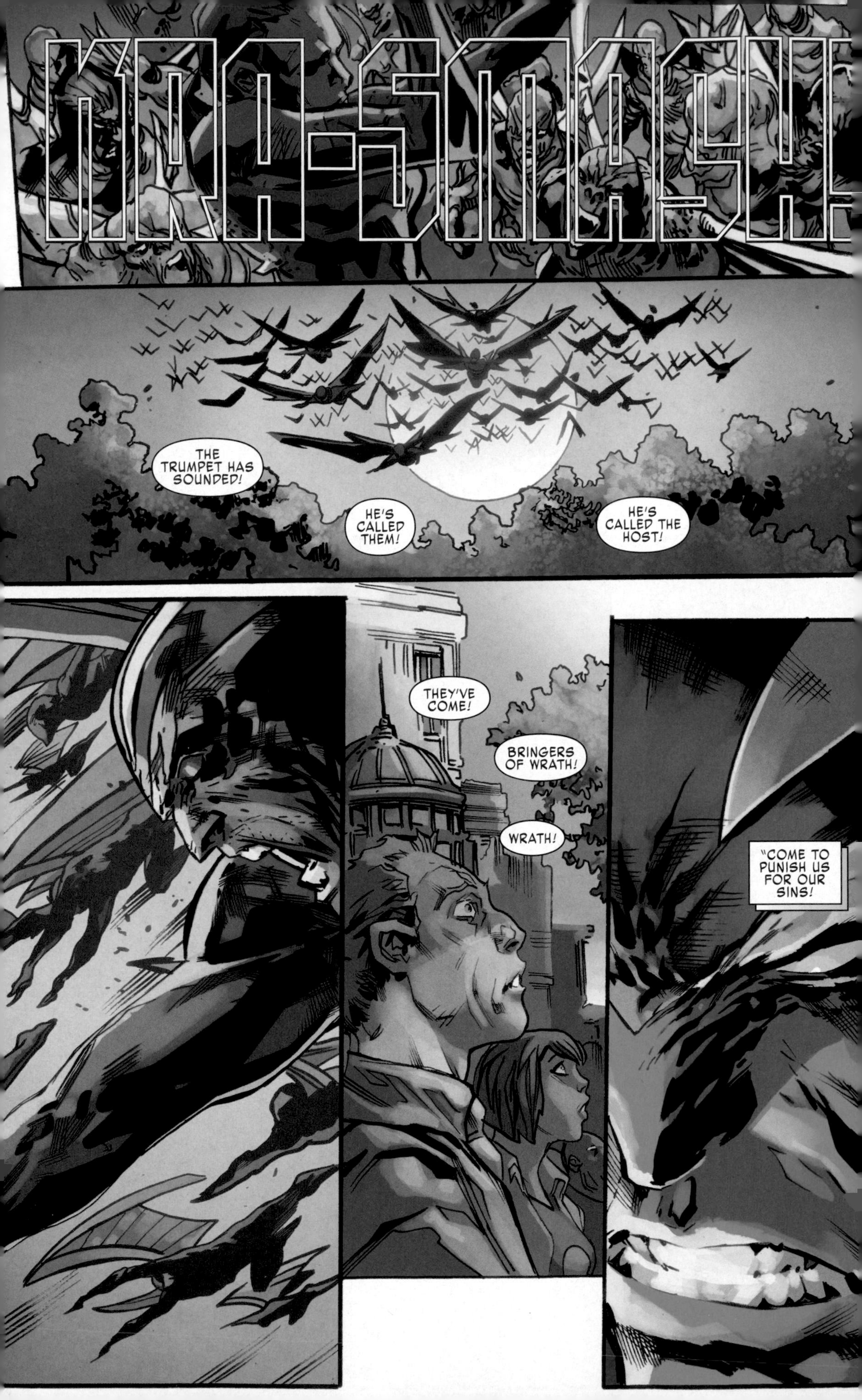
KRA-SMASH!
THE TRUMPET HAS SOUNDED!
HE'S CALLED THEM!
HE'S CALLED THE HOST!
THEY'VE COME!
BRINGERS OF WRATH!
WRATH!
"COME TO PUNISH US FOR OUR SINS!

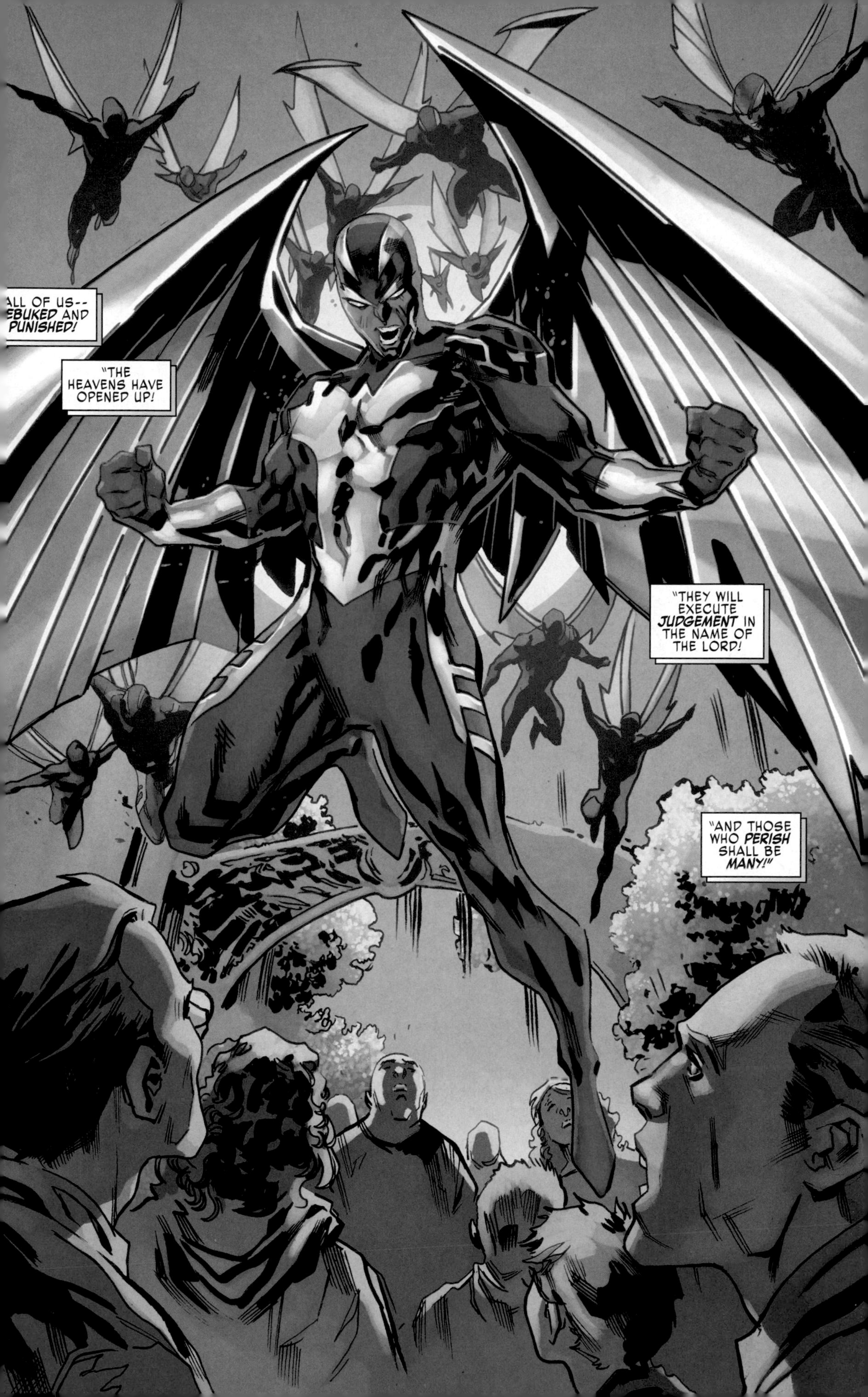
ALL OF US--
EBUKED AND
PUNISHED!
"THE HEAVENS HAVE OPENED UP!
"THEY WILL EXECUTE JUDGEMENT IN THE NAME OF THE LORD!
"AND THOSE WHO PERISH SHALL BE MANY!"

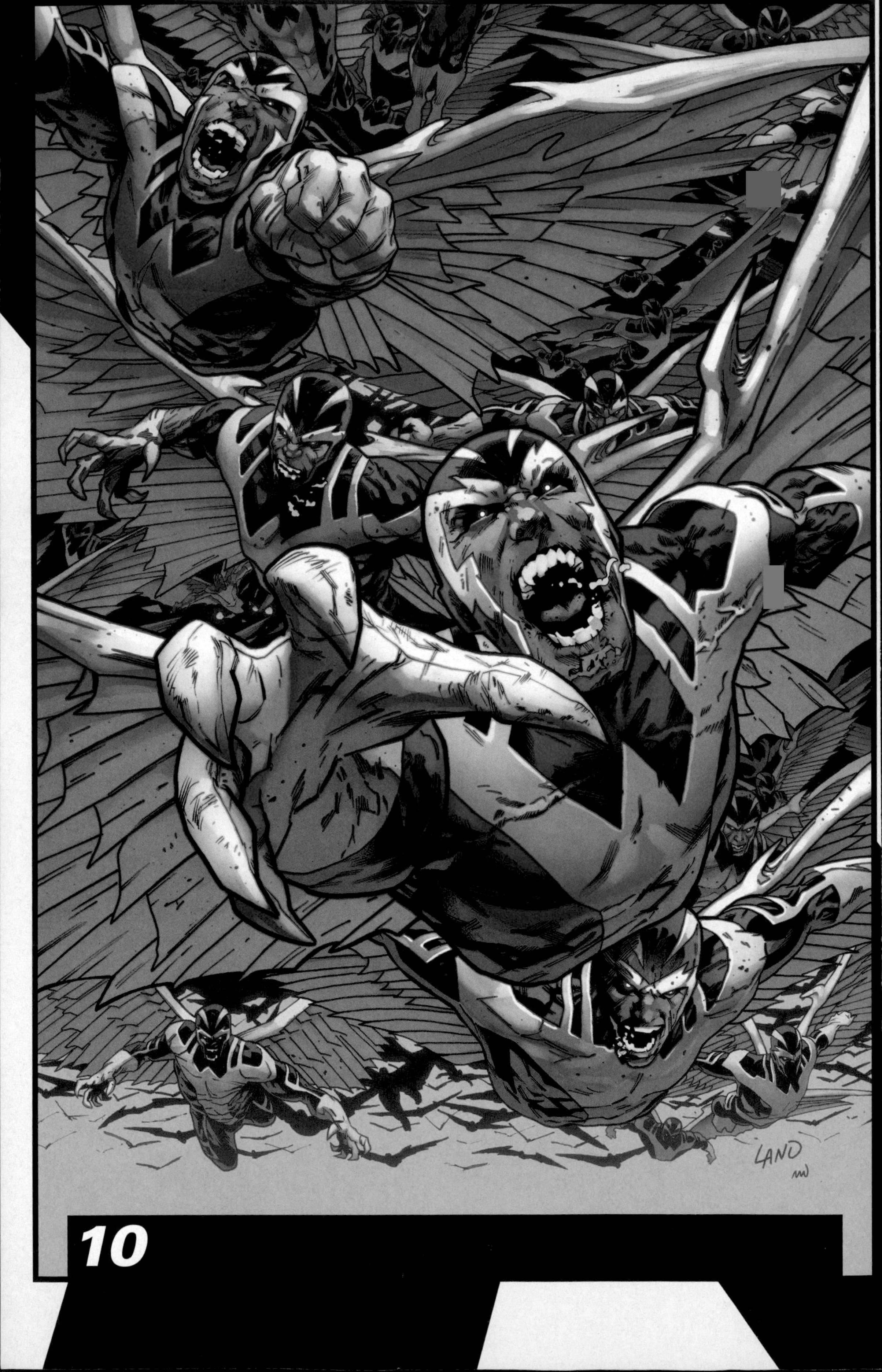
LAND

10

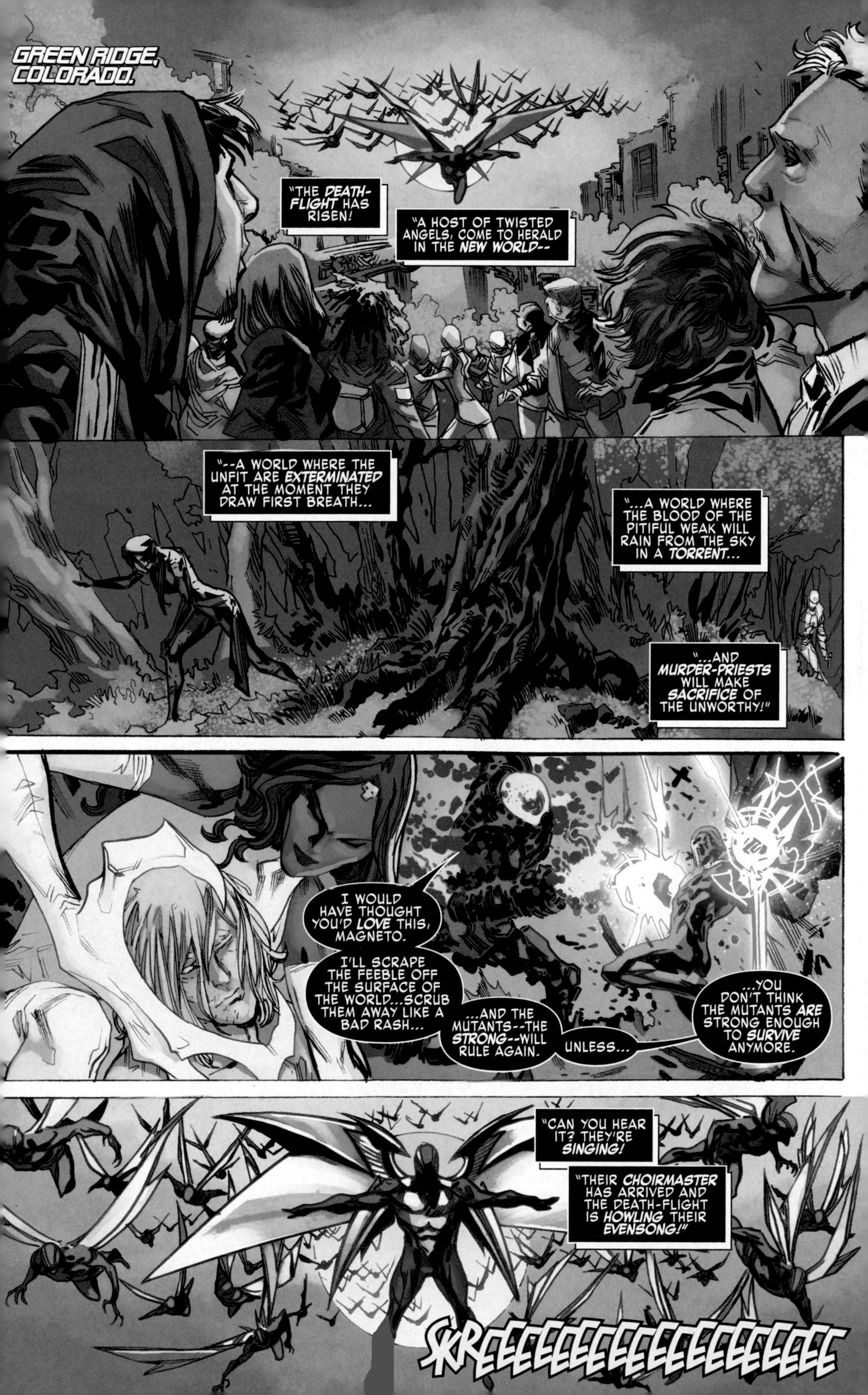
GREEN RIDGE, COLORADO.
"THE DEATH-FLIGHT HAS RISEN!
"A HOST OF TWISTED ANGELS, COME TO HERALD IN THE NEW WORLD--
"--A WORLD WHERE THE UNFIT ARE EXTERMINATED AT THE MOMENT THEY DRAW FIRST BREATH...
"...A WORLD WHERE THE BLOOD OF THE PITIFUL WEAK WILL RAIN FROM THE SKY IN A TORRENT...
"...AND MURDER-PRIESTS WILL MAKE SACRIFICE OF THE UNWORTHY!"
I WOULD HAVE THOUGHT YOU'D LOVE THIS, MAGNETO.
I'LL SCRAPE THE FEEBLE OFF THE SURFACE OF THE WORLD...SCRUB THEM AWAY LIKE A BAD RASH...
...AND THE MUTANTS--THE STRONG--WILL RULE AGAIN.
UNLESS...
...YOU DON'T THINK THE MUTANTS ARE STRONG ENOUGH TO SURVIVE ANYMORE.
"CAN YOU HEAR IT? THEY'RE SINGING!
"THEIR CHOIRMASTER HAS ARRIVED AND THE DEATH-FLIGHT IS HOWLING THEIR EVENSONG!"
SKREEEEEEEEEEEEEEEEEEEEE

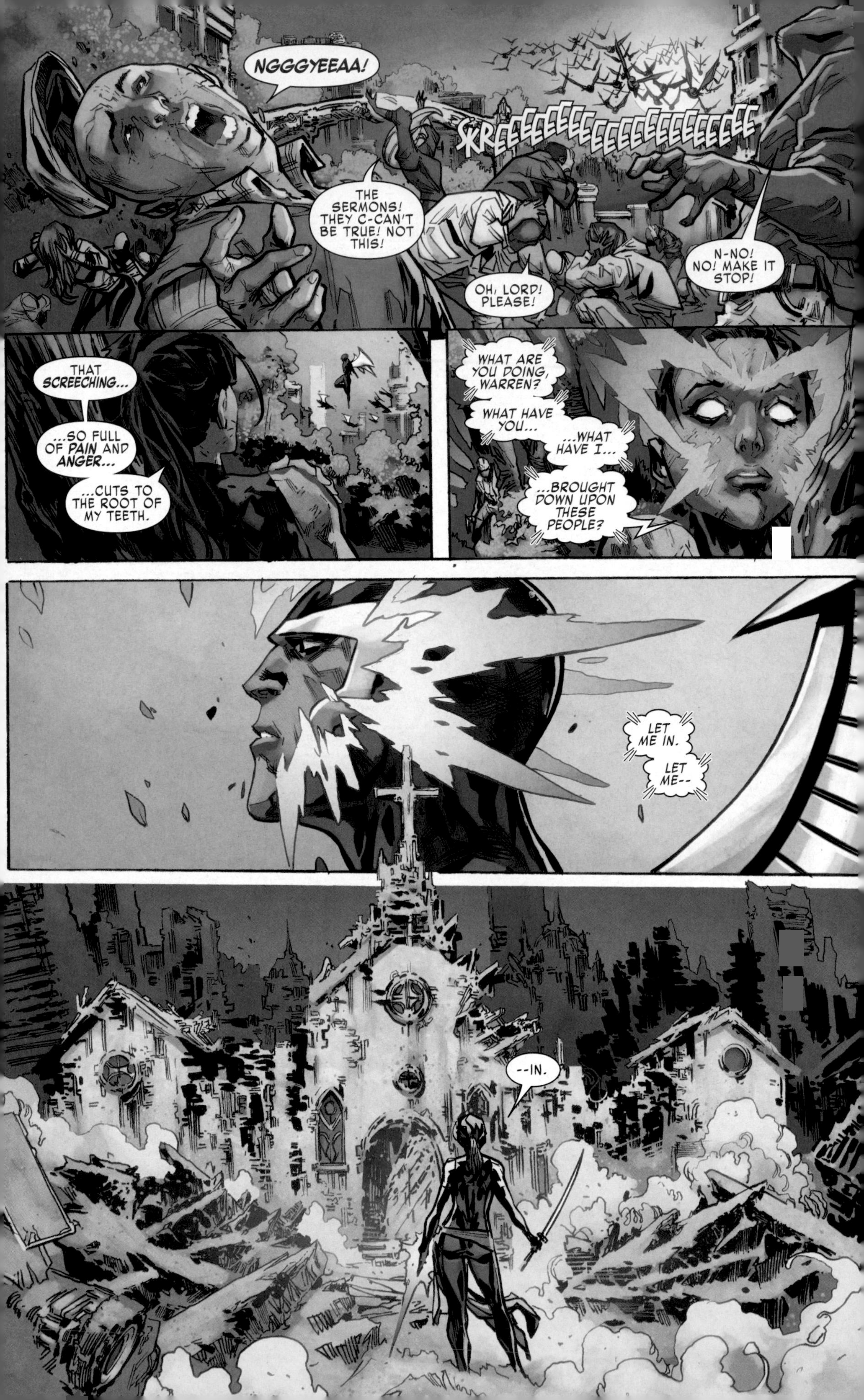
NGGGYEEAA!
SKREEEEEEEEEEEEEEEEEEEEEEEE
THE SERMONS! THEY C-CAN'T BE TRUE! NOT THIS!
OH, LORD! PLEASE!
N-NO! NO! MAKE IT STOP!
THAT SCREECHING...
...SO FULL OF PAIN AND ANGER...
...CUTS TO THE ROOT OF MY TEETH.
WHAT ARE YOU DOING, WARREN?
WHAT HAVE YOU...
...WHAT HAVE I...
...BROUGHT DOWN UPON THESE PEOPLE?
LET ME IN.
LET ME--
--IN.

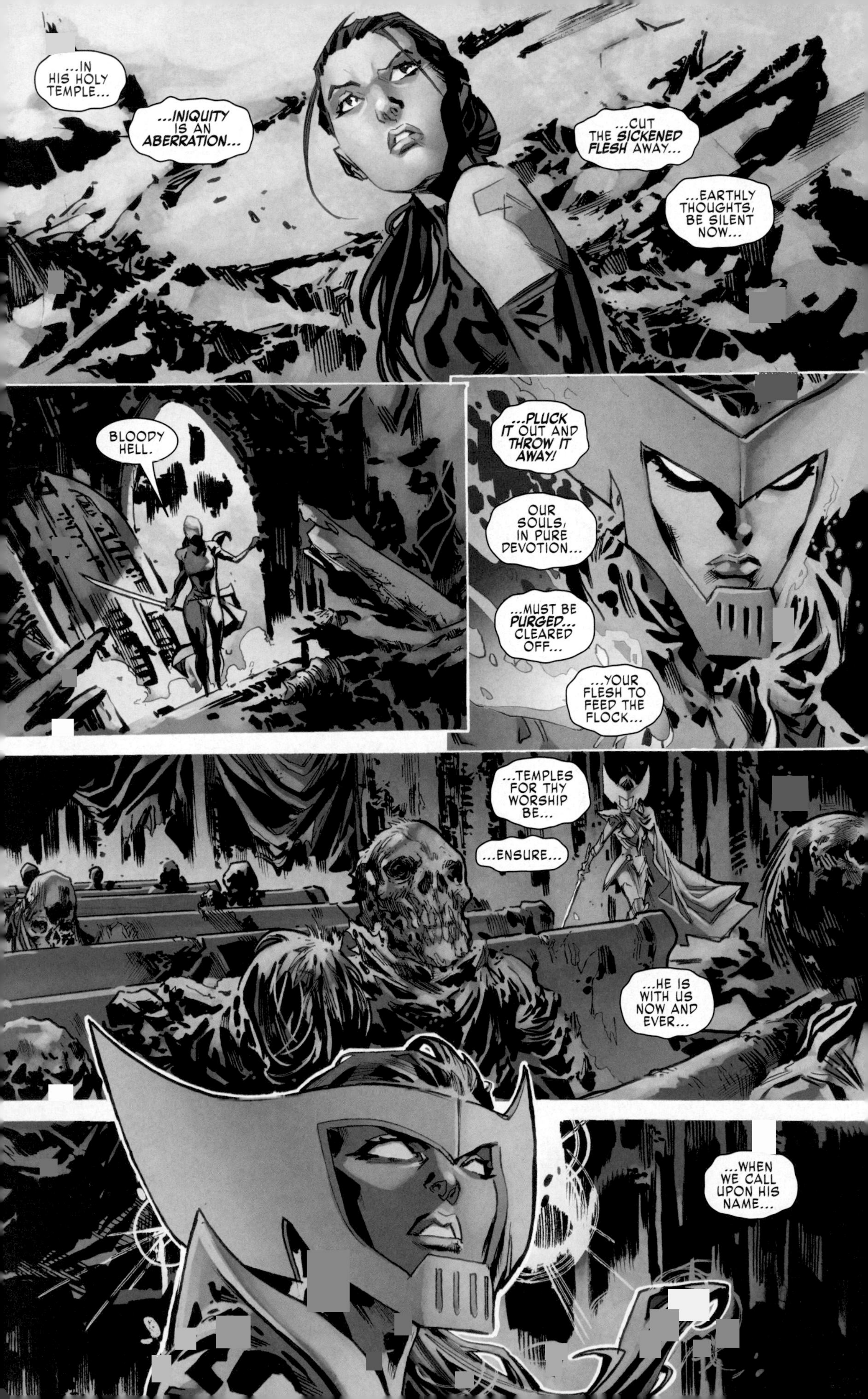
...IN HIS HOLY TEMPLE...
...INIQUITY IS AN ABERRATION...
...CUT THE SICKENED FLESH AWAY...
...EARTHLY THOUGHTS, BE SILENT NOW...
BLOODY HELL.
...PLUCK IT OUT AND THROW IT AWAY!
OUR SOULS, IN PURE DEVOTION...
...MUST BE PURGED... CLEARED OFF...
...YOUR FLESH TO FEED THE FLOCK...
...TEMPLES FOR THY WORSHIP BE...
...ENSURE...
...HE IS WITH US NOW AND EVER...
...WHEN WE CALL UPON HIS NAME...

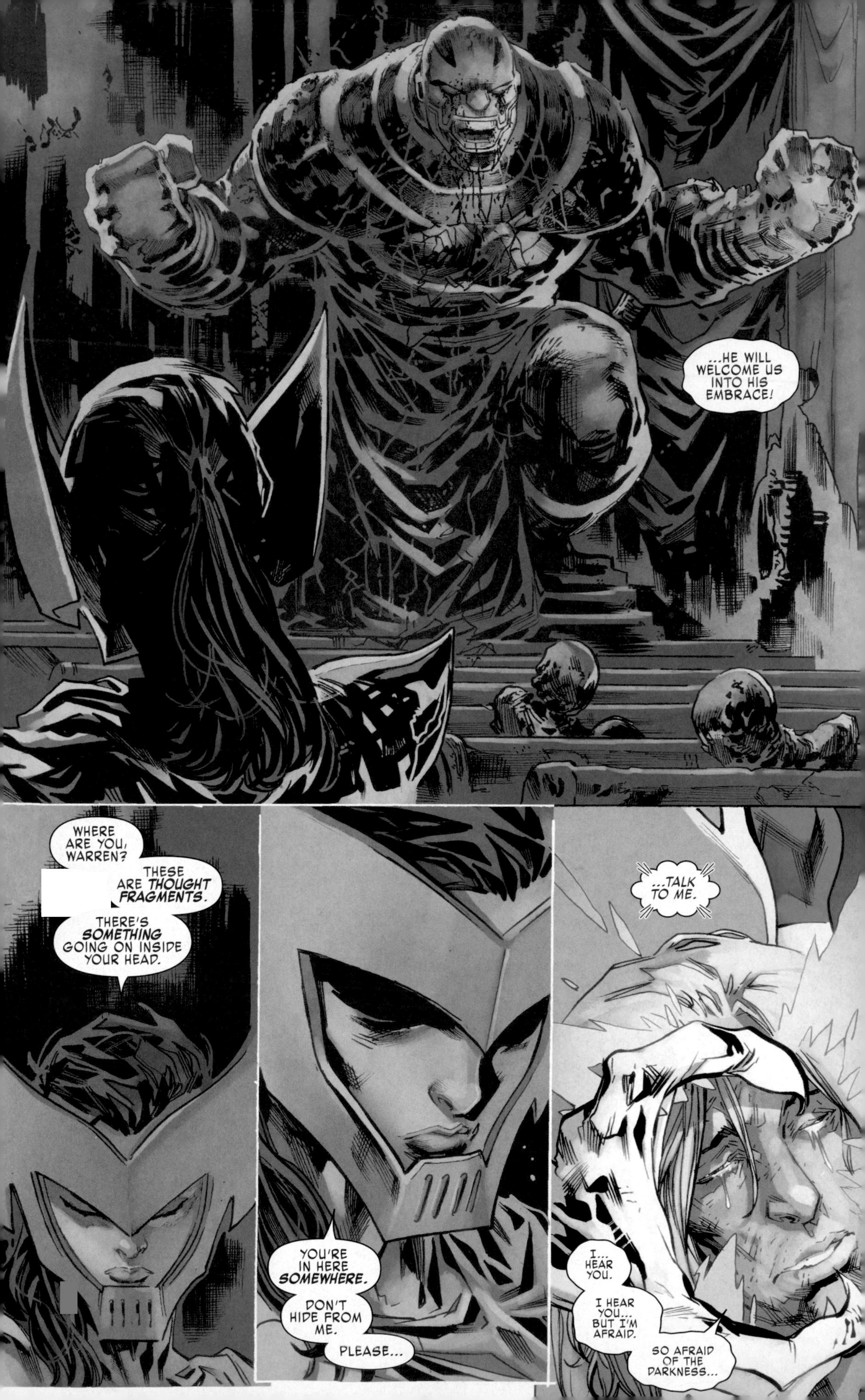
...HE WILL WELCOME US INTO HIS EMBRACE!
WHERE ARE YOU, WARREN?
THESE ARE *THOUGHT FRAGMENTS*.
THERE'S *SOMETHING* GOING ON INSIDE YOUR HEAD.
YOU'RE IN HERE *SOMEWHERE*.
DON'T HIDE FROM ME.
PLEASE...
...TALK TO ME.
I... HEAR YOU.
I HEAR YOU... BUT I'M AFRAID.
SO AFRAID OF THE DARKNESS...

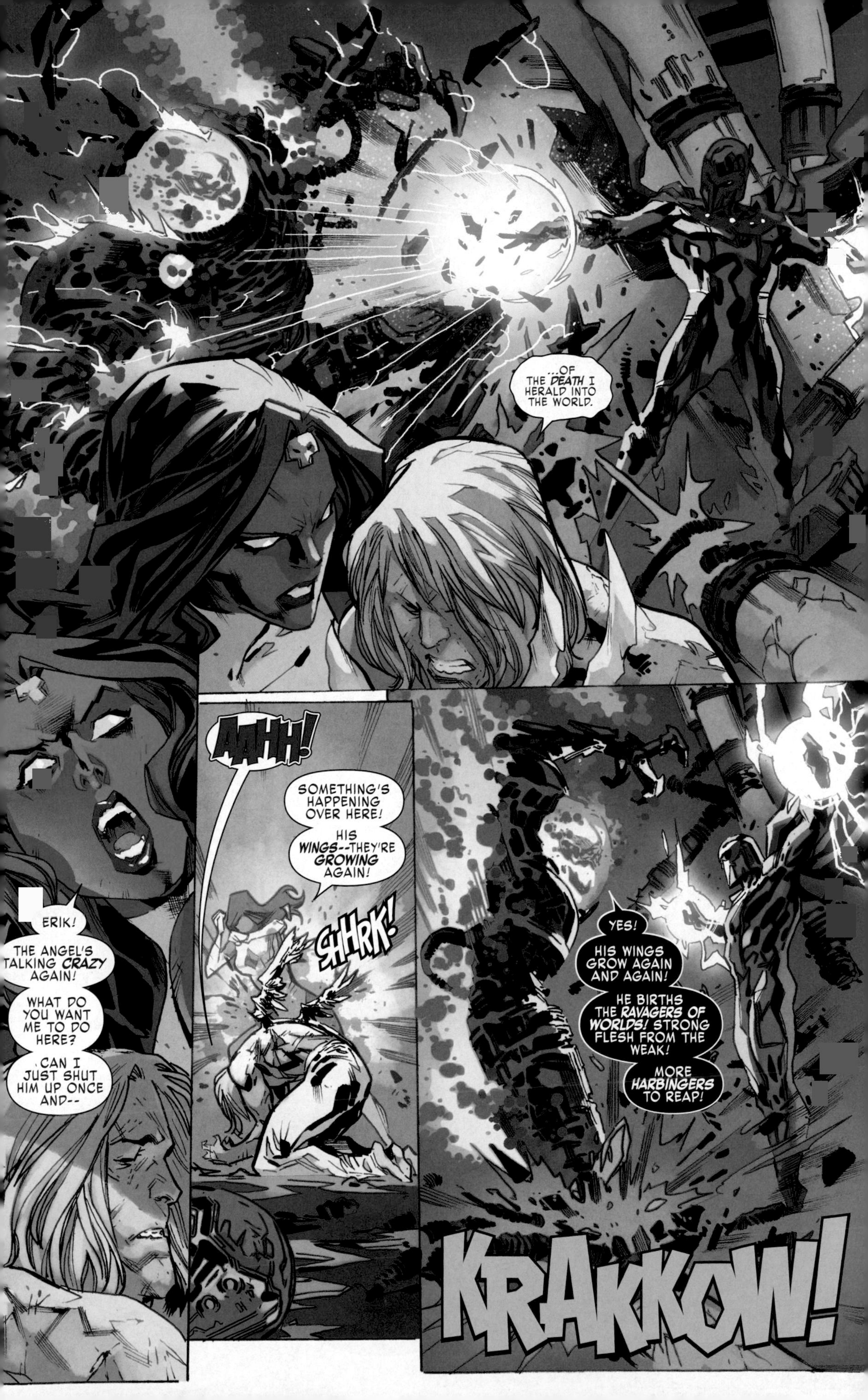
...OF THE DEATH I HERALD INTO THE WORLD.
ERIK!
THE ANGEL'S TALKING CRAZY AGAIN!
WHAT DO YOU WANT ME TO DO HERE?
CAN I JUST SHUT HIM UP ONCE AND--
AAHH!
SOMETHING'S HAPPENING OVER HERE!
HIS WINGS--THEY'RE GROWING AGAIN!
SHHRK!
YES!
HIS WINGS GROW AGAIN AND AGAIN!
HE BIRTHS THE RAVAGERS OF WORLDS! STRONG FLESH FROM THE WEAK!
MORE HARBINGERS TO REAP!
KRAKKOW!

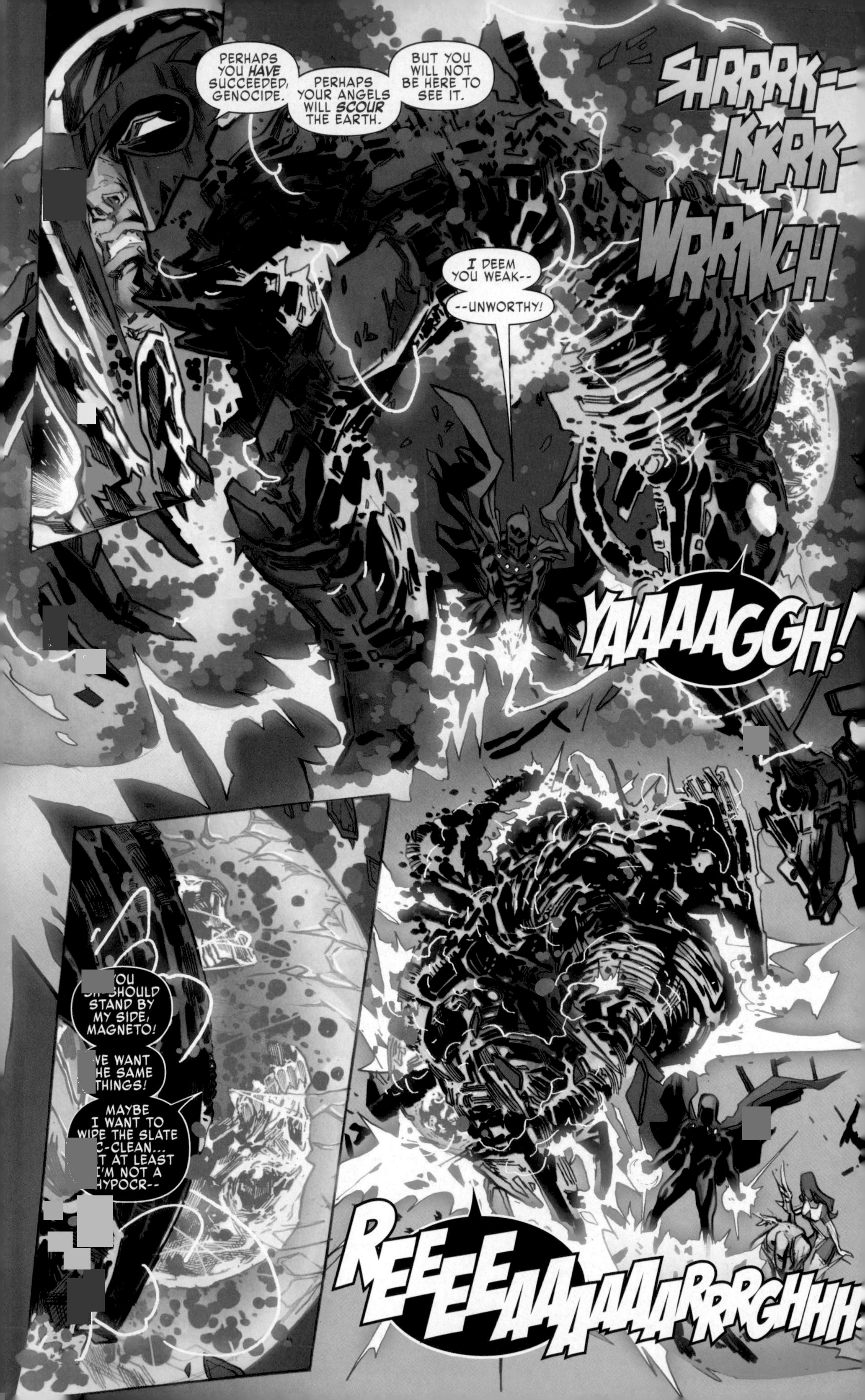
PERHAPS YOU HAVE SUCCEEDED, GENOCIDE.
PERHAPS YOUR ANGELS WILL SCOUR THE EARTH.
BUT YOU WILL NOT BE HERE TO SEE IT.
SHRRRK-- KKRK
WRRNCH
I DEEM YOU WEAK--
--UNWORTHY!
YAAAAGGH!
[redacted]OU [redacted]-SHOULD STAND BY MY SIDE, MAGNETO!
[redacted]E WANT [redacted]HE SAME [redacted]HINGS!
MAYBE I WANT TO WIPE THE SLATE [redacted]C-CLEAN... [redacted]T AT LEAST [redacted]'M NOT A [redacted]HYPOCR--
REEEEAAAAAARRRGHHH

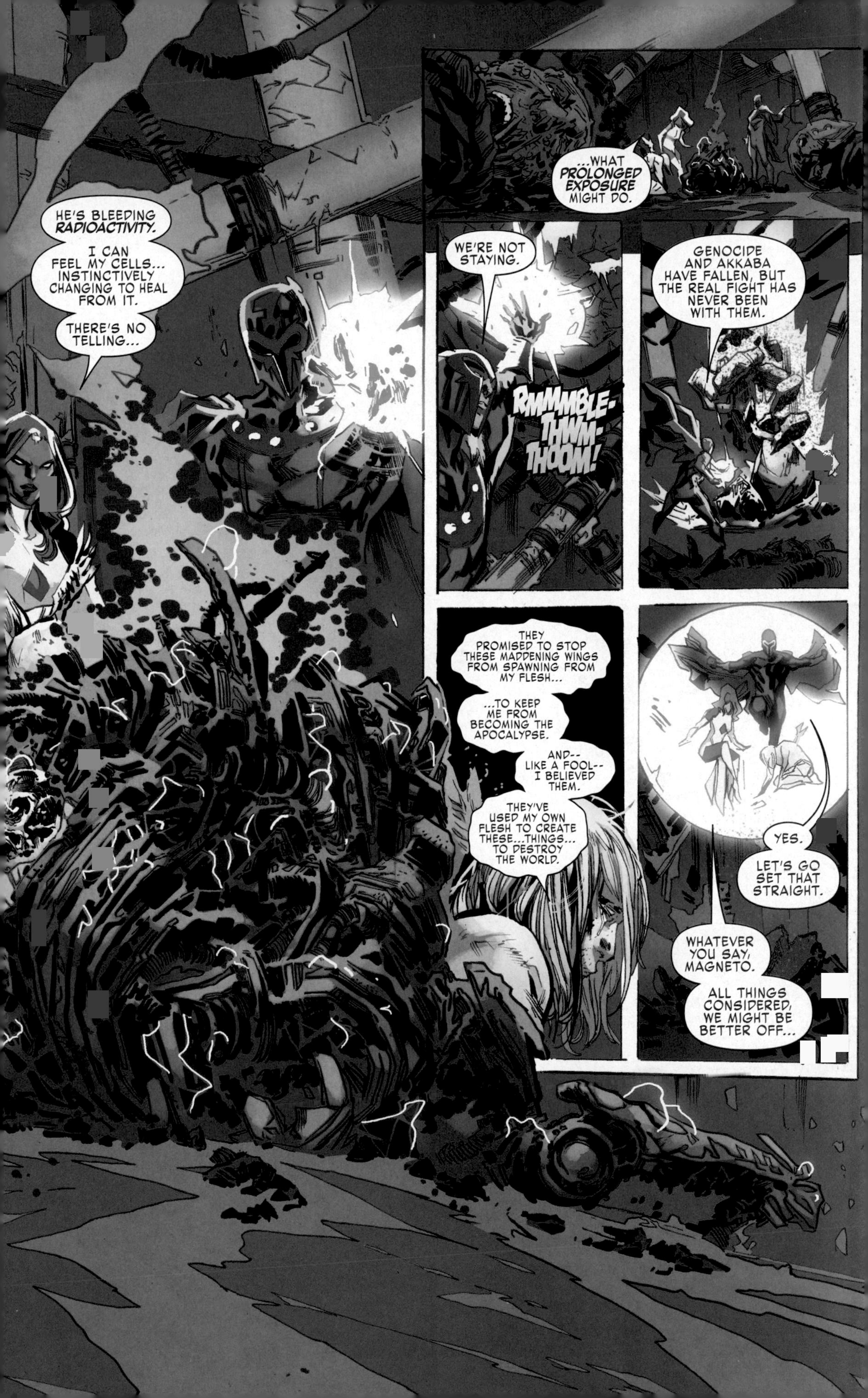
HE'S BLEEDING *RADIOACTIVITY.*
I CAN FEEL MY CELLS... INSTINCTIVELY CHANGING TO HEAL FROM IT.
THERE'S NO TELLING...
...WHAT *PROLONGED EXPOSURE* MIGHT DO.
WE'RE NOT STAYING.
RMMMBLE-THWM-THOOM!
GENOCIDE AND AKKABA HAVE FALLEN, BUT THE REAL FIGHT HAS NEVER BEEN WITH THEM.
THEY PROMISED TO STOP THESE MADDENING WINGS FROM SPAWNING FROM MY FLESH...
...TO KEEP ME FROM BECOMING THE APOCALYPSE.
AND--LIKE A FOOL--I BELIEVED THEM.
THEY'VE USED MY OWN FLESH TO CREATE THESE...THINGS...TO DESTROY THE WORLD.
YES.
LET'S GO SET THAT STRAIGHT.
WHATEVER YOU SAY, MAGNETO.
ALL THINGS CONSIDERED, WE MIGHT BE BETTER OFF...

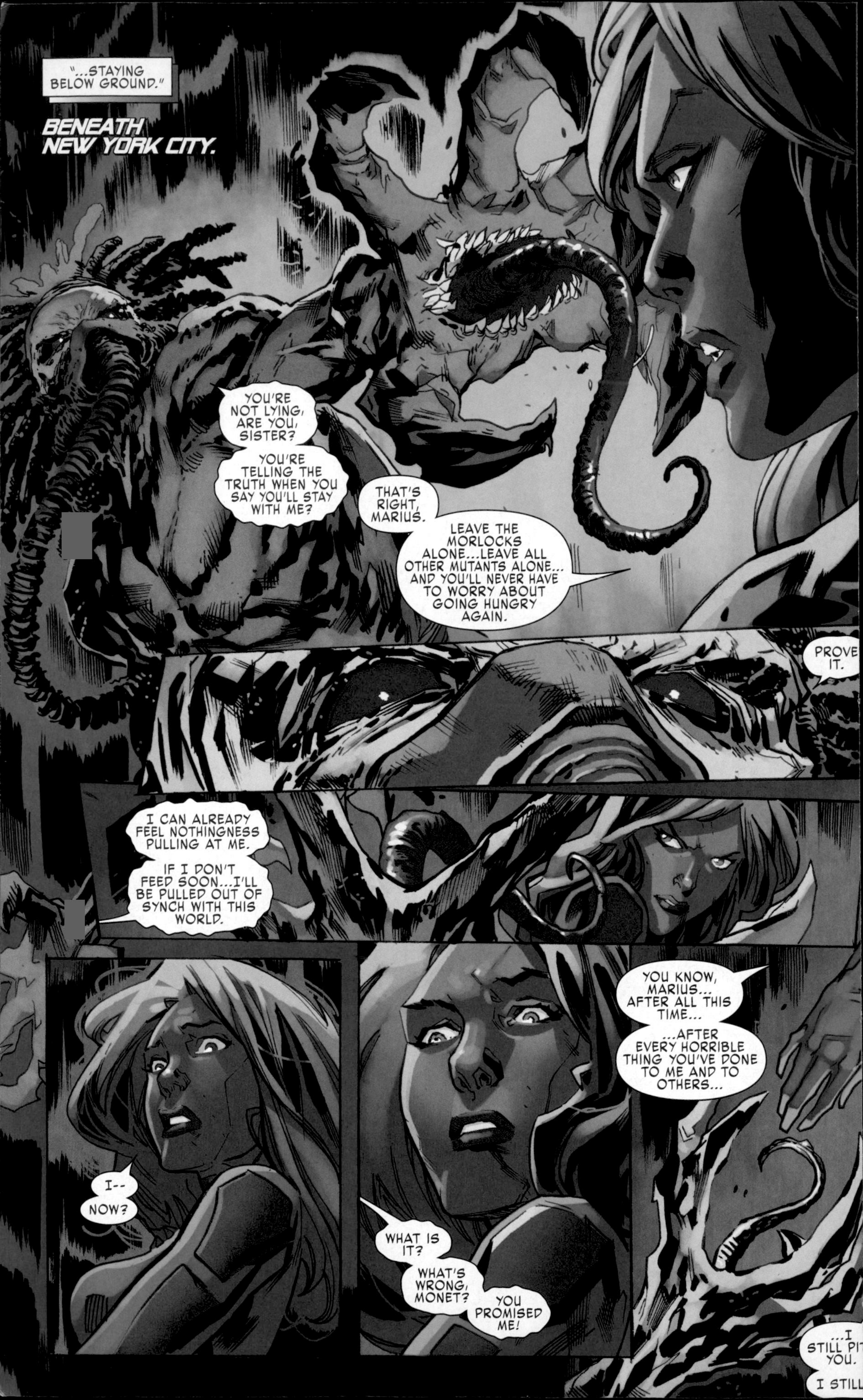
"...STAYING BELOW GROUND."
BENEATH NEW YORK CITY.
YOU'RE NOT LYING, ARE YOU, SISTER?
YOU'RE TELLING THE TRUTH WHEN YOU SAY YOU'LL STAY WITH ME?
THAT'S RIGHT, MARIUS.
LEAVE THE MORLOCKS ALONE...LEAVE ALL OTHER MUTANTS ALONE... AND YOU'LL NEVER HAVE TO WORRY ABOUT GOING HUNGRY AGAIN.
PROVE IT.
I CAN ALREADY FEEL NOTHINGNESS PULLING AT ME.
IF I DON'T FEED SOON...I'LL BE PULLED OUT OF SYNCH WITH THIS WORLD.
I--
NOW?
WHAT IS IT?
WHAT'S WRONG, MONET?
YOU PROMISED ME!
YOU KNOW, MARIUS... AFTER ALL THIS TIME...
...AFTER EVERY HORRIBLE THING YOU'VE DONE TO ME AND TO OTHERS...
...I STILL
YOU.
I STILL

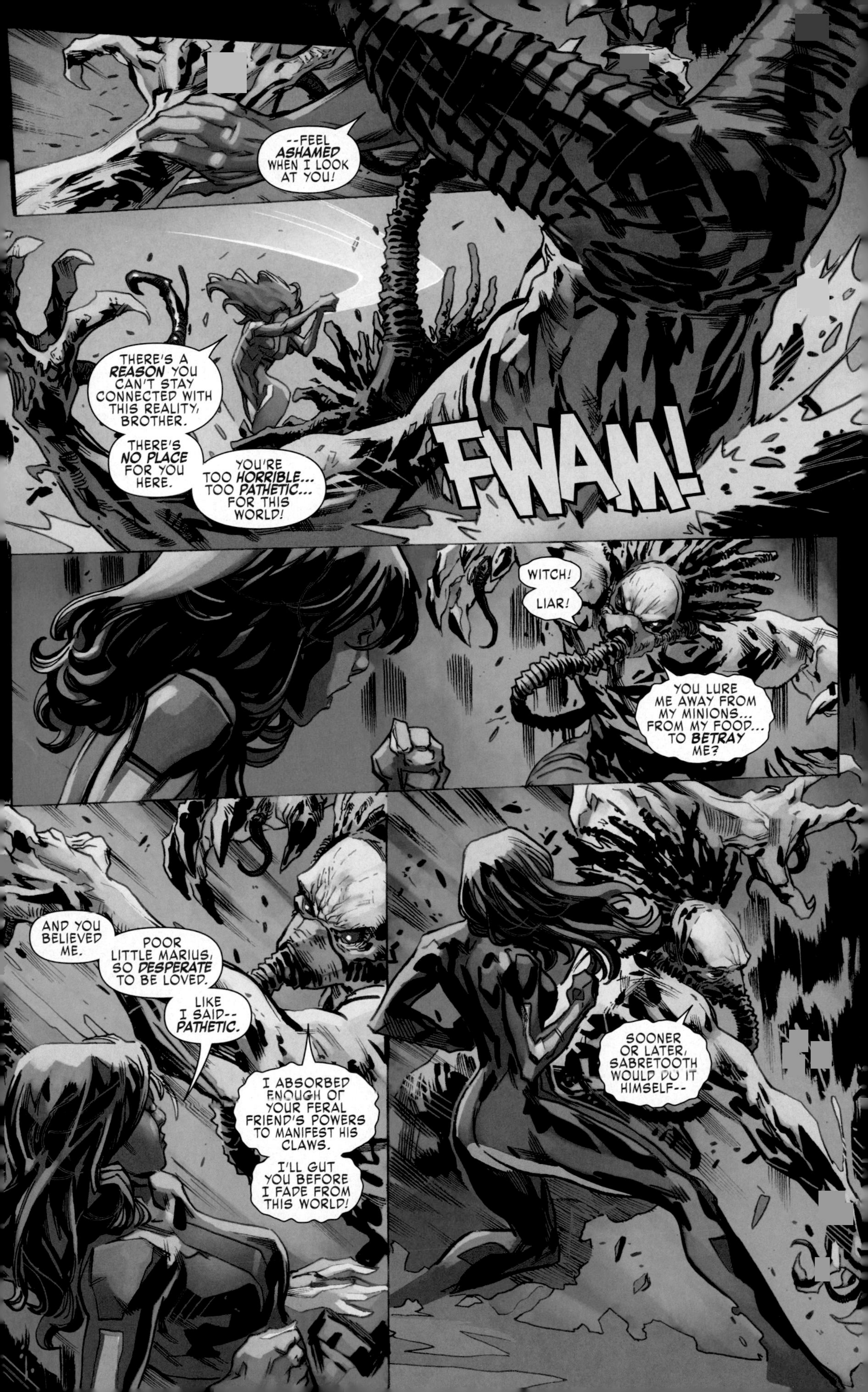
--FEEL ASHAMED WHEN I LOOK AT YOU!
THERE'S A REASON YOU CAN'T STAY CONNECTED WITH THIS REALITY, BROTHER.
THERE'S NO PLACE FOR YOU HERE.
YOU'RE TOO HORRIBLE... TOO PATHETIC... FOR THIS WORLD!
FWAM!
WITCH!
LIAR!
YOU LURE ME AWAY FROM MY MINIONS... FROM MY FOOD... TO BETRAY ME?
AND YOU BELIEVED ME.
POOR LITTLE MARIUS, SO DESPERATE TO BE LOVED.
LIKE I SAID-- PATHETIC.
I ABSORBED ENOUGH OF YOUR FERAL FRIEND'S POWERS TO MANIFEST HIS CLAWS.
I'LL GUT YOU BEFORE I FADE FROM THIS WORLD!
SOONER OR LATER, SABRETOOTH WOULD DO IT HIMSELF--

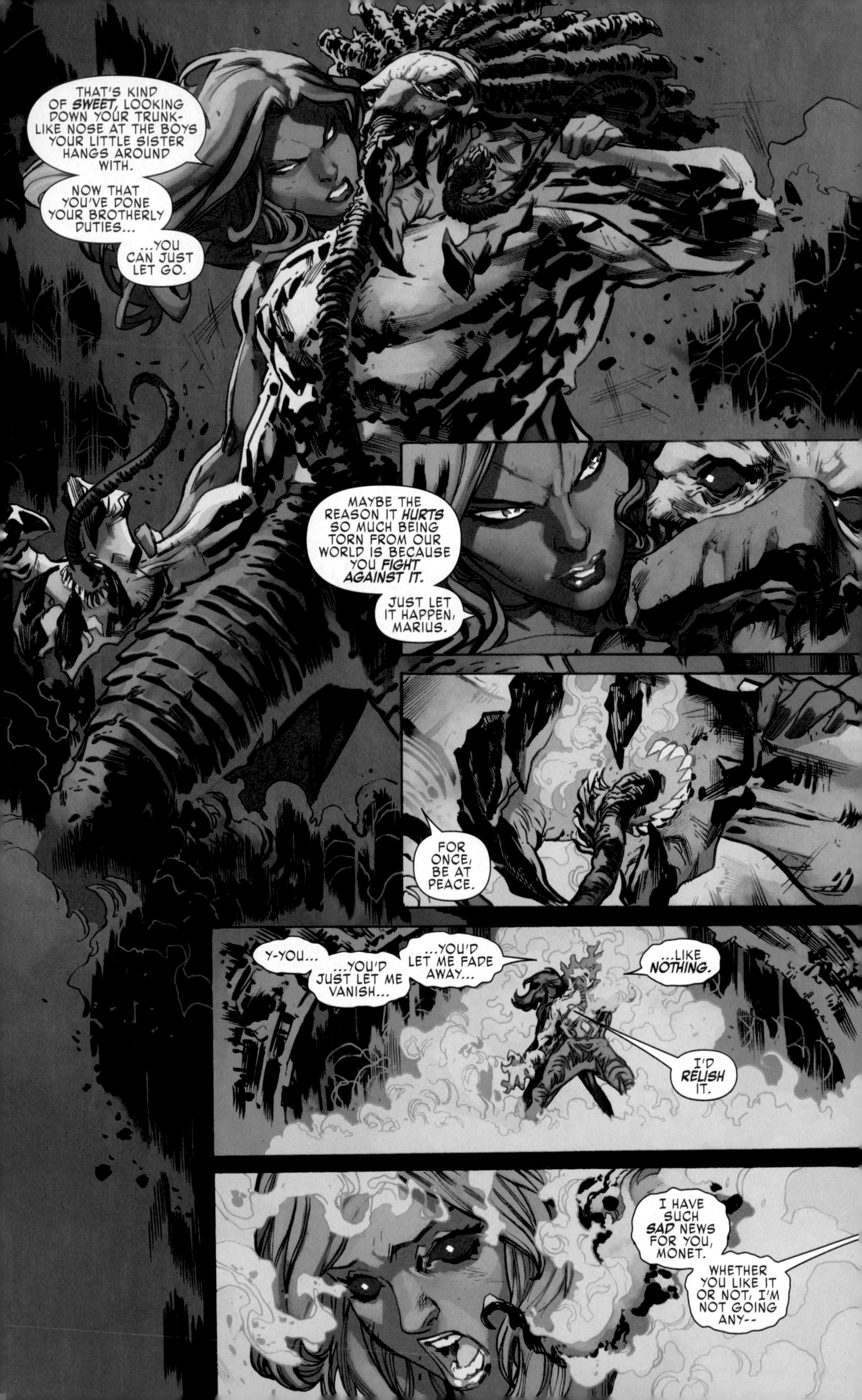
THAT'S KIND OF SWEET, LOOKING DOWN YOUR TRUNK-LIKE NOSE AT THE BOYS YOUR LITTLE SISTER HANGS AROUND WITH.
NOW THAT YOU'VE DONE YOUR BROTHERLY DUTIES...
...YOU CAN JUST LET GO.
MAYBE THE REASON IT HURTS SO MUCH BEING TORN FROM OUR WORLD IS BECAUSE YOU FIGHT AGAINST IT.
JUST LET IT HAPPEN, MARIUS.
FOR ONCE, BE AT PEACE.
Y-YOU...
...YOU'D JUST LET ME VANISH...
...YOU'D LET ME FADE AWAY...
...LIKE NOTHING.
I'D RELISH IT.
I HAVE SUCH SAD NEWS FOR YOU, MONET.
WHETHER YOU LIKE IT OR NOT, I'M NOT GOING ANY--

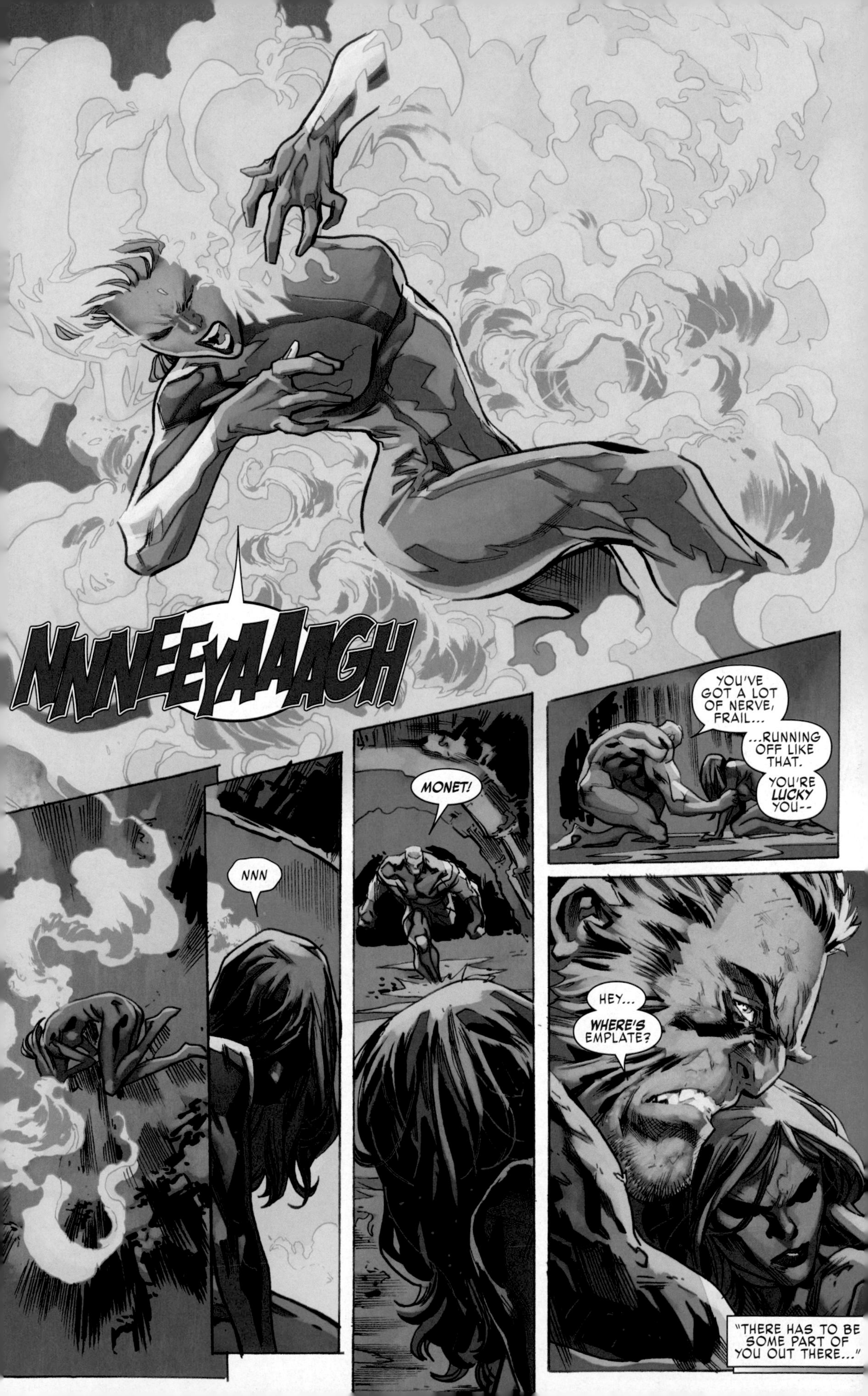
NNNEEYAAAGH
NNN
MONET!
YOU'VE GOT A LOT OF NERVE, FRAIL...
...RUNNING OFF LIKE THAT.
YOU'RE LUCKY YOU--
HEY...
WHERE'S EMPLATE?
"THERE HAS TO BE SOME PART OF YOU OUT THERE..."

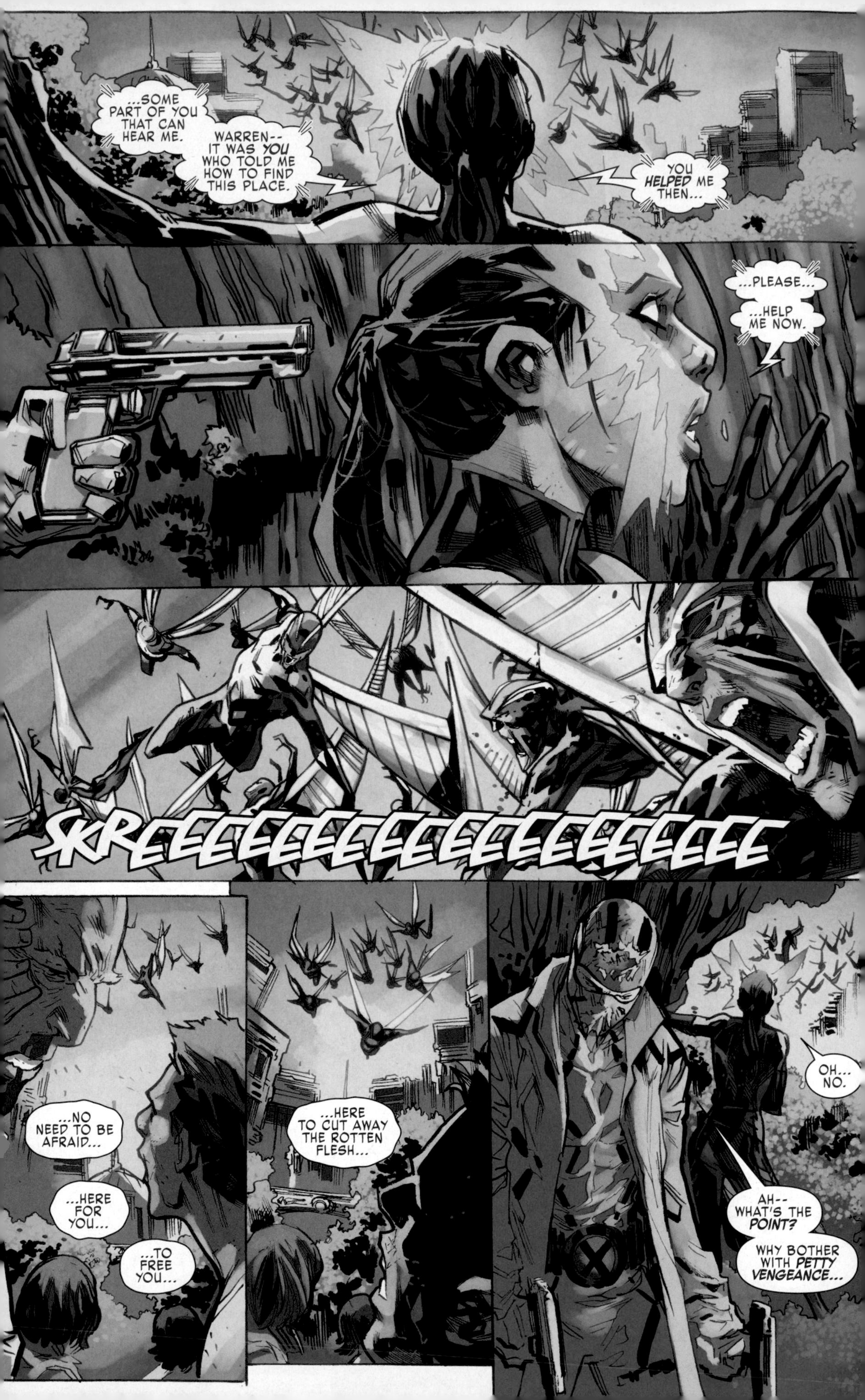
...SOME PART OF YOU THAT CAN HEAR ME.
WARREN-- IT WAS YOU WHO TOLD ME HOW TO FIND THIS PLACE.
YOU HELPED ME THEN...
...PLEASE...
...HELP ME NOW.
SKREEEEEEEEEEEEEEEEEEEEE
...NO NEED TO BE AFRAID...
...HERE FOR YOU...
...TO FREE YOU...
...HERE TO CUT AWAY THE ROTTEN FLESH...
OH... NO.
AH-- WHAT'S THE POINT?
WHY BOTHER WITH PETTY VENGEANCE...

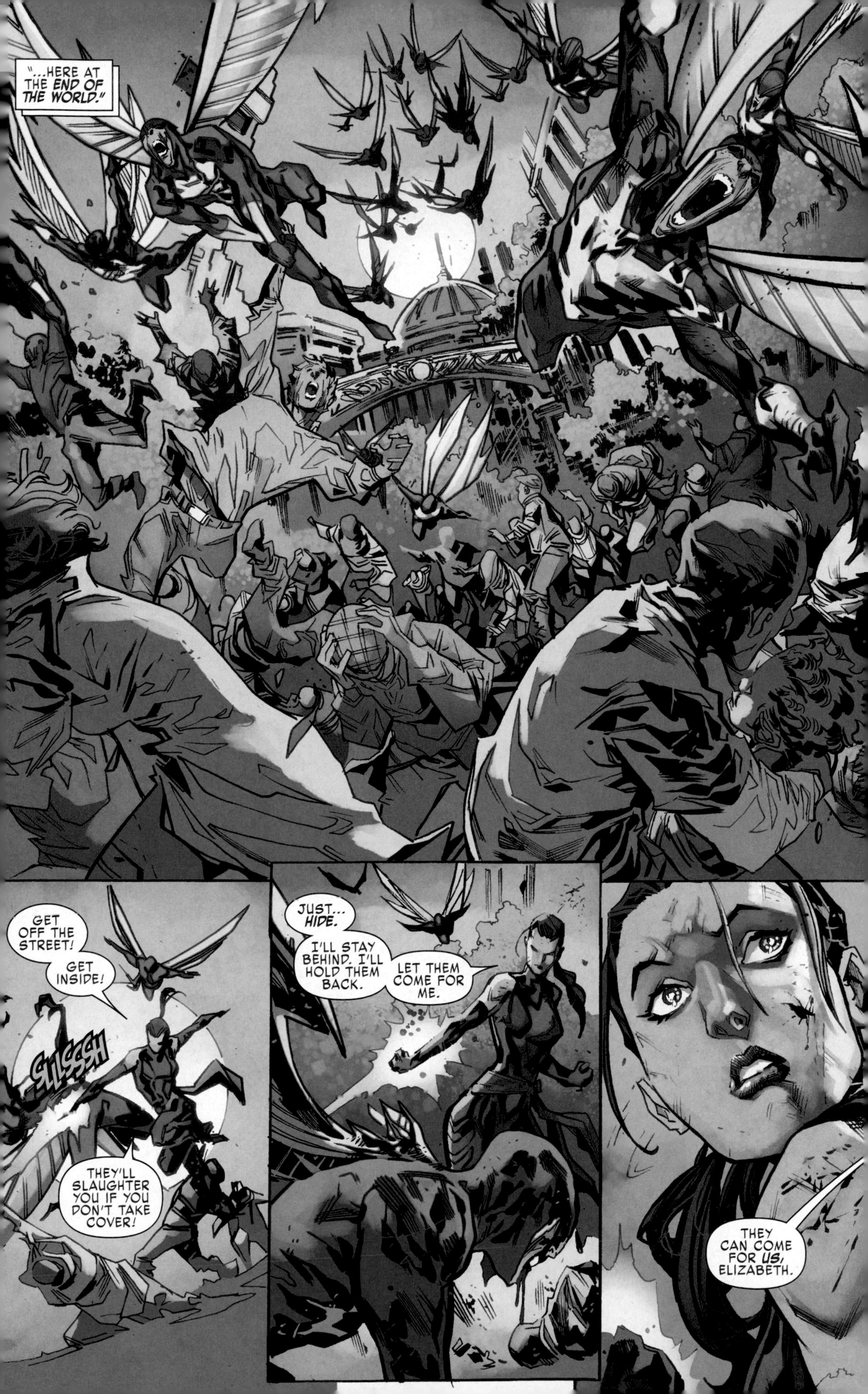
"...HERE AT THE END OF THE WORLD."
GET OFF THE STREET!
GET INSIDE!
SHLISSSH
THEY'LL SLAUGHTER YOU IF YOU DON'T TAKE COVER!
JUST... HIDE.
I'LL STAY BEHIND. I'LL HOLD THEM BACK.
LET THEM COME FOR ME.
THEY CAN COME FOR US, ELIZABETH.

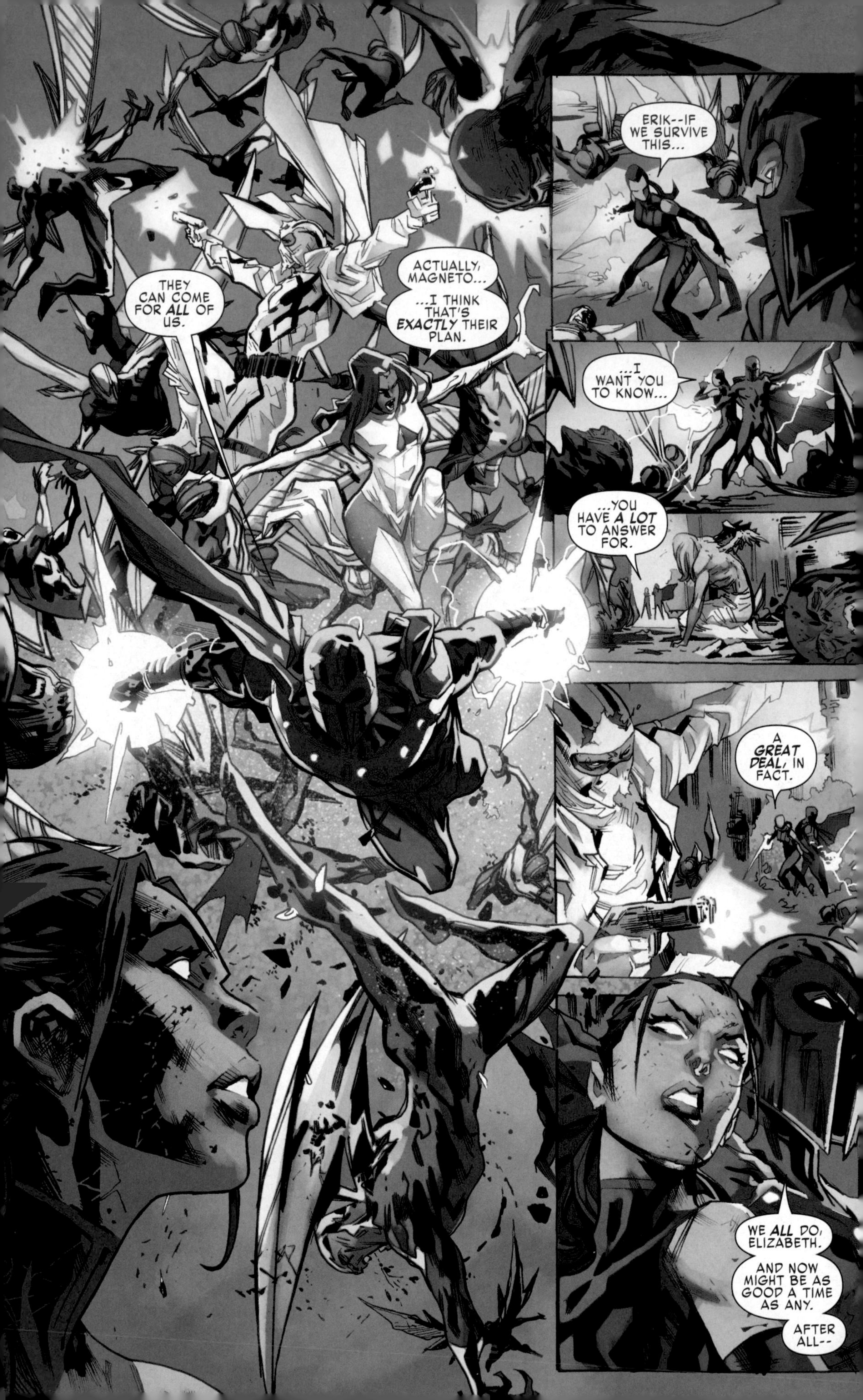
THEY CAN COME FOR ALL OF US.
ACTUALLY, MAGNETO...
...I THINK THAT'S EXACTLY THEIR PLAN.
ERIK--IF WE SURVIVE THIS...
...I WANT YOU TO KNOW...
...YOU HAVE A LOT TO ANSWER FOR.
A GREAT DEAL, IN FACT.
WE ALL DO, ELIZABETH.
AND NOW MIGHT BE AS GOOD A TIME AS ANY.
AFTER ALL--

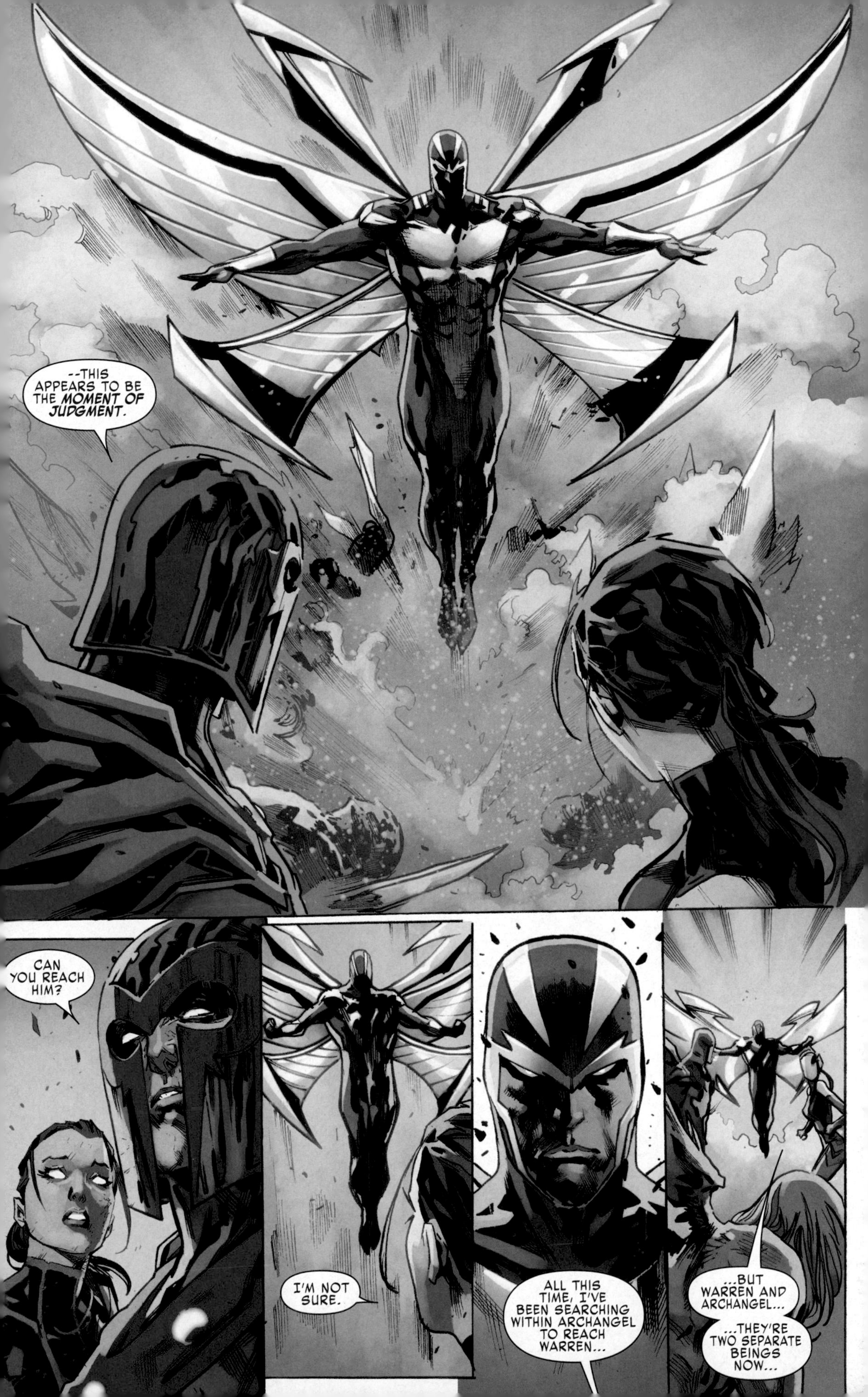
--THIS APPEARS TO BE THE *MOMENT OF JUDGMENT*.
CAN YOU REACH HIM?
I'M NOT SURE.
ALL THIS TIME, I'VE BEEN SEARCHING WITHIN ARCHANGEL TO REACH WARREN...
...BUT WARREN AND ARCHANGEL...
...THEY'RE TWO SEPARATE BEINGS NOW...

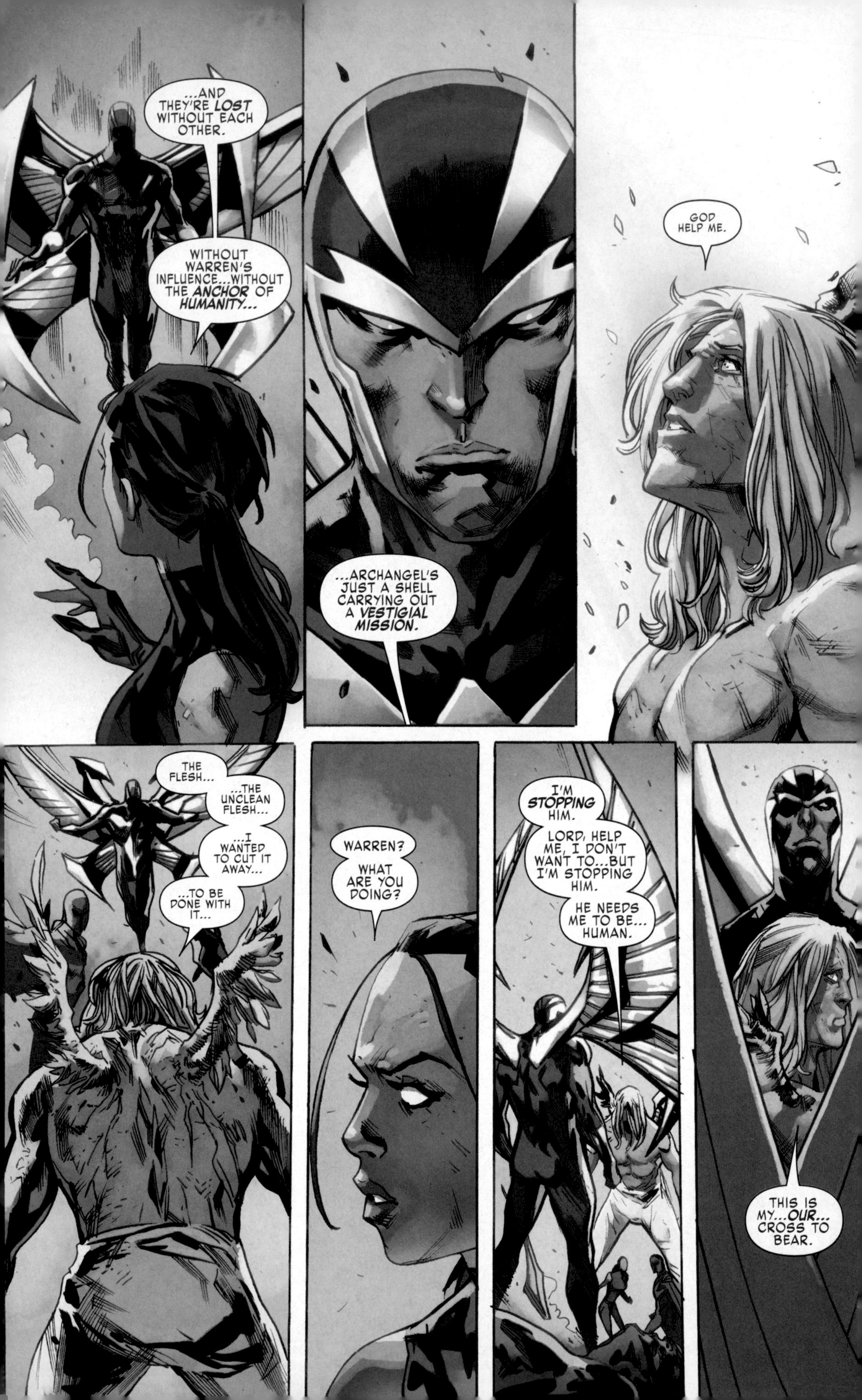
...AND THEY'RE LOST WITHOUT EACH OTHER.
WITHOUT WARREN'S INFLUENCE...WITHOUT THE ANCHOR OF HUMANITY...
...ARCHANGEL'S JUST A SHELL CARRYING OUT A VESTIGIAL MISSION.
GOD HELP ME.
THE FLESH...
...THE UNCLEAN FLESH...
...I WANTED TO CUT IT AWAY...
...TO BE DONE WITH IT...
WARREN?
WHAT ARE YOU DOING?
I'M STOPPING HIM.
LORD, HELP ME, I DON'T WANT TO...BUT I'M STOPPING HIM.
HE NEEDS ME TO BE... HUMAN.
THIS IS MY...OUR... CROSS TO BEAR.

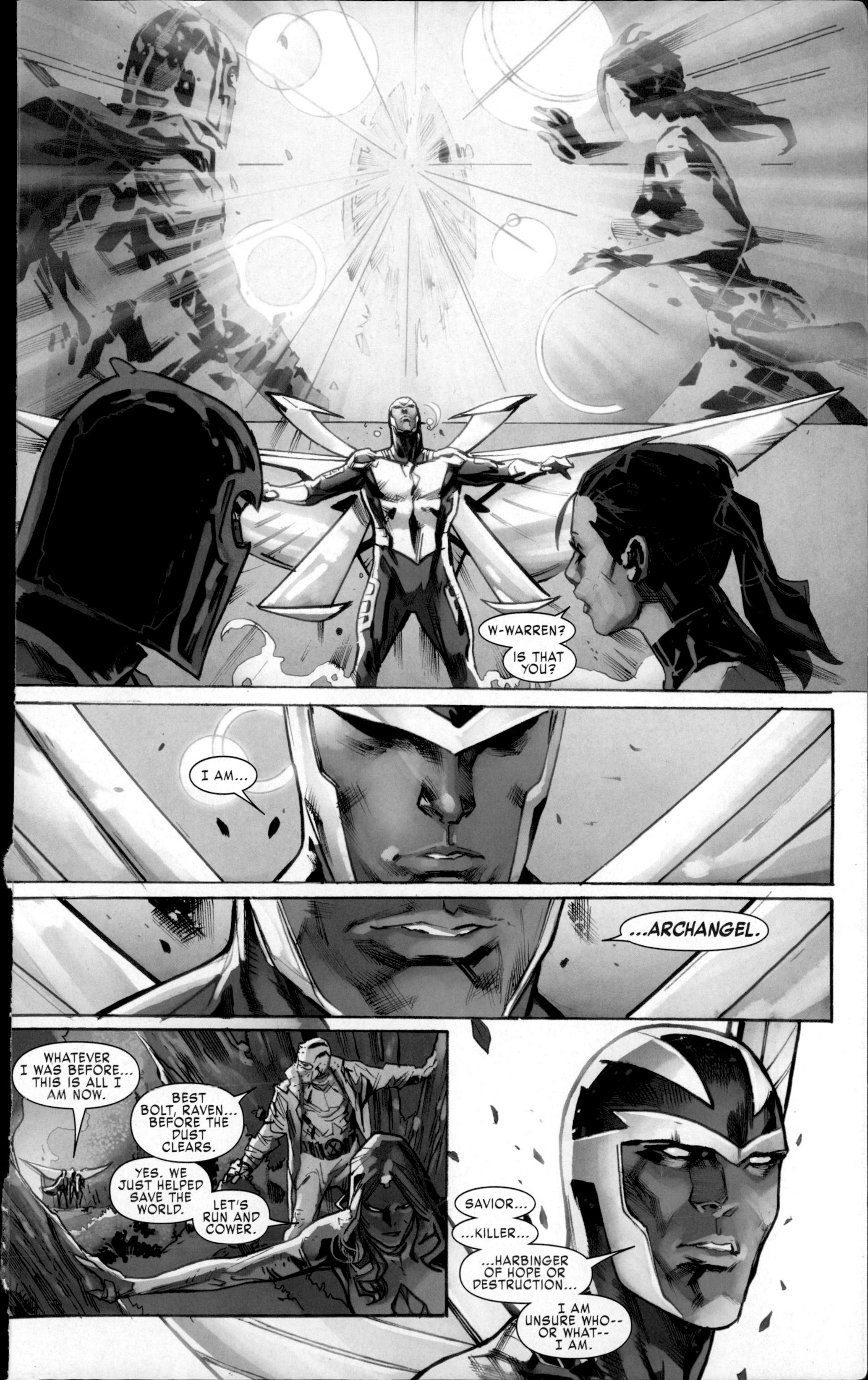
W-WARREN?
IS THAT YOU?
I AM...
...ARCHANGEL.
WHATEVER I WAS BEFORE... THIS IS ALL I AM NOW.
BEST BOLT, RAVEN... BEFORE THE DUST CLEARS.
YES. WE JUST HELPED SAVE THE WORLD.
LET'S RUN AND COWER.
SAVIOR...
...KILLER...
...HARBINGER OF HOPE OR DESTRUCTION...
I AM UNSURE WHO-- OR WHAT-- I AM.

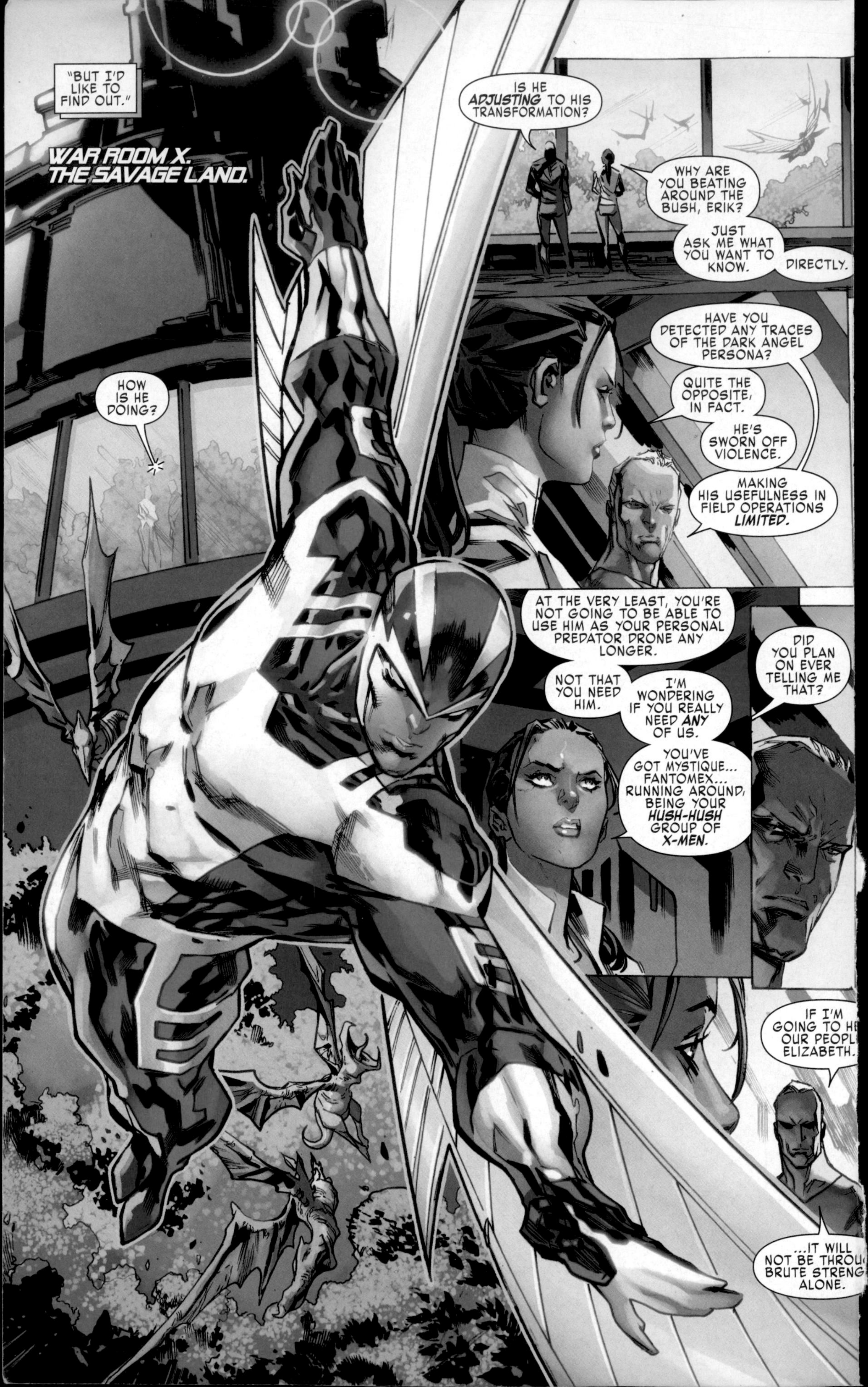
"BUT I'D LIKE TO FIND OUT."
WAR ROOM X. THE SAVAGE LAND.
HOW IS HE DOING?
IS HE ADJUSTING TO HIS TRANSFORMATION?
WHY ARE YOU BEATING AROUND THE BUSH, ERIK?
JUST ASK ME WHAT YOU WANT TO KNOW.
DIRECTLY.
HAVE YOU DETECTED ANY TRACES OF THE DARK ANGEL PERSONA?
QUITE THE OPPOSITE, IN FACT.
HE'S SWORN OFF VIOLENCE.
MAKING HIS USEFULNESS IN FIELD OPERATIONS LIMITED.
AT THE VERY LEAST, YOU'RE NOT GOING TO BE ABLE TO USE HIM AS YOUR PERSONAL PREDATOR DRONE ANY LONGER.
NOT THAT YOU NEED HIM.
I'M WONDERING IF YOU REALLY NEED ANY OF US.
YOU'VE GOT MYSTIQUE... FANTOMEX... RUNNING AROUND, BEING YOUR HUSH-HUSH GROUP OF X-MEN.
DID YOU PLAN ON EVER TELLING ME THAT?
IF I'M GOING TO HE OUR PEOPL ELIZABETH.
...IT WILL NOT BE THROU BRUTE STRENG ALONE.

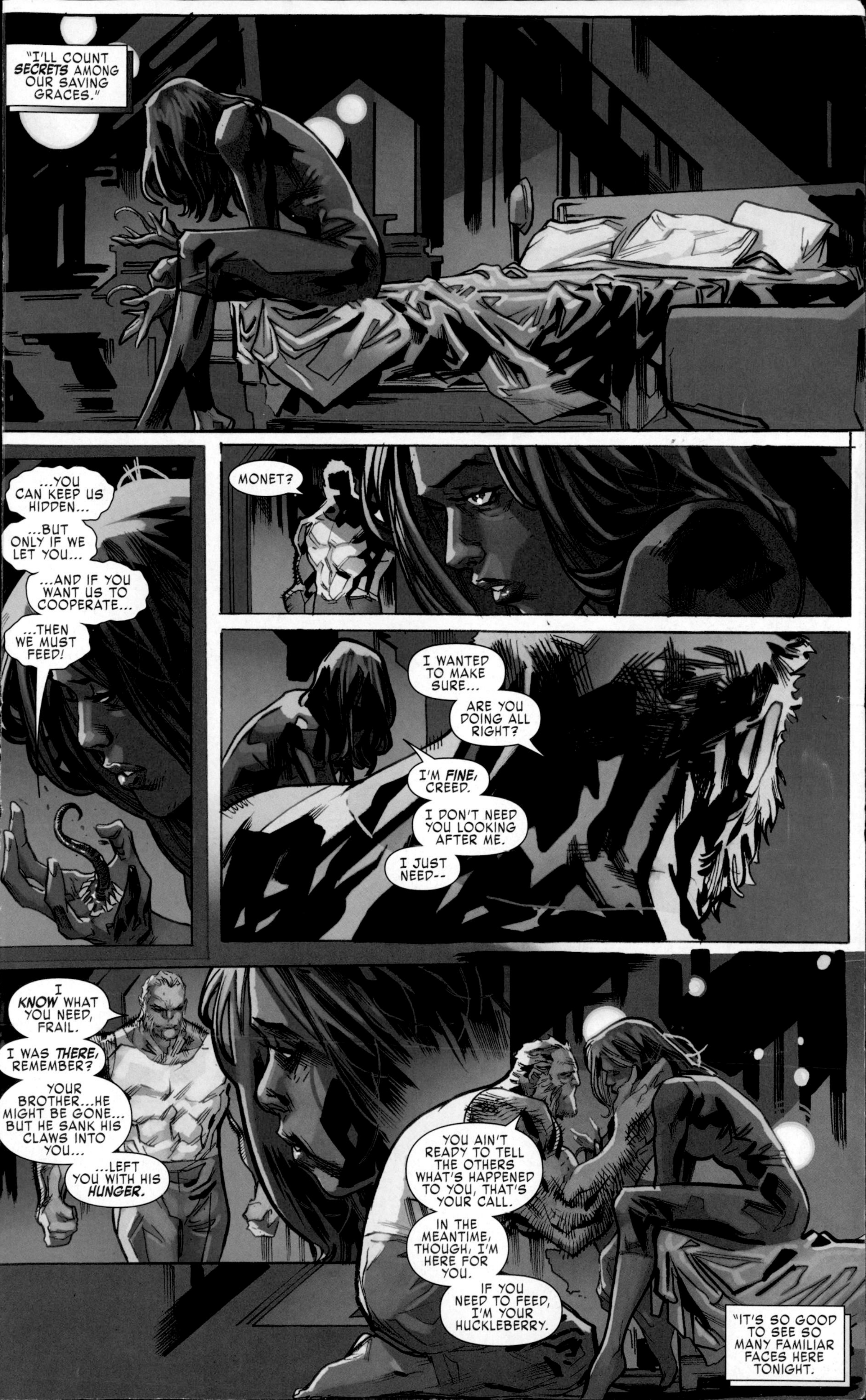
"I'LL COUNT SECRETS AMONG OUR SAVING GRACES."
...YOU CAN KEEP US HIDDEN...
...BUT ONLY IF WE LET YOU...
...AND IF YOU WANT US TO COOPERATE...
...THEN WE MUST FEED!
MONET?
I WANTED TO MAKE SURE...
ARE YOU DOING ALL RIGHT?
I'M FINE, CREED.
I DON'T NEED YOU LOOKING AFTER ME.
I JUST NEED--
I KNOW WHAT YOU NEED, FRAIL.
I WAS THERE, REMEMBER?
YOUR BROTHER...HE MIGHT BE GONE... BUT HE SANK HIS CLAWS INTO YOU...
...LEFT YOU WITH HIS HUNGER.
YOU AIN'T READY TO TELL THE OTHERS WHAT'S HAPPENED TO YOU, THAT'S YOUR CALL.
IN THE MEANTIME, THOUGH, I'M HERE FOR YOU.
IF YOU NEED TO FEED, I'M YOUR HUCKLEBERRY.
"IT'S SO GOOD TO SEE SO MANY FAMILIAR FACES HERE TONIGHT.

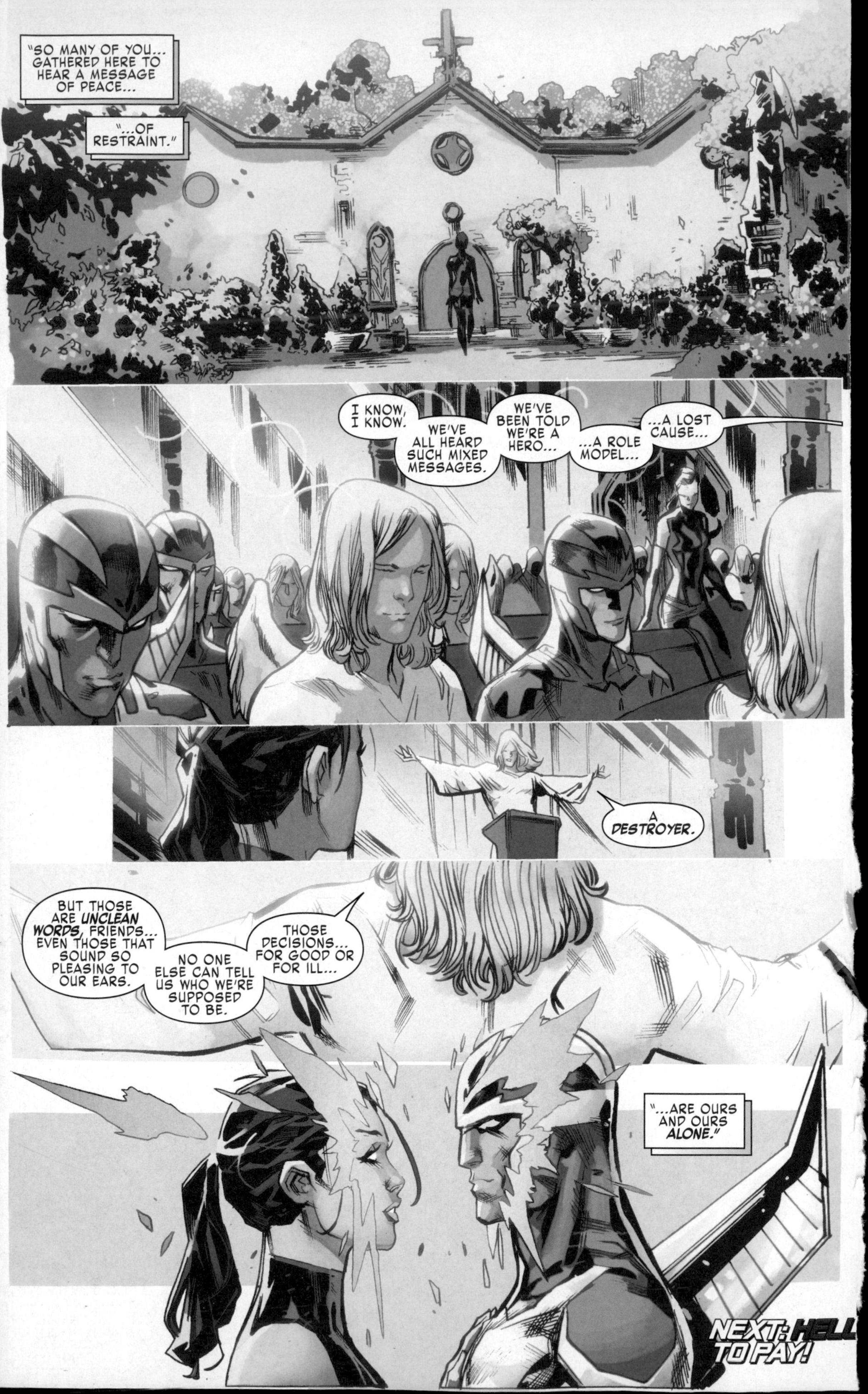
"SO MANY OF YOU... GATHERED HERE TO HEAR A MESSAGE OF PEACE...
"...OF RESTRAINT."
I KNOW, I KNOW.
WE'VE ALL HEARD SUCH MIXED MESSAGES.
WE'VE BEEN TOLD WE'RE A HERO...
...A ROLE MODEL...
...A LOST CAUSE...
A DESTROYER.
BUT THOSE ARE UNCLEAN WORDS, FRIENDS... EVEN THOSE THAT SOUND SO PLEASING TO OUR EARS.
NO ONE ELSE CAN TELL US WHO WE'RE SUPPOSED TO BE.
THOSE DECISIONS... FOR GOOD OR FOR ILL...
"...ARE OURS AND OURS ALONE."
NEXT: HELL TO PAY!